Books in the series Music in American Life:

Only a Miner: Studies in Recorded Coal-Mining Songs
ARCHIE GREEN

Great Day Coming: Folk Music and the American Left
R. SERGE DENISOFF

John Philip Sousa: A Descriptive Catalog of His Works
PAUL E. BIERLEY

The Hell-Bound Train: A Cowboy Songbook
GLENN OHRLIN

Oh, Didn't He Ramble: The Life Story of Lee Collins as Told to Mary Collins
FRANK J. GILLIS AND JOHN W. MINER, EDITORS

American Labor Songs of the Nineteenth Century
PHILIP S. FONER

Stars of Country Music: Uncle Dave Macon to Johnny Rodriguez
BILL C. MALONE AND JUDITH MC CULLOH, EDITORS

Git Along, Little Dogies: Songs and Songmakers of the American West
JOHN I. WHITE

A Texas-Mexican Cancionero: *Folksongs of the Lower Border*
AMÉRICO PAREDES

San Antonio Rose: The Life and Music of Bob Wills
CHARLES R. TOWNSEND

Early Downhome Blues: A Musical and Cultural Analysis
JEFF TODD TITON

An Ives Celebration: Papers and Panels of the Charles Ives Centennial Festival-Conference
H. WILEY HITCHCOCK AND VIVIAN PERLIS, EDITORS

Sinful Tunes and Spirituals: Black Folk Music to the Civil War
DENA J. EPSTEIN

Joe Scott, the Woodsman-Songmaker
EDWARD D. IVES

Jimmie Rodgers: The Life and Times of America's Blue Yodeler
NOLAN PORTERFIELD

Long Steel Rail: The Railroad in American Folksong
NORM COHEN

Sing a Sad Song

The Life of
HANK WILLIAMS

SECOND EDITION

Roger M. Williams

with a Discography by Bob Pinson

UNIVERSITY OF ILLINOIS PRESS

Urbana   Chicago   London

Manufactured in the United States of America

Library of Congress Cataloging in Publication Data

Williams, Roger M.   1934-
    Sing a sad song.
    (Music in American life)
    Includes index.
    1. Williams, Hank, 1923-1953.   2. Country musicians
    —United States—Biography. I. Title.
ML420.W55W5   1980   784.5'2'00924 [B]   80-15520
            ISBN 0-252-00844-8 (cloth)
            ISBN 0-252-00861-8 (paper)

Contents

Preface   vii

Sing a Sad Song   1

Afterword   255

Discography BY BOB PINSON   261

Index   305

Preface

Hank Williams is one of the most remarkable figures in the history of American show business. He was the finest songwriter country music has ever produced and one of its finest performers. Composer-orchestra leader Mitch Miller calls him "an absolute original" and classes him with Stephen Foster as an American songwriter. Williams' own recordings sold many millions; other artists' recordings of his songs sold many millions more. He broke once and for all the artificial barrier between country and popular music, with such memorable songs as "Your Cheatin' Heart," "Hey, Good Lookin'," and "Jambalaya," which were warmly accepted by artists and fans in both fields.

Williams has been hailed as a folk poet, a "hillbilly Shakespeare," and his best work, with its poignant simplicity and unblushing emotion, is indeed poetic. He was in effect a modern troubador, creating songs from the loves and joys and frustrations of his own life.

Although he has been dead for twenty years, Hank Williams and his music live on in a manner unparalleled in American popular culture. His own recordings, re-issued time and again, continue to sell to a body of fans and followers that has swelled to an estimated fifteen million. His songs, which Mitch Miller describes as "so indelible, so timeless they can take any kind of musical treatment," continue to take every kind, including jazz and soul. His popularity is so enduring and his influence so pronounced that many people express surprise when told Hank Williams is no longer living. The life, intertwined with the music, has become legend.

This book stems primarily from my interest, as a working journalist, in the fascinating story of a fascinating man. The idea for it was born in an offhand way, over lunch at the Vanderbilt University cafeteria. My luncheon companion was Joseph Sweat, then in charge of Vanderbilt's public relations department. A few years earlier, as a reporter covering Nashville's show business beat, Joe had become intrigued by the larger-than-life stories told about Hank Williams, and I was intrigued when he told them to me that day. "There must be a book in this," I thought to myself later, and indeed there was. I thank Joe for putting me onto it.

Throughout these pages, I avoid using the term "hillbilly music," not only because it is passé but because it carries a snide, mocking connotation. I find "country music" an acceptable alternative. As used in this book that does not mean traditional folk music from rural America but rather the carefully composed, stylized music we associate with Nashville, the Grand Ole Opry, and those "country and Western" stations that are on every radio band from Key West to Puget Sound.

My debts to various persons and institutions for help in this project are great, the more so because a number of prime sources of information proved uncooperative. My greatest debt is to three men whose recollections and guidance were invaluable: Wesley Rose of Acuff-Rose music publishers, Jerry Rivers of Hank's old band, and J. C. McNeil of Mobile, Alabama. Rivers deserves an extra measure of thanks. He gave hours of his time without hesitation, and he was a good companion as well as a good "source."

Also generous with their time were Taft and Erlene Skipper of Hank's hometown, Georgiana, Alabama, and Jack Cardwell, a jovial country music man from Mobile. Members of the old band—Don Helms, Sammy Pruett, Hillous Butrum, Bob McNett, and Lum York—were all very helpful. So were such Nashville figures as Roy Acuff, Vic McAlpin, Minnie Pearl, Ray Price, Oscar Davis, Harry Stone, Sam Hunt, Jimmy Rule,

Jack Stapp, Bill Williams, Irving Waugh, Aaron Shelton, Carl Jenkins, Trudy Stamper, Edwin Craig, Everett Corbin, and the late Red Foley. In Shreveport, Frank Page, Paul Howard, and Billie Jean Horton Berlin were kind and cooperative. So too were Sol Handwerger of M-G-M Records and Robert Shelton of the New York *Times.*

Attorney Robert Steward and Circuit Judge Richard Emmet, both of Montgomery, Alabama, sorted out for my benefit the tangled litigation that has taken place since Hank's death.

Atlanta doctors Sidney Isenberg and Vernelle Fox provided insights on problem drinking, patterns of family development, and related matters that were most valuable in evaluating the life and experiences of my subject. I am particularly grateful to Dr. Isenberg, who was overly generous with his time. A third Atlanta doctor, John T. Godwin, provided modern medical interpretations of heart disease due to alcoholism.

Special thanks are due my good friend George McMillan, who took time out from a demanding writing project of his own to offer suggestions and constructive criticisms, and to Connie Young, who typed long, late hours to get the manuscript in shape.

The Nashville *Tennessean* and *Banner,* the Alabama *Journal,* the Montgomery *Advertiser,* and *Billboard* magazine opened their files to me, and various staff members offered personal observations as well. The Alabama Department of Archives and History, and its director, Milo B. Howard, Jr., proved a fine source of information. Tuskegee Institute's Archives on Negro Life and History provided contemporary accounts of two Butler County lynchings.

1

On the night of June 11, 1949, a tall mournful-looking young man clutching a guitar pushed his way through a stage full of musicians and stood at the microphone of Nashville's Ryman Auditorium. The young man was Hank Williams, and the show was the Grand Ole Opry, the premier showcase of country music.

The Grand Ole Opry caters to name "artists," as they are called in the trade, and the program was loaded with them that night: Red Foley, Minnie Pearl, Roy Acuff, to name a few. Hank Williams was enough of a name to get a one-song guest shot on the Opry, but he was nothing more. He had been working out of Montgomery and Shreveport, way stations on the country music line, and he had recently recorded a song that was a far bigger hit than he was.

The song was "Lovesick Blues," written by a Tin Pan Alley-style songwriter. Hank usually sang his own compositions, but none of them had had the success of "Lovesick Blues." What else to sing, then, than that?

When he was introduced to the audience, Hank received little applause. The name did not command more. Then, with a pickup group of musicians poised behind him, he hunched his gangling frame and sang:

"I got a feelin' called the blu-oo-oo-oo-oo-ues
Since my baby said good-by . . ."

His voice was lost in a roar as the audience recognized the song and then the singer. "The minute he started that song, he got a standing ovation," recalls Wesley Rose, his long-time publisher, who was in the crowd that night. Hank reacted like a born entertainer. His eyes flashed, his long, thin mouth broke into a grin.

He moved even closer to the mike. He buckled his knees and began to sway, and his voice took a rich, throbbing quality that blended perfectly with the bluesy lyric.

The audience that hardly cared if it got any of Hank Williams now couldn't get enough of him. Highly popular artists often encore with another chorus or two at the Grand Ole Opry, but this audience brought Hank back a half dozen times. The venerable Opry has never seen anything like it, before or since. Time and again he sang the closing line, "I'm lo-o-onesome, I got the lovesick blues," and headed off stage, only to be called back by the clapping and shouting out front. Finally, master of ceremonies Red Foley, to get the show moving again, had to wave the audience into relative silence and make a little speech. At the age of twenty-five, Hank Williams was a country music star.

Just three years later, he was a broken man, his body ravaged, his spirit weak. One-half year after that, at the age of twenty-nine, he was dead.

2

Georgiana, Alabama, is a drowsy gathering of small stores and nondescript houses bisected by the tracks of the Louisville & Nashville Railroad. It is sixty miles south of Montgomery, one hundred and fifteen miles north of Mobile, meaning it is practically nowhere. The stores and houses have seen better days. The Amana movie theater, abandoned and crumbling, stands near the old-fashioned Citizens' Bank, which opens Saturday to serve Saturday-come-to-town folks. On opposite sides of the tracks stand the town's two modern buildings, the hospital and the city hall, the latter startlingly out of place with its alternating rows of brick and translucent glass. On an average day the dominant sound is likely to be the hum of a diesel engine, which nearly drowns out the singing of the birds.

Many of the streets have no street signs and, one almost believes, no names. "I was born and raised in Georgiana and I don't know the name of the first street," chuckles one oldtimer, only half in jest. "Shucks, it took the WPA to put numbers on these houses." Away from the railroad tracks, the streets are as quiet as nameless, numberless streets should be. The town has been effectively bypassed by a couple of new highways, and along the old main road, people on their porches wave at cars that pass by, figuring that anyone traveling that road is bound to be a neighbor. In summer, youngsters hunker down beside the road with a bushel basket of fresh vegetables, hoping to make a sale or two to pay for a trip to the movies that night.

Georgiana is one of the two significant towns in Butler County. The other is Greenville, the county seat. Together they form a central shopping area for a typical south Alabama county. It is made up of small farms, few of which could be called prosperous, which grow a little cotton, a fair amount of tobacco, and a variety of vegetables. What little industry is present is, for the most part, low paying and prone to cutbacks in the work force.

Butler County, due more to fate than to design, has escaped almost entirely the racial unrest that has cropped up in other parts of the Alabama black belt. "About all we've had," says a Georgiana resident, "was a bunch of darkies from Greenville who come down here a couple of years back. One of 'em had a white woman with him, and they all paraded through the streets. They ordered drinks in the drugstore, then went to the bank and another store to try to get 'em to hire some nigras. Didn't change nothin', and they ain't been back since."

Over the decades, however, Butler has had its share

of racial excitement. There were three lynchings in the county between the turn of the century and 1920. The first of them took place in Georgiana in 1901, and the old-timers there still talk about it: the Negro victim was hung from the footbridge across the railroad tracks for allegedly assaulting a young white girl; the girl died only a couple of years ago. In 1915, a white mob captured a black man accused of burglary, hung him from a tree and cut off his ears. Five years later, a black mill hand named Select Reeves, who allegedly had murdered his boss, was taken from his captors by a large bunch of masked men, "riddled with bullets of all calibers" (according to a local newspaper account), and thrown into a swamp.

Butler County's most dramatic bit of violence, however, came in the late 1930s and involved only white men. A native son held up a couple of stores in Georgiana, kidnaped a pair of insurance men, and lit out for Florida. When he ran out of gas, he hog-tied the two hostages and shot them down in cold blood. At his trial, the story goes, the killer said, "I'm sorry I killed that young feller. He begged so hard to live. But that big one—he was mean, he had it comin'."

Georgiana wasn't much when Hank Williams was growing up there, but it was more than it is now. The railroad, always the nerve center of Georgiana, was a mighty important thing then, in the 1920s and early '30s. One hundred or more men earned their living from the railroad, making it by far the biggest employer in town. Operations on the Louisville & Nashville's Montgomery and Mobile Division were controlled from Georgiana. There was a lot of traffic to control. Fourteen express passenger trains traveled through Georgiana each day, along with four locals and twenty to thirty freights. The sounds of whistles and rumbling engines echoed through the town day and night.

Important as it was, the railroad took a back seat to a Baptist preacher when it came to naming the town.

The Reverend Pitt S. Milner, who settled in the area just before the Civil War, did the naming. By the time the railroad arrived, Milner was already the most prominent citizen in the settlement. There was talk of naming the place Pittsville, in his honor, but he opted instead for Georgiana, a hybrid concoction of the names of his native state and his daughter, Anna, who had drowned in a pond behind his big white house on the hill.

Elonzo H. Williams, Hank's father, was a railroading man, but not for the L&N. Lon Williams, in the years Hank was a small boy, drove locomotives for the W. T. Smith Lumber Co., a big south Alabama timbering outfit in those days; one of the locomotives he drove for Smith now stands beside the highway just north of Georgiana, where it serves as the town's lone tourist attraction.

Lon Williams' family traces its roots way back into south and central Alabama. His father farmed for a time in Lowndes County, which many decades later achieved world-wide notoriety as the site of the civil rights slaying of Viola Liuzzo and Jonathan Daniels. His father was also a Civil War veteran—on the Union side. He joined the U. S. Navy before the war broke out, went AWOL in Boston, was caught in Richmond, and spent the war on a Union ship. "He still got an honorable discharge," Lon recalls, with a chuckle. "A lot of my old uncles said they were sorry they didn't join the Union side in the beginning." Lon's mother was a farm girl named Ann Autry, also from Lowndes County.

Lon stayed in school till the sixth grade, then quit to become a water boy in the lumber camps that flourished in that area of the state. He worked his way up to sawing logs and driving oxen, then to running the locomotives that haul the logs to the sawmills. Locomotive driving became his chief occupation for the next twenty-five years—in Mississippi, in Louisiana, in Florida, and finally back in Alabama. "I had lots of different jobs," he says, " 'cause that's the way I wanted it. A company gets to feel it owns a man. I always felt I was a free man and could go off and work somewhere else."

Along the way in his lumber company work, Lon Williams met a young woman named Lillian Skipper. They were married in 1918, just before Lon entered the Army. Lilly, as everyone called her, was dark-haired, husky, and self-reliant. She came from the same sort of stock as Lon; the Skippers had been black-smiths and farmers and loggers who were, in the words of one of the current members of the clan, "just ordinary people."

Yet one gets the feeling around Georgiana that the Skippers were better than the Williamses. A visitor asking about Hank Williams is invariably told, in a tone of respect, "His mother was a Skipper." To be sure, the Skippers are still quite prominent, though "ordinary," people in the Georgiana area.

In 1923, when Lon was thirty-two years old, he and Lilly settled in Mt. Olive, a tiny community a few miles west of Georgiana. They leased a plain but sturdy house for eighty dollars a year and opened a store in half of it. They also bought a three-acre strawberry patch, for twenty-five dollars an acre, and went into the berry business. They had a year-old baby, a girl named Irene. It was hard going, but they were used to hard going. That was life in rural south Alabama, and Lon and Lilly Williams had never known it any other way.

Their son was born September 17, 1923, soon after the Williamses got established in Mt. Olive. In their modest circumstances, his birth must have been a mixed blessing, but Lon did things up right. He had both a doctor (for a fee of thirty-five dollars) and a Negro midwife in attendance. "I had money in the bank when the boy was born," says Lon, who is very sensitive to stories of how Hank Williams grew up in poverty. "I was makin' one hundred fifty, one hundred sixty dollars a month, which was good pay. I paid that doctor by check, drawn on my account at the Butler County Bank."

Lon, who has been known to embellish a story, tells

one about the difficult time he had contacting the doctor when Lilly was ready to deliver. The problem, he says, was a party line, which to hear him tell it must have had as parties every resident of rural south Alabama (if indeed rural south Alabama had telephones in 1923).

"I picked up the receiver and rang the doctor," says Lon, "and all over Butler and Covington counties you could hear phones going click, click, as everybody else picked 'em up to see what was goin' on. I yelled into the phone, 'I wish every God damned one of you would go to bed. I want a doctor.' You could hear them phones hangin' up all over the countryside. Click, click. I got Dr. Langford then. Next day one of our neighbors said to me, 'You sure did sound mean on that phone last night.' I told her, 'If you'd have been in bed where you belonged, you wouldn't have heard it.' "

Lon and Lilly had a sturdy country name picked out for their son—Hiram. Hiram Hank, they named him. (Actually, through someone's error, it is "Hiriam" on the birth certificate.) The Hiram didn't last with anybody but his father, who has always called him Hiram or "the boy." The Hank didn't catch on immediately either. For a while, to his playmates, he was Herky or Skeets. But the boy himself took a fancy to Hank; it sounded more casual and more manly. When he came of age, he changed the name legally to Hank.

The house in which Hank was born was built in a favorite south Alabama style. It was a "double pen" structure, with two pens, or units, joined together by an eight-foot-wide hall running front to rear. On one side of the hall was the store, on the other side the living quarters, a total of six rooms. A porch ran across the front of the whole building, which was made of sealed logs. "You couldn't tell they were log houses," says Lon Williams with a bit of pride. Then he adds with disgust: "Somebody once put out a book showing a picture of a house I wouldn't keep hogs in and saying the boy was born in it."

From the start, Hank was a thin and none too healthy

boy. His sister, Irene, describes him as "pretty frail.
He was no athlete. Everytime he tried sports, it seemed,
he broke something." One such effort, perhaps at ice
skating, resulted in a ruptured disk, contributing to
back problems that were to plague him most of his
adult life.

"Hank never was as healthy as he should've been,"
says Taft Skipper, a cousin, who speculates that his
frailty may have stemmed from the poor baby formulas
his mother fed him. "But he had a lot of nerve. He
would try most anything. He wanted to be a regular
boy. He was pretty independent and liked to go his own
way."

Another cousin, J. C. McNeil, who spent a great deal
of time with young Hank, remembers him as "a real
loner. He never was a happy boy, in a way. He didn't
laugh and carry on like other children. It seemed like
somethin' was always on his mind."

During Hank's adolescence, the family moved con-
tinually. Usually the reason was to abandon a fading
job or business opportunity in favor of a new one. This
was by no means unusual for the time. As Taft Skipper
points out, "During the Depression, out of fourteen
hundred people working for W. T. Smith around Butler
County, there probably weren't over a dozen who owned
their own homes. It was mighty hard with the low wages.
If you didn't own it, chances are you moved around a
good bit."

Until 1935, all the Williams family's moves were in
the area around Georgiana: to Garland, where Lon had
another little store and another patch of strawberries
(he lost the berries in a freeze) and where Lilly ran
the first of several boardinghouses; to Chapman, where,
back on the lumber company payroll as a locomotive
driver, he saved up enough money to buy a house; to
Ruthven Mill, a W. T. Smith lumber camp; to McWilliams, where Lon now lives and where a battered metal
sign proclaims the settlement as Hank Williams' boyhood home.

In 1930, when the family was living in McWilliams,

Lon Williams entered a veterans hospital in Biloxi. He says he was suffering from gas inhaled during his World War I service. Lilly believed the problem was "shell shock," an all-purpose injury term that came out of the Great War (in World War II it was "battle fatigue"). Some relatives now hint broadly that his problem was more emotional than physical, and the length of his stay in veterans hospitals—roughly ten years—indicates they are probably correct.

Whatever the cause, the effect was certain: the Williams household was left without a man, and seven-year-old Hank was left without a father. Lon Williams never again was a real part of the family. During his years in the hospital, Lilly and the children visited him occasionally, but the visits, one senses, were brief and cheerless.

Lon's departure only formalized a family structure that already had been well established. Lilly always wore the pants in the family. Large in stature, with mannish features and a dark complexion, she was a lioness. She was tough talking and decisive, accustomed to making decisions and executing them as well. "Lilly was a pretty rough woman," says one long-time acquaintance, "and high-tempered too. Not the kind who's at home in a drawing room."

For a woman like this to choose a man like Lon is understandable, perhaps inevitable. Lon is small, unassuming, plodding in a dogged sort of way. He was no bum; he was a worker. Yet he was incapable of establishing himself in one place or one job. He moved from one to another—troubled by the Depression and perhaps by his war disabilities—without ever making much of any of them. The family fortunes rose and fell, and Lon seemed powerless to stabilize them. That task fell to Lilly, who was far better suited to it than her husband. She helped him direct his modest enterprises, the successes as well as the failures. She became the dominant force in the family, the great steadying, comforting influence for her children. This process, apparent enough when Lon was still in the home, became more and more pronounced as his absence from it continued.

The effect of all this on young Hank can at least be conjectured. It made him ever more dependent upon his mother, creating a confusion in parental role that worsened as he approached manhood and that probably prevented him from ever fully realizing himself as an adequate male.

As hard as Lon's and Lilly's relationship was on the children, it was even harder on their marriage. Taft Skipper, who saw a lot of the family when he was a youngster, says Lilly treated Lon well in his pre-hospital days: "She was just as kind to him as she could be. He had a bad case of nerves, so she'd bring him coffee in bed—that black, thick Luzianne brand—and try to keep us kids quiet for his sake." Lon, for his part, says Skipper, "always done the best he could. He worked and helped support his family, and he only quit when he had to go to the hospital."

True enough, but that was no remedy for the basic weaknesses of the marriage. There is no evidence that Lilly was distressed when Lon entered the hospital or that she was particularly concerned when his confinement dragged on year after year. Somewhere along the way, the bonds of their marriage simply dissolved, and when Lon was released from V.A. care, around 1940, there was no serious attempt at reconciliation.

Lon by this time was as bitterly jealous as Lilly was indifferent. He believed, so he says today, that his wife had "tried to get a commitment against me, to keep me in the hospital"; that she was stepping out on him with another man; and even that she tried, in cahoots with the man, to do away with him after his release. The marriage was sick when Lon went away, and it was stone dead when he returned.

Although young Hank was frail and something of a loner, he compensated for it by being self-assertive and resourceful, traits he inherited from his mother. He worked, and worked hard, from early childhood. The family didn't always need what little money he could provide, but Hank himself needed it if he was to have any of the good things a boy wants. His father recalls him selling peanuts at a logging camp at the age of three. Even if that is stretching it by a year or two, the story bespeaks a certain resourcefulness. "I bought the peanuts from a farmer, and the boy sold 'em," says Lon. "He even knew how much was owed him, and on payday he'd collect. I remember one time a logger told him, 'I don't owe you that much' and he told the man, 'I'm gonna go get my daddy.' The man laughed and said, 'Wait a minute, son. I'll give you your money.' "

Adds Lon defensively: " 'Course he didn't *have* to sell peanuts for a living. Anybody who tells you that is crazy."

Hank continued selling peanuts for years. He also shined shoes, delivered groceries, and did whatever odd jobs he could to make a few cents.

Hank's musical experience also started at the age of three. He sat on the bench with his mother when she played the organ at the Mt. Olive Baptist Church, next door to their double pen home. Whether from this experience or not, he developed a love for and understanding of the old four-square hymns. They greatly influenced the songs he later wrote, and some people think his hymns are the finest work he ever produced.

Lilly herself had a fair amount of musical talent. She accompanied the singing of the Mt. Olive Church congregation each Sunday. A few musical genes may even have passed through her to Hank from her father, John Skipper. Old John, the present-day Skippers recall, was good at "composin'," making up simple songs which he would sing, unaccompanied but with gusto, to friends. Hank's first instrument was a harmonica, which he got for Christmas when he was six. "He like to run me nuts with that thing," says Lon, "runnin' it back and forth in his mouth."

But Hank's musical interest did not really develop until he was about eleven. Until then he showed scarcely more musical aptitude than other boys his age. Also, his family would have been hard-pressed to provide him any kind of serious instrument or lessons. When Lon entered the hospital, the Williamses were left in poorer financial circumstances than ever. They soon moved from the Mt. Olive house to Garland, where the family picked strawberries for a short time. Then they moved into Georgiana, the largest town in that part of Butler County, when Lilly landed a job in a WPA cannery.

The family rented a house on a nice street a stone's throw from the cut that carries the L&N tracks through Georgiana. The house was built on stilts and was so high off the ground you could walk under it. Their next-door neighbor was one of the town's most prominent men, Herman Pride, the former mayor and postmaster, who still lives in the same house. On a hot summer day not long ago, Pride and his wife sat on their spacious front porch (she cutting up fresh string beans) and reminisced about young Hank Williams. "He was a nice-lookin' little old boy," said Pride, "right lively but not smart alecky. And he was crazy about cowboy things. We used to call him 'two-gun Pete,' all decked out in his hat, belt, and boots. He used to run along the brick wall in front of my place till I thought sure he'd break his neck. He had other kids doin' it, too, but they never fell that I know of."

It is hard to find in Georgiana an unqualified good word for Lon Williams, who is generally regarded as something of a no-account, but almost everybody agrees his wife Lilly was a fine woman. This is mainly because of the manful way she struggled to support her children, but it is also because she showed a sense of humanity in doing it. One of her jobs was as nurse in the hospital of Dr. J. Crawford Watson, who is described as "the most famous surgeon in this part of the country."

"You can say what you please," says Mrs. Pride firmly, "Mrs. Williams was one good woman. I remember one day, when she was working at Dr. Watson's hospital, somebody told her about a little boy who was sick, not from poverty but from filth. The doctor said if somebody didn't do something for the boy he'd die. Mrs. Williams went out with me every morning to look after the boy. None of us got any money for it, but she did it just the same."

Another of Lilly's jobs was helping allot the carloads of food and cloth that were sent to Georgiana to ease the pains of the Depression. "People were so poor then you can't imagine," says Mrs. Pride. Poor as the Williamses were, they were decently off by Depression standards. Lilly's WPA cannery job, one of the "created jobs," as old-timers in Georgiana call them, earned her about a dollar a day, pretty close to what common laborers were getting at the time.

"We were poor people," recalls Irene Williams, "but we weren't in poverty. No matter what anyone says, we never begged." Irene is irritated by the rags to riches legend that has persisted about Hank. She is fiercely proud of the family's resilience, its ability to cope with misfortune.

"They lived pretty good," says Taft Skipper. "Nothing extra, but plenty to eat and wear. Lilly was a good manager. She was an excellent cook too. She could cook anything in the Southern style—biscuit pudding, you name it—and she could take ordinary things and make some real good dishes out of them."

Soon after the Williamses moved into the house next door to Herman Pride, the place burned to the ground. They lost everything except what they were wearing when the fire struck—a pajama top of Hank's, a pajama bottom of Irene's, a gown of Lilly's. "Some townspeople took up a collection for us," Irene recalls, adding sardonically, "It was led by a well-to-do lady who kept all the clothes that came in without any holes in them and some of the money too. At least we didn't see much of the money."

The family found another house across town, on Rose Street. Lilly eventually turned it into a boarding-house, which seemed to her a sensible way for a widow to add to her income. Soon after they took possession, though, she instituted another cost-cutting scheme, a vegetable garden. She enlisted the aid of relatives and assorted volunteers in hacking a garden out of a small plot of land adjoining the house, and soon the plot was sprouting butter beans, peas, okra, and other delicacies of the Southern soil.

The day they moved into the new house, Hank and Irene, as well as Lilly, went out to make some money. Hank was not yet seven, and his earlier "work" had been mostly for fun. Now it was mostly for real; anything he could contribute to the family, now virtually without possessions, would be a help.

Irene roasted some peanuts and put them in little paper bags. Hank took them out on the streets of Georgiana. He also took a can of shoe polish and a rag, and anyone passing up the peanuts was offered a shine instead. Each sold for a nickel. No one recalls just how good a seller or shiner Hank was, but by the end of the day he had made thirty cents. With it, he bought stew meat and rice (ten cents each), potatoes and tomatoes (five cents each). He presented the food triumphantly to his mother and exclaimed, "Momma, fix us some gumbo stew. We're gonna eat tonight!"

Next day Hank made another thirty cents. This time he gave way to boyish desire and spent the money for firecrackers and caps. When he came home later than usual, Lilly gave him a paddling, setting off, the story goes, a miniature fireworks display in his seat pocket.

For the next few years, young Hank Williams dug for every nickel he could get. The loungers at Austin Reid's barbershop remember him as an undersized but alert kid who would do any small job or run any errand for a few cents. "He was a little bitty feller, with legs no bigger'n a buggy whip," says Reid. "He hung around here a lot, looking for food and cigarettes. If he did something for you, you could give him anything—a nickel, a piece of candy, a few peanuts. If you tossed a cigarette butt away, he'd dive for it 'fore it hit the floor. Still, he was a happy boy."

Adds Reid: "Last time he come to Georgiana he had two Cadillacs with him and a shirt I 'spect cost more'n my whole suit of clothes. If he'd just left the liquor alone. . . ."

The fact is, Hank Williams was drinking liquor by the time he was eleven years old. That seems shocking today, but it was not unusual in the rural South of the 1920s and '30s. There was always wine and beer, not to mention moonshine, available, and country kids just naturally took a few nips when they could. It was an adventure, and it gave you a funny, sorta dizzy feeling afterward.

"You'd sneak out and get what you could," chuckles Jack Cardwell, a Mobile disk jockey who was a contemporary of young Hank's in south Alabama. " 'Course if your old man caught you, he'd tan you good."

Drinking, in the South at that time, was a sport enjoyed by all ages and sexes, national Prohibition and local dry laws notwithstanding. Moonshine was the regional drink. It sold around Georgiana for anywhere from thirty-five to seventy-five cents a pint, and it varied in quality all the way from hideous to rather tasty.

(The manufacture and consumption of 'shine is still very big business in the South, despite the gradual repeal of laws banning tax-paid or "regular" liquor. Georgia is the number one moonshine state, and Atlanta is known as the moonshine capital of the world for its activity as a sales and distribution center. In Georgia alone, during the federal government's "Operation Dry," 5,200 stills with a mash capacity of over 4.3 million gallons were seized in the three years preceding November 1968. Seizures over the South as a whole amounted to about three times those numbers during the same period, and heaven knows how many operations continue undetected. Interestingly, price is no longer a key factor in consumption of moonshine, at least not in the cities. The consumer in the "shot houses," the hideaway bistros that serve 'shine by the shot, pays almost as much for it as he would for regular liquor. He does so out of habit, because of the kick he gets from breaking the law, and because he plain likes the stuff.)

Drinking, in young Hank's time, often was less frowned upon than smoking for such restricted minorities as women and children. Jack Cardwell recalls that, around Butler County thirty or forty years ago, "No woman but a hen house hussy would smoke. But ninety-eight per cent of 'em dipped snuff. Dippin' was okay. If they couldn't afford to buy snuff, they'd make it by mixing sugar and cocoa."

Although he probably had tasted booze even earlier, Hank had his first major experiences with it during a year he lived with his cousin J. C. McNeil. That was in 1934. The McNeils lived near Fountain, in neighboring Monroe County, in a "camp car," a railroad boxcar converted into a house. The camp car was a common sight around Alabama lumber camps in those days. The companies provided them, free or at minimal cost, to loggers and their families. They were primitive dwellings, but they offered the advantage (to the company) of being mobile; when logging operations shifted to a new site, the cars could be hooked to a locomotive and transferred with the other equipment.

Hank came to live with J. C. McNeil so J.C.'s sister could live with the Williamses and attend high school in Georgiana. The McNeils' camp car, located in the Pool lumber camp, was barn red and mounted on concrete slabs. It actually consisted of two boxcars, arranged in an L shape. Most of the facilities were outside: the well, the toilet, the wood to be burned in the stove and heater.

"It wasn't too bad a place to live," says J. C. McNeil, whose father worked at the camp. "We enjoyed it as kids. There was lots of woods to play in, and we worked a big garden with butter beans, peas, corn, and okra. We were poor, but we never did go hungry. Of course, never did nobody have much extra either."

Actually, by the standards of those Depression days, the McNeils and other lumber camp families were pretty well off. They were on salary, and most of them lived like they knew where their next dollar was coming from. Their wives and children were decently dressed. They could afford a little entertainment now and then. A good many of them even had cars, mostly old Model T's that were kept in bare running condition. "The camp people," says Taft Skipper, "all had a little money to spend. But the country people were extremely poor, tryin' to scratch a living out of cotton, corn, and a few pigs and chickens."

The camp cars, he recalls, were not bad places to live. "They were in good condition and pretty comfortable. All they had for heat was an old wood stove, but you could stay warm. The surroundings were all right too. The yards usually were kept well swept and the cars painted."

Moreover, there was a spirit of community around the camps. Everybody worked for the same company, and deadening as that might be in today's white collar world, it had advantages in the south Alabama of the 1930s. There was no lack of friends for socializing with and calling on in time of need. There were plenty of kids, and late afternoon would find them playing hopscotch in the dust of the camp or cowboys and Indians in the nearby woods. There were plenty of churches too (the rural South has been short of many things but never of churches), and Mrs. McNeil, a devout Methodist, marched J.C. and Hank off to services every Sunday morning.

A favorite recreational pastime was organizing dances and parties on Saturday nights. Sometimes the loggers would pay a bunch of musicians to come to one of their houses; other times they would drive to a dance hall in a nearby town. Either way, the children usually went along. So did the booze, and the two had a way of getting together before the evening was far along.

The youngsters' technique was simple and highly effective. Since consumption at the party itself was frowned upon, bottles were stashed outside—in the automobile, in the bushes, or in some other supposedly safe place—and reclaimed for repeated whistle wetting as the evening progressed. The youngsters always got their share. "We'd watch where they hid the stuff," says McNeil, "and we'd dig it out and get as drunk as hoot owls on it." The parents didn't like that, of course,

but they weren't so concerned that they stopped bringing either their children or their booze to the parties.

Hank's drinking in this fashion, it must be empha-
sized, was not unusual for that time and place. And it
had little to do with later severe problems with alcohol.
Those problems grew out of emotional conflicts far
more deep-seated and complex than secretive nips at a
bottle of moonshine.

All this time, Hank remained a thin, lonesome sort
of boy. "He'd go along with the gang," says McNeil,
"but he never would get interested in nothin'. Say, a
baseball game. That's a boy's pride and joy, but Hank
didn't much care about it."

Hank the loner had a good number of fights, standing up to boys who, in McNeil's words, "laid some
abuse on him." Frail as he was, he was no coward. He
also was no wallflower when it came to girls. "He was
a woman go-getter," says McNeil. "He'd go after anybody's gal, and that would lead to more scraps. That
don't go over too good with country boys, you know."

The year with the McNeils may well have been the
best of Hank's boyhood. It was a more pleasant, more
stable household than the one run on a shoestring by
Lilly Williams. Mrs. McNeil was more relaxed and less
overbearing than Lilly, and she and Hank got along
well. Her husband was an amiable fellow who took part
in many of the boys' activities. This was of critical importance to young Hank, who had spent the past four
years of his childhood without a father. McNeil provided Hank with the fatherly interest and direction he
badly needed, and he also provided a happier house
than the boy had ever known.

There were economic benefits as well. Walter McNeil,
compared to Lilly Williams, was earning good money.
He made six dollars a day as locomotive operator at
the camp. He did not see much of his pay in cash form,
because the company issued "black money," or scrip,
to its employees. The idea, as developed by countless
company towns, was to get the employees to spend
their money in the company store, where the company

could make a profit on them. The workers at the Pool lumber camp didn't like the system, but they accepted it as part of their lot.

Hank, J.C., and J.C.'s younger brother wandered all through the woods around Fountain, hunting rabbits and squirrels with Walter McNeil's single-barreled shotgun. They set out lines in the creeks to catch catfish. They went to a one-room schoolhouse, where Hank was an indifferent student. They went to nearby Fountain, to a little amusement park, where J.C.'s mother swapped vegetables for tickets so the boys could ride the merry-go-round.

They also got into boyish trouble. One night at a church social, Hank and J.C. laid plans to pilfer some sandwiches. The idea was for a boy inside the church to place a plate of sandwiches close to the window, so a confederate could reach up and snatch it.

"We reached in and yanked something out of the window," laughs McNeil, "but it wasn't sandwiches. It was a sack full of chinaware. It got all smashed, and the boy inside squealed. Well-to-do people owned the stuff, and to hear 'em talk you never could replace it. Daddy made me stick my head between my legs, and he gave me a real hiding. Then Hank said. 'Uncle Walter, I was as much into it as J.C., so you might just as well whip me with him.' And he did, too.

"My Daddy made us both go 'round selling milk and peanuts till we made up every dime of that broken chinaware. That wasn't nothin' new for us, though. Hank and I were always shining shoes and selling stuff. On a good day we'd make maybe forty cents apiece. Sometimes we'd make just enough to get to the movie show, then we'd come back and make some more."

One of the boys' favorite pastimes was hiking to see Uncle Ed—Ed Skipper, Taft's father. Uncle Ed was a hunter, and J.C. and Hank often pressed him to take them coon and possum hunting. "We went over to his place so much we must've been puttin' ourselves on them," says McNeil. "I can just imagine them sayin', 'Yonder come those damn little devils again.'"

Uncle Ed had a farm, and the boys helped him with chores from time to time. Once Hank spent several days picking potatoes and later complained to Mrs. McNeil, "You know, he didn't offer me tater one" in the way of payment. "He didn't, either," says McNeil, "but then we didn't work much. We were more a bother than a help. And Uncle Ed was good to us when it came to huntin'. He'd get up at three in the morning sometimes to go with us."

Hank learned a good deal during his year with the McNeils. He saw more of adult life than he had ever seen before. And, though it didn't seem important at the time, he got a long exposure to country music, at the Saturday night dances in and around the logging camp. It stuck to his ribs like Mrs. McNeil's fried chicken, and before two years were out he too was a country musician.

3

There are several different versions of how and when Hank Williams learned to play the guitar. Some stories practically have him born with a guitar in his hand. Others assign to various people the credit for buying him his first guitar, giving him his first lessons, and so forth.

Lilly Williams always said flatly that she bought her son his first guitar and arranged for his first instruction.

But almost inevitably with a famous man and memories dimmed by time, Georgiana legend credits people other than Lilly with starting Hank down the road to musical immortality. One is Fred Thigpen, who used to be the town's Ford dealer and who now lives there in retirement. Thigpen says he bought Hank's first guitar, getting it for about $2.50 at the jewelry-instrument store owned by Jim Warren.

"Hank hung around my Ford place a lot," says Thigpen. "He was a li'l ole boy, kinda like you'd throw away. I fed him a good deal, and sometimes, when he'd slip away to my place early in the morning, I'd tune in a music program on the radio for him; Jimmie Rodgers, I believe it was. He wanted a guitar, so one day I told him, 'You find one that don't cost too much and I'll buy it.' He came back, told me about the one at Warren's, and we got it." Thigpen doesn't remember anything about the instrument except that it was "dark color, not too big" and that Warren sold it to them at a bargain price.

According to Georgiana's old-timers, Hank hung around Jim Warren's store a good deal. Some say it was Warren, not Fred Thigpen, who gave Hank his first guitar. Whether he did or not, Hank apparently liked to be around Warren as well as the instruments he had in his store.

Jim Warren, who is dead now, was one of Georgiana's most interesting individuals. He was a good old-timey musician, proficient on guitar and fiddle, and he lived behind his store. A bachelor, he befriended a black family, maintaining a house for them outside of town. The Ku Klux Klan was quite strong around Butler County in those days, and the Klan took exception to Warren's association with blacks. There was angry talk that Warren was sleeping with the woman of the family. Warren denied that but retorted that even if he was he'd be no worse than a preacher he knew.

"The Ku Klux beat Warren up one time," recalls Herman Pride, the former mayor. "He wound up sending the Negro family up to Selma, but he stuck it out in Georgiana, even though the town was ashamed of him." If young Hank knew of Warren's reputation, and he probably did, it didn't keep him from seeing and liking the man.

Georgiana credits a sprightly old man named Cade

Durham with giving Hank his first lessons on the guitar. Durham himself is rather vague on the subject—he remembers little to distinguish Hank from his dozens of other pupils—but says steadfastly that he did teach the boy guitar. Perhaps the town has convinced him he must have done so. After all, he has taught the last few decades' worth of Georgianans.

Durham had his own string band for years, with Russell Foster and the Hancock boys, Johnny and Allen; one of the best string bands in the South, as he recalls it. Hank heard the Durham band play numerous times at the Rhodes Brothers dry goods store, where country entertainment was provided to drum up business. Durham still teaches guitar and fiddle. His wife allows as how, although she could never play either of those instruments, "I could always make a bass fiddle talk. They ain't but three strings to worry about."

Back in young Hank's time, Durham taught at his house on Meeting Street, in a sitting room decorated with assorted fiddles, guitars, and mandolins. His fee was fifty cents an hour, "and I gave 'em a pretty good show for it." His method, with beginners like Hank, was to teach basic chords. He showed his pupil the chord formations on the guitar, then played the melody of a song on his fiddle while the pupil "chorded" with a flat pick behind the fiddling. The songs were of no special type—just whatever Durham knew plus whatever he could get in sheet music at Georgiana stores. "I'd saw out old fiddle tunes like 'Corinna' and some little old blues numbers," he says.

"Miz Durham used to pet young Hank and treat him like one of our own children. All I done was just start him off on the guitar. He had the talent."

According to J. C. McNeil, one of the most reliable sources of information on Hank's boyhood, Hank learned his first few guitar chords from Mrs. McNeil the year he lived in the camp car at Fountain. She had an instrument, and the boys watched avidly as she strummed the chords to simple country songs. (J.C., now a carpenter in Mobile, still plays and sings, particularly his cousin's songs.) Hank's interest increased a little more each Saturday night, as he watched the string bands perform at the logging camp dances.

Lilly Williams maintained she bought Hank his first guitar, after the family had moved from Georgiana to Greenville. "I promised him the instrument to make him work hard in school," Lilly wrote in a newspaper story published shortly after Hank's death. " 'If you make good grades, I'll give you the guitar,' I said.

"The guitar cost me three dollars and fifty cents, secondhand. I paid fifty cents a month on it until it was paid for. Hank gave me money from his peanut sales and shoe-shining work to help pay for it.

"But the instrument which brought Hank fame was a bad-luck article for him the first day.

"The little fellow was overcome with joy when I brought the guitar home from the music store.

"He jumped and shouted to the top of his voice.

"Belatedly, he ran into the yard and swung the gate.

"He leaped on a young calf that was lying just outside the yard and twisted the calf's tail.

"The yearling bawled with fright. He leaped into the air and before Hank knew what was happening the calf had thrown him to the ground, breaking his arm.

"It almost broke his heart too, for he couldn't play his guitar with a broken arm.

"Three days later, though, when he could wiggle his fingers, Hank was trying to chord the guitar."

Whatever the Thigpens, the Durhams, *et al.,* did for Hank Williams musically, they didn't do nearly so much as a black street singer called Tee-tot. Rufe Payne was his real name, but everyone knew him as Tee-tot. He lived in Greenville, up the tracks from Georgiana, and he scratched out a living singing on the streets of both towns and giving occasional, impromptu lessons.

There were other street singers around that area, including a man named Dove Hazelip, who'd survived a gunshot wound in the forehead. But Tee-tot was the best known. J. C. McNeil describes him as "just a good old common nigger. His hands were so long they came to his knees. All niggers got some kind of rhythm and good timin', and he sure had it."

Tee-tot came to Georgiana a couple of times a week, most often on Saturday. If he couldn't catch a ride, he'd travel the fifteen miles by train, catching the L&N's local number five on Saturday morning. Sometimes he had an engagement—a church supper or a black dance. More often, he just played and sang on the sidewalk, in barbershops, anywhere he could attract a few people who might part with some small change. They would put the money, a nickel or dime at best, in his battered hat, and he'd keep on singing.

"There was always a crew of little boys around him," says Herman Pride, "followin' him from store to store." One of the boys was Hank Williams, already captivated by the sound of a blues guitar and a lonesome song.

How much actual playing and singing Hank did during his years around Georgiana is difficult to determine. Old-timers, with their talent for embellishment, tend to remember him as a right prominent young musician at that time. For instance, Fred Thigpen, who says he bought Hank's first guitar, also says, "I heard him sing his first song. It was 'Railroad Blues.' He crawled up on the steps of a mail crane, down at the railroad station, and sang it. He was twelve or thirteen at the time."

Whether he was playing it or not, young Hank was known as a kid who liked music. He was spending an increasing amount of time around string bands and guitar pickers. One of the string band men who remembers him is the Reverend Oscar D. Cardwell, a hell-raising lumberman from Georgiana who "got the call" to become a Baptist preacher at the age of sixty. Reverend Cardwell was a fiddle player with lots of showy tricks ("I never could play tol'able well, but I was a good showman"), and he used to gather with a few of the boys at the "radio shack" (the town's one radio station), located over Johnson's grocery store in Georgiana.

The big attraction at the radio shack was noise.

Whether the band was actually broadcasting or not, it would play into an amplifier system turned up sufficiently loud to send the sound halfway across town. Hank stopped there often, probably as much to see the microphones and what not as to hear the music. "He was a thin boy, with legs that looked like pipe-stems," says Reverend Cardwell. "He didn't play an instrument when he'd come in, but when somebody played somethin' that suited him, he'd get on the floor and dance up a blue breeze."

Perhaps the first instrument Hank played in public was what people then called a jazz horn, a kazoo sort of thing you could play a tune on simply by humming into it. He often got in a few licks on the jazz horn when he accompanied the McNeils to logging camp dances. During the same period, his mother remembers, his tooting on the instrument became so popular that dancers would request him to play and then pass the hat for him when he did.

Hank was confident enough during that year with the McNeils to try a little street singing of his own. The street in this case was the platform of the Fountain railroad station. Hank and J.C., when Walter McNeil would let them, would go to the station to meet incoming trains. "He'd sing up a storm," says J.C., "not for money, just for fun. Mostly things like, 'On one cold winter night/Not a star was in sight/And the cold wind was whistling down the line.' The people gettin' off the trains didn't fluster him a bit. He wasn't at all bashful."

Jack Cardwell, the Mobilean who grew up in that era, recalls doing the same thing at Georgiana's Greyhound bus stop. Cardwell, however, was doing it for money. "I remember how I got started," says Cardwell. "My brother had him an old Martin guitar. 'Jimmie Rodgers' old guitar,' it was supposed to be. Heck, all of 'em were Jimmie Rodgers' old guitar in those days. Rodgers was the biggest thing going. Momma taught my brother three chords plus the words to 'My Old Pal of Yesterday.' He started playing for the buses that came in, so as soon as I learned that song I lit out for the bus station too. I was at Jackson's filling station. And when that bus came in, I was right there, strummin' and singin' like I'd been doin' it for years. I was about eight, and sometimes I'd make me forty, fifty cents that way."

Young Hank also had a few singing lessons, as part of a church program. J.C. took lessons with him, " 'cause anything Aunt Lilly tried to do for Hank, mother tried to do the same for me. They were sisters." Although the lessons involved music, they were not popular. "We'd do a few do, re, mi's, then we'd head out for the woods or Uncle Ed's."

Hank did not actually get together musically with Tee-tot in Georgiana. That came about a year later, when the Williamses moved to Greenville. Hank had his own guitar then, and a strong determination to learn to play it well.

Hank and J.C., whose family had relocated near Greenville, took what amounted to lessons from Tee-tot —two or three lessons for a dollar, with the money provided by their mothers or by little jobs the boys did to pick up change. "The main thing was keeping time," recalls J.C. "That's what Tee-tot kept pointing out to us. We sang and played what he did. We didn't know many songs of our own."

Tee-tot took a liking to Hank, and he showed the boy everything he could. When there was no money to pay him for a lesson, Mrs. Williams gave him a meal instead. Tee-tot died not long afterward, with scarcely a hint of what a huge success his young protégé would turn out to be.

Greenville was, by Butler County standards, a metropolis. It was the county seat and had a population four times as large as Georgiana's. Although it is on the Louisville & Nashville's Montgomery and Mobile Division, Greenville has not been so dominated by it as has Georgiana. A courthouse square, rather than railroad tracks, is the center of town.

Lilly Williams moved her family up to Greenville, in

the summer of 1935, in hopes of gaining financial stability. She had pretty well decided that running a boardinghouse offered the best opportunity for a women with two children. She set one up near a cotton gin in Greenville, and it proved quite successful. At the same time, she continued doing odd jobs, such as nursing and sewing.

At about this time, Lon Williams claims, the federal government made Lilly a lump sum payment of "several thousand dollars" for his military service-connected disabilities. "They talk about 'no support' from me," snorts Lon. "Where in hell was my money goin' to then?"

Hank's sister Irene scoffs at the "lump sum payment" story. She says the family got very little from Lon's disability and made ends meet strictly on its own. "The only several thousand dollars my mother had she worked like a dog for and saved," says Irene.

When Lilly did get a small military service pension, says Irene, she got it at her own behest, not Lon's. "We got it through Lister Hill, who was running for the U. S. Senate. He came through town one day, and I met him in a jewelry store while he was campaigning. 'My ma wants to see you very badly,' I told him. He went home with me and sat on our front porch talking to my mother. Then he got her a pension."

Young Hank by this time was a tall, painfully thin boy with a shock of brown hair, a sad mouth and sadder eyes, and ears that stuck out much too far. He wore steel-rimmed glasses. (Either his vision improved or he didn't need glasses badly, for he never wore them in later life.) He was a quietly happy boy, still not a joiner and still not a student, but content to go his own way at his own pace.

Irene, thirteen months older than her brother, was also tall but huskier than he. She had far more of her mother's looks, with a full face, dark brown hair, and arching brows. Everyone remembers Irene as being more forceful than Hank, not always pleasantly so. Mrs. Lilly McGill, then a schoolteacher in Georgiana, who barely remembers Hank ("He was so ordinary he merges with the crowd in my memory"), has a clear recollection of Irene: "She was much more forward, with a good bit of braggadocio."

The Williamses lived in Greenville for only a couple of years, and with one exception they were relatively uneventful years for Hank. The exception was music, which was occupying more and more of his time and interest. It was in Greenville that Hank really learned how to play the guitar. And it was in Greenville that he wrote his first songs.

His guitar teacher now was Tee-tot alone. Hank hung around the street singer as much as he could, observing his techniques, listening to his songs, talking to him about the music. Tee-tot was quite eclectic in his musical tastes. He played only popular stuff, to be sure, but within that broad genre everything from hymns to jazz to ragtime to mountain ballads.

Hank was not interested in instrumental virtuosity on the guitar; at least he never achieved it. He was interested in the guitar as a backup for songs. What Hank learned from Tee-tot was not cross picking or Travis picking or Carter Family picking or any other style of playing melody on the instrument. Rather, he learned chords, chord progressions, a few bass runs, and the simple, driving style of accompaniment that suited the songs he was to write.

More important, he learned a lot about the "feel" of a song: how to make a blues sound blue or a funny song sound funny. Tee-tot was a professional entertainer. If he wasn't entertaining, he got damned few coins in his hat. So he had to know how to put a song across, not in the sense of a Sammy Davis, with elaborate stage productions and a captive audience, but in the sense of the wandering minstrel who must gather his own audiences as he goes. Tee-tot, in his job, didn't have to be good so much as he had to be appealing. Young Hank learned audience appeal from him, and he honed it to perfection. At his best, there never was a performer with more appeal to an audience than Hank Williams.

Whether or not Hank picked up any songs *per se* from Tee-tot is open to conjecture. Some people say he did. His father, for instance, says he learned both "My Bucket's Got a Hole in It" and "I Can't Buy No Likker" from the black. Perhaps so. In any event, there is no question that Tee-tot had a profound influence on Hank's style of playing and singing. That means he had a profound influence on his songwriting too, for Hank wrote songs with his own performing style very much in mind.

Although Hank received few formal "lessons" from Tee-tot, the street singer was constantly passing along the sort of tips (new chords or new runs or new versions of songs) one guitar player can give to another. Lilly Williams, who already had visions of her son as a professional musician, recognized the value of Tee-tot's instruction, and she treated him kindly. "He was rewarded with food from my kitchen," she later wrote.

According to Lilly, Tee-tot "just worshipped" young Hank. That is rather doubtful; more likely it was Hank who worshipped Tee-tot. But there was a warm personal relationship between black man and white boy, and it was so apparent that Tee-tot sometimes worried about it. "Little white boss," he would say, "these here white folks won't like me takin' so much keer a-you."

In later years, when he was urged to take music or guitar lessons, Hank refused. He would play his own way, he said, the way Tee-tot had taught him. And as big as he became in the music world, Hank never hesitated to credit the street singer with getting him started. When he was riding the crest in 1951, for instance, he told Montgomery *Advertiser* columnist Allen Rankin: "All the musical training I ever had was from him. . . . I never have read a note or written one. I can't. I don't know one note from another."

Hank didn't do much songwriting during this period, but he did do some. A Greenville schoolmate, Flora M. Heartsill, has recalled his writing this little ditty:

I had an old goat,
She ate tin cans.
When the little goats came,
They were Ford sedans.

Doggerel, yes, but with a certain imagination. Perhaps a great songwriting career is evident in those four lines.

All the while, Hank was becoming a performer. Never bashful, he now seemed positively anxious to perform. Taft Skipper recalls spending the night with the family in Greenville and Lilly "wanting us to listen to Hank sing and play. We did, and he was pretty good." He was also pretty set on what he wanted to be in life—a musician. From Greenville on, Hank seldom did any other kind of work.

4

On July 10, 1937, the Williamses moved again, this time to Montgomery, the first capital of the Confederacy. The financial picture was still cloudy at best, and Lilly figured a big city offered better possibilities. She also figured it offered a better chance for her musician son to build a professional career.

Montgomery, then a sleepy, arch-Southern city of seventy-five thousand, had at least two radio stations that broadcast live country music, WSFA and WCOV. It also had a number of night spots and theaters that featured the country sound, plus a constantly changing cast of musicians, forming and re-forming bands and serving as a grapevine for information on available jobs. Finally, Montgomery was the center of the bustling little music business that provided country bands to play at schools, dance halls, private parties, and so forth all around south and central Alabama. Clearly, it was the place for young Hank to be.

The family took up residence at 114 South Perry Street, the site of the present county health department. Lilly immediately turned it into a boardinghouse and dropped most of her sideline occupations to try to make it a success. Irene went into the pre-packaged lunch business. She made lunches each morning and sold them around town—at the fire station, at the police station, at the old Montgomery curb market. She also sold cosmetics door to door.

Hank kept on with his shoe-shining and peanut selling. But they were occupying less and less of his time now, while music was occupying more and more. One sure sign was his trading in the old $3.50 guitar Lilly had gotten him in Greenville. The new instrument was a good one, a Gibson with a sunburst finish; that is, stained dark except for a yellowish-orange "sunburst" on the top. Hank was very proud of the new guitar, and was certain, as all guitarists are, that it improved his playing at least a few hundred per cent. Lilly had to pay some cash on the trade-in deal, so the Gibson became Hank's Christmas present for that year.

Montgomery's Empire Theater, in those days, ran a regular amateur night. Hank had seldom been in a theater to watch a movie, let alone to perform. But he'd written a song called the "WPA Blues," and he decided to sing it at the Empire's amateur night.

Decked out in boots and a cowboy hat and toting his Gibson sunburst, Hank took the stage at the Empire. His song was no masterpiece (it has never been published), but the theme really hit home. The crowd grinned and clapped delightedly as the skinny youngster sang:

> I got a home in Montgomery,
> A place I like to stay.
> But I have to work for the WPA,
> And I'm dissatisfied—I'm dissatisfied.

Hank won first prize that night—the magnificent sum of fifteen dollars. It was more money than he'd ever had in his life. It didn't stay with him long, just as it didn't years later when the sums were reckoned in the thousands. He blew the whole fifteen dollars on an impromptu celebration, treating all his friends. That was to become another Hank Williams' trait; as long as there was money, Hank always spent it freely.

" 'WPA Blues,' " his mother later said, "was the first song Hank ever composed. How little did the crowd know, the truthfulness and sincerity in the words to that song! Hank had had the WPA blues so long that the song was a cry of despair. . . . And the crowd loved it —as they have ever since. They loved it because it was not only Hank's cry, but that of their own and of the people they knew and loved. Hank won the contest. He had discovered the secret. And he never let it go."

Hank himself once told columnist Allen Rankin his basic songwriting rule was, "If you're gonna sing, sing 'em something they can understand."

Hank followed up his Empire Theater success with a visit to radio station WSFA. He auditioned for a singing spot and got one, on a program featuring Dad Crysel's band. "The Singing Kid," he was dubbed. Before long, he had a program of his own, a twice-weekly, fifteen-minute segment on which he strummed his guitar and sang country songs. The two shows together paid only fifteen dollars, but getting them was by far the most important thing that had happened in his budding musical career.

WSFA was Montgomery's premier station, with a signal that carried across the southern half of Alabama and into neighboring states. Its programs created a demand for the entertainers featured on them, giving those entertainers a ready-made audience for in-person appearances—"show dates," as they are called in the business. When he began singing on WSFA, the name Hank Williams began meaning something to the folks in Evergreen and Monroeville and Troy, and that, in turn, meant a great deal to him.

The boys in Dad Crysel's band were not unhappy to see Hank get his own show. They got so many requests for him to sing they didn't have time to play their own numbers.

Hank's favorite songs were Roy Acuff numbers. Acuff, the "Smoky Mountain Boy," who wrote such country classics as "Wabash Cannonball" and "The Great Speckled Bird," was just then making a name for himself around Knoxville. Anything Acuff sang, Hank sang too, belting it out in his best imitation of the intense Acuff style. A bass player-comedian named Shorty Seals used to sing duets with Hank on the show. Hank carried the melody and Shorty a wailing country harmony.

In those days every country singer worth anything, and many who weren't, had his own band. A band, with its fiddler and steel guitar player and comedy acts, made a much more attractive and salable package than a lone singer with a guitar. So Hank Williams, at the age of thirteen, formed a band. A string band, it was called, because, as in almost all country music groups, there are no horns or drums or reed instruments, just stringed instruments of one sort or another.

To form his string band, Hank got together with another aspiring young musician, Smith Adair, who went by the nickname "Hezzy." Yielding to his fascination with things Western, he gave the band the name Drifting Cowboys. It proved a happy choice, for Drifting Cowboys remained the name of Hank's band right to the end. (The name has become so popular and so strongly identified with Williams that the men who played under it in Nashville regrouped under it later, sixteen years after his death.)

One picture taken in the WSFA studio of an early Drifting Cowboys band shows four fresh and self-conscious faces posing, instruments at the ready, for the camera. With the exception of the middle-aged fiddle player, Mexican Charlie Mays, they were all young. There was a small stocky bass player, Shorty Seals; a "steel man," Boots Harris, with the same skinny face, stick-out ears, and prominent Adam's apple as Hank himself; a well-built, dark-haired, rather handsome lead guitarist, Indian Joe Hatcher; and Hank Williams, standing a head taller than the others in cowboy boots and fancy trousers with a stripe down the side. The fancy Western uniforms the band later wore were not in evidence. The boys in those days were lucky to be able to afford a pair of cheap boots and a cowboy hat.

Hank did not use the band all the time. On the radio shows, he usually appeared alone, just strumming his guitar and singing. But for his show dates, he invariably brought along the Drifting Cowboys.

They played schoolhouses, hoedowns, barbecues, parties, and what were loosely called honky-tonks— roadhouses or dance halls, mostly, where boozing and brawling were as much a part of the evening as dancing. Irene Williams was Hank's first manager. She soon gave way to Lilly, who, with her characteristic drive, worked hard at the job. She booked the show dates, made sure the band got to them on time (often driving the car herself) and, most important, collected the gate receipts.

Admission to a show, whether a school program or Saturday night dance at a honky-tonk, was usually a quarter. Lilly either collected the admission money or stayed close by the person who did, and she was un-compromising in her insistence that everybody pay. "Aunt Lilly wouldn't even let us relatives in the door unless we paid," says J. C. McNeil ruefully. "She controlled the money."

Adds McNeil: "Aunt Lilly was a tough woman. Everybody's always lookin' for money, I know, but she was lookin' for more than that. She wanted to make something out of Hank, for his own sake. She knew if she didn't push him, he'd never make it."

A number of the musicians who played with Hank in his Montgomery days take a less charitable view of Lilly. They see her as a domineering, grasping mother interested in "making something" out of her son more for what it would do for her than for him. "She had an interest in Hank, all right," Sammy Pruett, a Drifting Cowboy almost continuously after 1944, says bluntly. "None of us dug her too damn much." Reminded that some people think Lilly really made Hank's career, Pruett snorts, "Bull shit."

The question of Lilly Williams' motives may never be answered conclusively. While she did want to capitalize on her son financially, she also desperately wanted him to make it big for a couple of less obvious reasons: to prove that a Williams really could amount to something in the world and to make her own years of sacrifice worthwhile. Through his Montgomery years, as well as later, Hank was essentially an emotionally immature person. He needed someone to help him from one step to the next, and Lilly was the helper. The most judicious judgment seems to be that although she did not make her son's career, she did give it a firm push.

What sort of show did those early Drifting Cowboys put on? A pretty good one. Although it was built around music, there was comedy too, corny stuff by today's standards but real gut-busting humor in the South of a quarter-century ago. Hank became, in his middle teens, an accomplished master of ceremonies, able to introduce the members of the band and keep up a patter between songs.

He also became a journeyman performer on a couple of other instruments. He learned to saw out a tune on the fiddle, and he learned the rudiments of the steel guitar. Although he never excelled at either the fiddle or the steel, and dropped them altogether when he became a star, they served a purpose in the early days. They helped Hank establish an identity in country music, where versatility in a performer is much admired.

Musically, the Drifting Cowboys band followed the wellworn paths of earlier country ensembles. It played a mixture of Nashville creations and what today is called folk music, that is, songs of obscure origin handed down from one generation to the next. There were lively, blue-grassy numbers, songs of lost love, humorous ditties, hymns of widely varying tempo and taste ("sacred songs," these are reverently called in the trade). There was also a smattering of songs by Hank himself; later, his own songs would comprise the great majority of those sung on every program.

The whole repertoire was treated in traditional fashion. The rhythms, 2/4 or 4/4 with an occasional waltz beat thrown in, were carried chunk-chunk by the bass and Hank's backup guitar. The lead guitarist played occasional breaks plus a variety of fancy runs and flourishes, while the steel guitarist and fiddler ventured a solo whenever they felt up to it. Nobody tried to be musically inventive. It would have been silly to try. Country music of the Nashville type is highly stylized, and the paying customers would be disappointed, to say the least, if it was presented in an unconventional way. Besides, Hank and the boys were trying to learn their chosen trade, and the best way is by copying, not altering, the material.

"Those boys were hard down good, I'll tell you," recalls the Reverend Oscar Cardwell, the late-blooming preacher from Georgiana. "They came to our place one time when the fellers gathered for music. Seemed like they were all teen-agers in the band, but they made the rest of us feel like sure-nuff country boys." Cardwell's own band wailed away at "Ragtime Annie," "Eighth of January," and "other good old fast numbers," while the Drifting Cowboys played slower, smoother stuff as well. Hank awed the old-timers with his singing: "We wasn't singing much, but he sang all night long."

Was there any drinking going on? "Everybody drank some at those affairs," says Cardwell. "I remember a time me and the band was out in an old car, with our instruments and a big tall jug. The car ran off into a ditch, spilling us and everything else out. We were half loaded already, so we just sat in the middle of the road with our jug and played music till somebody come along. We got 'em to help us lift our car out of the ditch, and we went on our way."

In their travels around south and central Alabama,

Hank and Hezzy and the boys tried to make it back to Montgomery after each show date. It was cheaper that way. When they couldn't get back, they stayed with somebody's kinfolk. On a couple of occasions they spent the night with Ed Skipper, the "Uncle Ed" who Hank had loved to visit as a boy around Georgiana.

"One time the boys played a theater in Evergreen and didn't have enough to go to a hotel," says Taft Skipper. "We put 'em up as best we could, although we were just livin' in a three-room apartment. Three or four of 'em slept on mattresses in the apartment, and Hank slept in the car. It couldn't have been too easy on him, 'cause he was as big right then as he ever got."

One of the band's favorite spots for show dates was Thigpen's Log Cabin, a dance hall located just outside Georgiana. It was run by Fred Thigpen, the Ford dealer, who had seen a lot of Hank as a boy and wanted to help him succeed as a musician. The Log Cabin is now a black night club, a low estate in the eyes of Georgiana's whites, but in those days, says Thigpen proudly, "it was the most famous place in this part of Alabama. It was a classy club. We advertised on the radio, and we had a lot of name bands. One time we even had Wayne King."

Hank and Hezzy and the Drifting Cowboys were not one of the Log Cabin's top attractions. They filled the dates Thigpen couldn't fill with better known bands. There were plenty of those, and the Drifting Cowboys did well at the place. "I give Hank everything he made," says Thigpen, "and I fed him too. I'd just collect the money and turn it over to him, or to his mother when she was along. He made plenty out of it, 'cause he usually drew a full house, being a local boy and all."

At Thigpen's Log Cabin and elsewhere on the honky-tonk circuit, a musician had to be tough and resourceful to survive. The typical dance hall devotee, once he got boozed up, was spoiling for a fight. An entertainer needed quick fists or swift legs or a beguiling tongue, or all three.

The problem was booze. None of the counties in

which the Drifting Cowboys played served liquor by the drink, and not many of them sold it by the bottle. The Bible Belt didn't, and still doesn't, approve of such a straightforward approach to the consumption of alcohol. But bootleg whisky, thanks to the traditional alliance between bootleggers and preachers, was for sale almost everywhere. So was moonshine.

Butler County, for instance, was legally dry, but bootleg stuff was available to anyone with the wits to ask for it at a gas station outside Georgiana. The cheapest whisky, and the kind most popular with the younger set, was "spot bottle," so called because of the identifying dot on the label. It was bottled in bond, which meant you probably wouldn't die or go blind, and it came in pints and half pints, perfect for drinkers of limited means.

The social code at the honky-tonks, reflecting the social code of most of the rural South, demanded sneak drinking. A man could get falling down drunk, but the whisky must not be seen in public. As at the lumber camp dances, therefore, it was secreted in sundry hiding places outside the honky-tonks: under the seats of cars, in bushes and the crooks of trees, in the drainpipe or the tall grass. Between dances the young bucks, and their more adventurous dates, would stroll outside to enjoy a snort or two. Occasionally booze got into the dance hall itself. The vehicle was sometimes a hidden flask, more often a soft drink bottle that carried an air of legitimacy. A favorite trick was to buy a Coca-Cola, drink half of it, fill the other half up with whisky and bring it back in to the dance. Whatever method was employed, slipping the thirst outside or slipping the thirst quencher inside, the result was the same: toward the end of the evening, a few patrons invariably got out of hand.

When the musicians were lucky, the fights stayed around the dance floor and away from the stage. The musicians were a highly visible group, however, so it was quite natural for the nasty types to include them as targets.

Hank had a way of becoming one of the targets. Maybe it was because he was the leader of the band. "I had to ruin some fairly good guitars over people's heads," he said in later years. That was the fate of his second guitar, the Gibson sunburst. The band was playing a dance hall in Fort Deposit, and at 1 A.M. they called it a night and started putting away their instruments. One of the patrons wanted the dance to go on, and he came at Hank with a knife to put his point across. Hank bashed him over the head with the guitar, then climbed out the window.

"I'm sorry, Mama," he told Lilly when he got home that night, "but it was either get the guitar broke or my head broke, so I picked the guitar."

Several years later, Hank broke another guitar in an act of self-defense. Again it was in Fort Deposit. A burly farmer got a snootful of moonshine and told his wife to quit yammering about what a great singer Hank Williams was. Then he turned toward Hank, sitting innocently on the bandstand, and declared, "I'm going to knock my wife's brains out next time I hear her listening to your bellowing on the radio."

"I don't blame you, friend, " replied Hank, trying to pacify the man.

"On second thought," said the farmer, "stand up and I'll knock *your* brains out right now."

Hank stood up—the better to swing his guitar. "Durn it," he said later, "I ruint a perfectly good twenty-five-dollar instrument on that fella's head."

Hank gave up using his hands for self-defense after he broke them a couple of times. A broken hand cuts a musician off from work for weeks. Guitars were costly too, however. Hank solved the problem neatly on one occasion by wielding the heavy steel bar used to fret the steel guitar. The trouble was, the intervention of a sympathizer almost got him into deep trouble.

"Hank was beatin' the guy on the temple with the bar," says Drifting Cowboy Sammy Pruett, "when another local guy, coming to Hank's assistance, almost cut the first guy in two. He had to hold his guts in.

They took Hank into court the next day, but the judge
let him off. Hell, it wasn't his fault."

On another occasion, the steel bar let him down, to a
point where it cost him a chunk of his eyebrow. As
Hank told the story years later, a man at a dance hall
who'd been baiting him all night finally grabbed him,
and the two of them tumbled onto the dance floor.
Hank had been playing steel guitar, so he still had the
bar in his hand. "I was poundin' him on the head with
the steel bar," Hank said, "and he was about to go
under. One more good blow woulda done it. But he
reached out and bit a plug outta my eyebrow, hair and
all." Hank bore the scar from that little tiff for the rest
of his life.

One of his closest calls occurred when he flattened
an assailant with a tire tool outside a dance hall. The
man wound up in critical condition, and the local authorities were determined to try Hank for murder if he
died. Fortunately, the man lived, and Hank was able
to wheedle his way out of a sticky situation.

When steel guitarist Don Helms and a couple of his
buddies joined the Drifting Cowboys in 1941, Hank's
first move was to provide them with portable protection.
"Follow me," said the leader. He went to a nearby
pawnshop and bought a blackjack for each new man.
"If you're gonna work in the joints I work in," he explained, "you'll need these." Helms was only fourteen
years old, which indicates how early a boy became a
man in the south Alabama of those days. "Those
joints," he recalls with a certain fondness, "were the
kinds of places where they sweep up the eyeballs every
morning."

The rough-housing in the honky-tonks convinced
Hank they were no place for a musician to play.
"People don't come to honky-tonks to listen to music,"
he complained. "They come to fight."

In later years Hank carried this policy a step further.
He refused to sing his sacred songs, or hymns, in places
where whisky was being consumed, and he got upset
when he heard them played on the jukebox in such

places. Roy Acuff felt the same way. "I won't sing a religious number when people are drinking," he said in 1953, after his show closed prematurely at New York's Hotel Astor Roof.

Young Hank always made it a point to see Acuff when his hero came to Montgomery for a show. "I guess in a way he idolized me as a country artist," says Acuff matter-of-factly. "He'd usually come by my dressing room, sit around, sing songs and play the guitar. He was just a little fellow, and he just hunkered around in the corner, waiting for a chance to sing. He'd sing some of my songs and sometimes one of his."

Was Acuff impressed? "Yes, in that he didn't try to copy anybody much. I guess he copied me more than anybody, but he was developing a style of his own."

Acuff took an interest in Hank. He occasionally stopped by the honky-tonks where the young man was working. "I'd sing with him sometime in those places." Why? "Well, I wasn't as big then as I am now, and I didn't have a lot of other businesses like I have now. I used to go out and listen to quite a few of the younger artists."

Consciously or unconsciously, Hank developed a style of singing containing elements of the distinctive Acuff style. As Acuff says, "We were especially similar in presenting songs. Each of us had a type of cry in our voice, and we sang with a lot of energy and feeling."

On stage and off, Hank was the prototype of the country singer. He talked slow and easy and made homey jokes. There was nothing phony about it, and his listeners knew that. He always dressed in the Western manner, not just because Nashville stars did so but because he'd been hung up on cowboys since childhood. At the age of seventeen, he even ran away to Texas to join a rodeo. All he got out of it was an injured back. The story is that he got half drunk, climbed aboard a bronc, and promptly got tossed. His back bothered him from then on. The injury led to a couple of operations and, eventually, to the steady consumption of pain pills.

It was in Montgomery, at about this time, that Hank composed his first serious songs. Few of them were ever published or recorded, but they taught him the techniques of songwriting. In addition, they helped him build a name in the country music field.

He turned out large numbers of songs, hoping to work them into his show on WSFA. "I used to write a new song each week and take it up to one of the program directors and sing it," he recalled later. "He'd say, 'Not good enough, boy.'" So Hank would sing the songs of Acuff and other established writers for another week. Meanwhile, he'd keep writing himself. Gradually, his own songs filled a larger and larger place in his repertoire.

The early songs were mostly sad, and they fell into the time-honored Nashville pattern—laments for unrequited love. Hank learned quickly, perhaps instinctively, that this was the theme to follow. "You know what makes songs, Mama?" he told his mother at age seventeen. "Love. It's love that makes the best songs."

If love was important, so was speed, especially when a fellow was trying to establish himself. Hank was quick with a new song. "He could compose a new song the quickest of anybody I ever knew," says a musician who played with him in the early days of the Drifting Cowboys. He remained, even in the days when he was turning out million sellers, an inspiration writer. He seldom labored over a song. He much preferred grabbing an idea and running with it. To him, songwriting was always an emotional, not an intellectual, exercise.

At least three songs from that period have survived. They typify the nondescript sort of stuff Hank was writing in his late teens. One is "Never Again [Will I Knock on Your Door]." It was a lilting waltz beat and a set of unimaginative, platitudinous lyrics. Then there is "I Don't Care [If Tomorrow Never Comes]," another song of lost love, with lyrics on a par with "Never Again." The best song from this period, and the one that had the greatest commercial acceptance, is "Six

More Miles," a maudlin number about accompanying "my darlin' " the six miles to her grave.

"Six More Miles" resembles an old Carter Family song, "Will the Circle Be Unbroken," a somber but highly singable number about a young man watching his mother's casket being taken away. ("Undertaker, undertaker, undertaker please drive slow/For that body you are haulin', Lord I hate to see her go. . . . Will the circle be unbroken/Bye and bye, Lord, bye and bye/There's a better home a-waitin'/In the sky, Lord, in the sky.") Hank probably knew that song, for the Carter Family was very popular in those days.

Country boys like Hank often sold songs, for whatever price they would bring. There was a good market in selling to name performers, who were always on the lookout for new songs as they traveled around playing show dates. Hank did some selling and some buying too, and it is probably true that a few of the songs he later published were reworked versions of songs he bought around Montgomery.

J. C. McNeil recalls being with Hank when he shopped for songs. The seller would come to his mother's boardinghouse, and Hank would listen critically while the song was played and sung. "People were callin' him on the phone all the time," says McNeil, "wantin' to sell him songs. I remember two-three guys came out to the house one day, but he didn't take any of the things they offered."

Perhaps the best song he ever sold was "Prayin' for the Day When Peace Will Come." He sold it to Pee Wee King, then an established star, when King came through Montgomery during the war. There are different stories about how much Hank received for it. One version says seventy-five dollars, which sounds much higher that the going rates. Comedienne Minnie Pearl says authoritatively it was ten dollars.

"I was with Pee Wee's band, and we'd gone to Dothan, Alabama, to do a show," says Minnie. "We went to the country radio station—it was a dreary day—and there was a man sitting there in an old beat-up cowboy hat, old boots, and a beat-up brown suit. It was Hank Williams. He wanted to sell a song. 'I'm prayin' for the day . . .' it went. He was obviously down on his luck, and Pee Wee bought it from him for ten dollars.

Minnie Pearl, who later became a good friend of Hank's, wasn't particularly impressed by the song or the fact that the writer wanted to sell it: "You run into lots of writers like that all along the line." But she was impressed by Hank. "Especially his eyes. He had the most haunting and haunted eyes I'd ever looked into. They were deep-set, very brown, and very tragic."

5

Hank had just gotten decently started in the music business when he ran up against two powerful forces— a woman and whisky. They were to become, together with his music, the strongest influences in his life.

For all his songs about love and heartbreak, young Hank had never formed romantic attachments with girls. He liked what they could provide, sex, but his emotions rarely went beyond that. Nobody recalls him even having a steady girl friend through his early and mid-teens.

All that changed when he met a girl named Audrey Mae Sheppard. She was a tall, rawboned, wavy-haired blonde, six months older than Hank. She had a long, angular face, rather like Hank's, and a prominent nose and mouth. Yet she was pretty in a country fashion. And, down inside, she bore an ambition that was to make Hank's life both successful and difficult.

Audrey was from the Enon community, several miles east of the little town of Banks, which is in turn about fifty miles southeast of Montgomery. She was the daughter of C. S. (for Charley Shelton) Sheppard, a farmer who, like his father and grandfather before him, scratched a living out of the south Alabama soil. Charley Sheppard raised cotton, peanuts, cows, and hogs and found it "pretty tough going" trying to raise a family too.

He had three daughters (a son died at the age of ten), and Audrey was the oldest. She got part way through high school before quitting. She was married in her teens to a local boy named Erskine Guy, who was about eighteen and helped his father farm. Audrey and Erskine had a daughter, Lycrecia, but their marriage lasted only a few years. They were divorced in early December 1944, in Audrey's home county of Pike. She retained custody of the child.

Audrey got a job in a drugstore in the town of Brundage. It wasn't long before she found another man —Hank Williams.

Hank and Audrey, the story goes, met at a medicine show in the town of Banks. Hank was selling patent medicine, and Audrey was a passer-by who succumbed to his manly charm. Ed Linn, in a 1957 article called "The Short Life of Hank Williams," tells the story this way:

"He was working as a musician-shill in a medicine show at Banks. . . . One day Audrey Sheppard, a tall, striking blonde, happened to be riding by with her aunt. Since neither had ever seen a medicine show, they decided to stop. After the show was out of the way, the owner put on his pitch, then sent his entertainers into the audience to peddle his nostrum.

"When he got to Audrey's car, Hank forgot his sponsor's product and went into business for himself. His sales pitch was good enough to get a date for the following afternoon. . . ."

However and wherever the two met, it is certain Hank quickly became infatuated with Audrey. Just why he did mystified his close friends. "Hank would always make a girl if he could," remarks one, "and he started

after Audrey. I can't figure out why he got so attached
to her, but it was like no other woman in the world
had one of those things."

At the outset, Audrey was somewhat less enchanted
with Hank. She was a little put off by his sloppy manner and his habit of getting drunk now and again. "If
you're going to go with me," she told him, "you're
going to have to leave whisky alone."

"Hank stayed on the wagon for a couple of weeks,"
wrote Linn in the *Saga* magazine profile. "Then, while
they were driving through town on one of their daily
afternoon dates, he asked her to stop the car. 'Audrey,'
he said, 'get me a bottle.' She refused.

"The next day . . . she found him drunk. That was
the way it went."

Audrey convinced Hank she was a singer, and before
long she joined the Drifting Cowboys as the female
vocalist. She wasn't much good, but Hank at that time
didn't care. He was crazy about the girl, and singing
with her, in front of an audience, for money, must have
seemed like paradise.

One Saturday night in December 1944, when they
were playing a show date in Andalusia, Hank and
Audrey decided to get married. The ceremony was
performed in a rural filling station by the station owner,
who served as a justice of the peace on the side. A
couple of the Drifting Cowboys acted as witnesses, and
the whole party had to pool its funds to pay the J.P.
Lilly Williams wasn't along on that trip, so she knew
nothing of her son's wedding until the couple returned
to the boardinghouse the next day.

The marriage ceremony apparently was invalid, because court records, in Pike and Covington counties,
show that Audrey wed Hank only ten days after her
divorce from Erskine Guy became final. Alabama law
requires at least a sixty-day waiting period, and the
requirement is printed on Audrey's divorce decree.
However, Alabama's permissive common law marriage
statute grants common law status to a man and woman
who merely live together and hold each other out as

husband and wife, with no minimum time period required; so there never was any real question that Hank and Audrey were "married."

The Williamses took up residence at Lilly's boardinghouse in Montgomery. Other members of the band stayed there too, some on a regular basis. It was an old, two-story frame house at the edge of the downtown area. Sparsely furnished but inexpensive, it attracted the usual cross section of boardinghouse clients. There were laborers and shop clerks. There were single girls, with and without visible means of support. There were loners and losers and rummies.

Lilly ruled this brood with a firm hand, taking no crap from nobody. One of her boarders recalls her as being "a heavy Marjorie Main. She was loud and a little overbearing, and she had a kind of fanatical religious crust."

Although Lilly liked Audrey, she tried to maintain her control and influence over her son. She still went along on many of the show dates, acting as a combined money collector and den mother. And she still came in for a share of the earnings. As Hank got older and more sure of himself, Lilly's share got less predictable. Within two or three years after his marriage, Lilly was getting no set figure or percentage, just whatever Hank agreed to give her.

Sometimes the division of spoils between mother and son led to heated disputes. "Lilly was a horrible woman" says a Montgomery man who knew the family. "She and Hank fought like cats, physically as well as verbally. When he came in drunk after playing a date, she'd roll him for his money, then accuse him of getting rolled by a girl. Then they'd have it out, and sometimes Hank would wind up smashing her."

Hank's fights with his mother were symptomatic of his growing resentment of her. She had dominated his life for years, and now that he was starting to make it on his own, he was trying to throw off the domination. He always retained a strong feeling of dependency toward his mother, but from the Montgomery days onward that feeling had to compete with one of resentment.

Concerned as she was about Hank's money, Lilly was more concerned about his drinking. Still in his mid-teens, Hank was becoming a chronic drinker. His mother tried to reason, wheedle, and shake it out of him, but she did not succeed.

Why did alcohol get a foothold with Hank when it did? His moonshine revelries back in Fountain could not have been responsible, not unless one accepts the theory that persons with an innate craving for alcohol are sure to become alcoholics once they taste it. The hectic, free-wheeling life of the honky-tonk musician is more to blame; drinking was a natural by-product of that sort of life. But the main reason has to be Hank's basic emotional deficiencies. He was proving himself incapable, even at early age, of coping with his life and problems in a straightforward fashion.

Hank set his drinking pattern early. He drank sporadically, with long, intermittent dry spells. When he got going, however, he seldom stopped until he was either unconscious or too drunk to lift the glass. That state did not take long to achieve, for Hank had a small alcohol capacity. He flew high on a couple of drinks, and a couple more usually finished him.

J. C. McNeil remembers seeing Hank drunk on numerous occasions during the early years in Montgomery. "Sometimes it would take him a couple of weeks to get over it," says McNeil. "He'd go two, three months without any trouble, and then he'd do it again. Hank would pile up in his room at the boardinghouse, and Aunt Lilly would try to taper him off. It got to the point where, if there was no other way, she'd get old Dr. Black to give him some kind of shot."

In those days, Hank was a friendly drinker. He loved to booze it up with the boys, usually the members of the band but often McNeil and other relatives who happened to be around. "Whisky was so much easier to come by in Montgomery," says McNeil. "Back in

Fountain a half cup of shine woulda knocked us for a row of stumps. But in Montgomery it was all around us, and we got to handle it better."

Perhaps the other boys did, but not Hank. He never did learn to handle it. The one thing he did get out of booze was a few songs. "He was more of a genius drunk than sober," chuckles McNeil. "He'd lay in bed drinking, and he'd call Irene and probably Audrey and quote songs to 'em." Oftentimes, the alcohol-inspired songs stood up under later inspection, and this persuaded Hank that his muse performed better under the influence. This pattern changed a few years later, when Hank, although drinking more than ever, decided it and writing did not mix.

Hank's group favored whisky—bonded stuff, now that they were out of the moonshine area—with Coke as a chaser. They drank some beer too, though Hank did not develop a real taste for it until later. There were no frills or amenities. A swig from the whisky bottle was followed by a swig from the Coke bottle. The trick was to get drunk but stay sober enough to get your share of the bottle.

One time in the early 1940s, Lon Williams, not long out of the veterans hospital, came up to Montgomery to see his son. He was surprised to find him in "a drinkin' place," getting loaded on beer. "I done my best to talk to him," says Lon, who says he himself hasn't touched a drop for over twenty years. "I never did buy him whisky." He didn't have to. Hank made out very nicely on beer.

On another occasion, Lon recalls proudly, Audrey called him in Butler County and asked his help. "She said she couldn't do nothin' with him—'he'll pay attention to you when he won't to me.' We paid a man ten dollars to run him down here. I give him a little wine to try to sober him up. It didn't really work. When he got up, he went up the road to the bootlegger's and got some more skinny. Miss Audrey and his mother come back and got him before he was sober." (Lon carefully distinguishes between the Audrey of those days and the

Audrey of today. In references to her then she is "Miss Audrey"; now she is "that woman.")

Lon saw Hank only occasionally after that, usually in the same boozy circumstances. "If he'd take a notion to get drunk and lay up here, I'd take care of him," says Lon. A sad father-son relationship, indeed, but understandable in light of a broken marriage and an imbalanced childhood.

All the while, the Drifting Cowboys were changing, mostly for the better. New members came and went, and the band gradually took on a more professional tone. The most significant additions were Don Helms, who joined the Drifting Cowboys in 1941, and Sammy Pruett, who came a couple of years later. Both were with the band during Hank's glory years in Nashville.

Helms, a handsome, blond-haired native of New Brockton, Alabama, was the son of a country fiddler. He learned to play fiddle and guitar, switched to steel guitar and formed his own band. At the age of fourteen, when he joined the Drifting Cowboys, he was already an accomplished steel man and a veteran of the honky-tonks, playing with a band called the Alabama Rhythm Boys.

One of the Alabama Rhythm Boys who knew Hank went to Montgomery to talk to him about prospects in the big city. Hank must have been unhappy with his current batch of Drifting Cowboys, for he agreed to hire the Rhythm Boys band intact. Helms quit school and came to Montgomery as part of the group.

Pruett came in through Helms. Helms had left the band to become a welder in the shipyards in Panama City, Florida. There he met Pruett, a native of Goodwater, south of Birmingham. Pruett knew only a few chords on the guitar and had never played professionally, but he and Helms began playing together for fun. When they heard that Hank was again looking for musicians, they quit their shipyards jobs and headed for Montgomery. With them was a bass and guitar player named Curly Corbin. Hank hired them all: Helms in his old job as steel man, Corbin as bass player, and Pruett, who was still rather unskilled, as a backup guitarist.

By this time, Hank, with a big assist from Lilly, had become a small-time businessman-band leader. Although he didn't make much in the way of profit, he kept his musicians on salary and took care of the band's expenses. The boys got five dollars apiece when they played a show date, which was three or four times a week; the shows usually lasted four hours. They also got room and board at Lilly's place if they wanted it. For obvious reasons, most of them did, but Pruett usually went home to Goodwater between jobs. "I could run back and forth on the bus for sixty cents," he recalls. "I made it okay on fifteen or twenty bucks a week. Hell, I had no expenses other than cigarettes."

They played the same places Hank had been playing since he formed the Drifting Cowboys a few years earlier: Greenville, Andalusia, Fort Deposit, Enterprise; dance halls, schoolhouses, honky-tonks of every description. The owner of the place got fifteen to twenty per cent of the gate receipts, Hank got the rest. Out of this, Hank had to pay the boys' salaries, the travel expenses, the lodging expenses at his mother's boardinghouse.

He also had to pay for his own failures to show up, which were becoming noticeably frequent. He would get loaded and have to spend the next few days drying out; in the process, several show dates might come and go. The band usually carried on without him, but the gate would be off and, worse, the manager or promoter would be reluctant to sign the boys up for additional shows.

When Hank was available, the Drifting Cowboys put on a good show. It invariably opened with a country fiddle tune, backed by guitar rhythm. Fiddlers drifted in and out of the band. When there was none, Hank himself did the fiddling. "He wasn't very good, but he had enough showmanship to carry it off," says Sammy Pruett. Then Hank would sing a couple of songs—he did all the solos—with the boys in the band sometimes coming in on the choruses.

Hank was the undisputed star of the show. The other boys, except when they played an instrumental solo, were strictly backup men. The one exception was the bass player, who doubled as a comedian. This dual role gave him special status, and no show was complete without a couple of routines from the bassist-comedian. Dressed in an outlandish uniform featuring baggy britches, he hammed it up throughout the show, with Hank and the other band members playing straight men and leading the laughs.

During one stretch, the bass player had a third function. That was when Cannonball Nichols filled the job. He was a part-time wrestler, which qualified him as protector of band members and instruments when the honky-tonk fights started. "He couldn't play bass for nothin'," says one of the old Drifting Cowboys. "But we kept him 'cause he knew some half nelsons. That gave the rest of us time to get the hell off the stage."

"It was fun in those days," says Helms. "We were doing something we'd always wanted to do and getting paid for it. Besides, it was a way out of working on a farm. I think we all felt, once we got out of the country, that if we ever had anything to do with a mule, it'd be to his damned face!"

For Hank Williams, however, it had to be more than fun. He'd been a serious performer, a professional, for several years, and he was trying to make it big. Proceeds of a couple hundred bucks in Andalusia or Enterprise didn't look very big. He was popular on WSFA, but apparently not popular enough to propel him on to greater things—the Louisiana Hayride in Shreveport, say, or the Barn Dance in Chicago or the Mecca of country music, the Grand Ole Opry itself. He was drawing as many as three hundred fan letters a day, but they produced neither money nor job offers. "You can't eat fan letters, Mama," he complained, "not even with ketchup on 'em."

Besides, the life he was leading was grinding him

down. There was too much hell raising, too many boozy blasts followed by too many layoffs while he sobered up. To his credit, Hank stayed in school through much of this time. He graduated from Abraham Baldwin Junior High School in Montgomery and went on to Sidney Lanier High School. He lasted only a few weeks at Lanier, quitting in the fall of his sophomore year. He was nineteen years old at the time, so his progress obviously had been halting.

In fact, Hank's classroom performance was never better than sub-par. He was not bright and he had little interest in the subjects taught in school. He seems to have been particularly immune to instruction in English. His grammar was bad throughout his life, and his pronunciation was not much better. He said "winder" for window, "hep" for help, "pitcher" for picture. Country musicians sometimes talk that way to add color to their act, but with Hank it was no put on.

What prompted Hank to drop out of school, however, was not so much the futility of his trying to cram an education into his head as the pressure of his life as a musician. He attended classes in Montgomery after staying up, playing and partying, most of the night before. That would have taxed a tough constitution, and for a frail young man like Hank it was too much. Something had to give, and school was the logical choice.

"I guess I kinda resisted formal education," he said ruefully in later years. "I picked and sang at night, and I reckon I must've slept through my classes."

Many Williams admirers are convinced the world is fortunate Hank did resist formal education, which might well have spoiled his great natural talent. There is a lot to that reasoning, though it smacks of the logic used by Mississippi's James K. Vardaman some seventy years ago in defending his refusal to educate the black. "Why squander money on his education," declared Vardaman, "when the only effect is to spoil a good field hand and make an insolent cook?"

Hank's health was also a factor in his decision to leave school. He was plagued by hookworm, a disease common to the rural South in those days, and his sister says it got so bad it impaired his vision.

By the fall of 1942, Hank was feeling depressed about his musical career. At nineteen, a veteran of six years of show business, he felt he was going nowhere. In addition, young musicians were getting called into the service, so he was having trouble keeping the Drifting Cowboys staffed with good people. In a single stroke, he quit high school and gave up the band. He then tried to enlist in the Army but was rejected because of the back injury he'd suffered trying to be a rodeo performer. In despair, he took a job at the Alabama Drydock and Shipbuilding Company in Mobile.

He started as a shipfitter's helper, one of the lowest positions at the yard. His pay was sixty-six cents an hour. It wasn't much, but at least it was steady; no more worrying about whether there'd be anything left after paying the band's expenses. After about six weeks, he was put into the welder training program. He became a welder and was making ninety-seven cents an hour when he quit.

Hank lived with an aunt in Mobile, and he kept a hand in country music while working at the yard. He played a number of little joints around the city but was not well known. Freddie Beach, a fiddle player who worked with Hank in Mobile, remembers him mainly for his determination to get back into entertainment full time and for his bad driving. "Hank went around in a 1935 Ford sedan," Beach says, "and it seemed like he was practically blind. I honestly don't think he had a driver's license."

Hank had some money in postal savings then, and he told Beach he had put it there to keep it away from his mother. "He said she was consistently taking money from him," says Beach. "I think that was really the reason Hank came to Mobile—to get away from her."

Lilly paints a different picture of the Mobile interlude. In her booklet, *Our Hank Williams,* she took credit for rescuing Hank from the shipyard and says he loved her for it. "I believed in Hank," Lilly wrote. "I knew he had what it took with his singing. So I rented a car and went to every schoolhouse and night club in the Montgomery area. I booked Hank solid for sixty days. Then the third week he had been 'out of the music business,' I went to Mobile and got him and put him back in it.

"When Hank saw the datebook for those shows he gave me the sweetest smile I've ever seen and said, 'Thank God, Mother. You have made me the happiest boy in the world.' "

Lilly is confused on time. If Hank did leave Mobile after three weeks, he came right back. Shipyard records show him working on and off at the yard until August of 1944, one year and nine months after he began. So his salvation, through Lilly or anybody else, did not come quickly.

Still, salvation did come, and that is the important thing. When Hank returned to Montgomery in 1944, it marked the end of his uncertainty. He never again deserted music.

6

Hank assembled another group of musicians under the name Drifting Cowboys and went back to work. When the war ended, guitarist Sammy Pruett rejoined the group. Steel guitarist Don Helms, also released from service, rejoined it soon after, and the band was again up to strength.

Things improved for Hank and the boys. Maybe it was the post-war boom, which provided money for such things as entertainment, or maybe the band was better. In any event, there were more, and more lucrative, show dates. Hank was paying the band members about ten dollars a day and giving them room and board at Lilly's place, yet he was managing to clear a good deal more money than before. It was, of course, still a risky business. "If it rained, or if there was a football game that night, we didn't draw as much," says Helms. "There were times when Hank didn't make anything. But a lot of times, after paying us, he'd come out with a hundred or a hundred fifty dollars." To Hank, that was really good money.

One of the band's regular dates was at a dance hall called the Journey's Inn in Camden, about sixty miles southwest of Montgomery. Hank's informal business dealings with the owner illustrates his ability to be a regular country boy and make a living too. The Journey's Inn had just opened (even the poverty-ridden Black Belt was being buoyed by the post-war prosperity) and was looking for entertainers. "Hank came by and we traded," reminisced the inn's owner, H. B. Hawthorne, after Hank's death. The band would play one night a week for dances, and Hank would plug the inn whenever he could; he did this on his WSFA show, by means of a song he dashed off called "The Journey's Inn Blues." Hawthorne, in return, guaranteed the band work and gave Hank a better-than-fair shake financially.

The normal split was eighty per cent for the band, twenty per cent for the inn, but Hawthorne boosted the band's share on bad nights. "Many a time the receipts were only about fifty dollars," wrote Hawthorne, "and I wouldn't take my cut out as I knew it cost them at least that much to come over from Montgomery and pay their expenses." Even on the fifty-dollar nights, Hank figured a job at the Journey's Inn was worth the long drive. It gave the band a showcase (it now would be called "exposure"), and besides, a little money was better than none.

Audrey Williams was very much part of the group. She took on some of Lilly's old tasks, such as arranging show dates, taking tickets, and handling the finances. She also sang and filled in on guitar when somebody didn't show up. In addition, when Hank was unable to appear, she made sure the rest of the band filled the date. On one occasion when Hank was absent, at the Journey's Inn, a patron tried to put the make on her. "She never gave him a look," according to H. B. Hawthorne. "My partner put him out of the building and told him to go home, which he did."

During this period, Hank began turning out songs on a fairly regular basis. Most of them were religious numbers. Hank, after his childhood, never demonstrated an interest in organized religion. But he had flashes of intense personal feeling about spiritual matters, which led to some of the finest songs he ever wrote. Further, he knew that "sacred songs" always find a ready market in country music.

"When God Comes and Gathers His Jewels" is a typical Williams product of the period. It sounds the themes of death and family sorrow, which always had great appeal for him. A haunting melody and a quite sophisticated metaphor—expressing death and ascension to heaven as a matter of God "gathering His jewels"—lift the song above banality.

Hank followed a standard country music theme in writing "Wealth Won't Save Your Soul." As the title implies, this is a warning to turn toward the Lord, and away from "earthly wealth," which will be "useless to you if you've strayed from the fold/For my friends it won't save your poor wicked soul."

There were also, of course, laments on the ageless problem of unrequited love. Hank was to write far better ones later, "Your Cheatin' Heart" and "Cold, Cold Heart," for instance, but the early, cruder pieces struck responsive chords in many a listener.

"My Love for You [Has Turned to Hate]" is an example. It reads like childish poetry, but in Hank's hands it doesn't sing that way. The secret is in the theme of the woman who done you wrong, which country music lovers have always found compelling, and in Hank's ability to bring the theme alive in performance. On record, he did it with the high, heart-breaking sound of his voice, which gave such songs a sense of real conviction. On stage, he added the personal magnetism of a born performer, particularly the "haunting and haunted eyes" that so impressed Minnie Pearl.

Through his songs and his relentless rounds of local show dates, Hank was attracting attention beyond the confines of south and central Alabama. Name musicians playing Montgomery were told to make sure they heard this kid Hank Williams. Sometimes they could hear him without going out of the auditorium, for Hank and his band were being booked on big shows as a supporting act. Their verdict was almost unanimous: the boy had talent and potential.

He also had the drinking problem, the same one he'd had for the past few years. He would go on a tear every so often and end up unconscious and unable to play his show dates. He missed some radio shows too, and the station had to fill in with transcriptions of previous shows. The word on all this got around quickly and before long most country music people who mentioned Hank also mentioned his problem. He was, they said, "unreliable."

"He was uncontrollable" says Oscar Davis, a Nashville-based promoter who handled a number of Montgomery shows on which Hank appeared. "One time I let him handle the advance ticket sales for a show. He got hold of the tickets and distributed them all over town—for his own benefit. It never got the money. He probably drank it up."

When Hank sang his "Me and My Broken Heart" on a show with headliner Ernest Tubb, Tubb was so impressed he told his manager: "That kid was the best thing in the show, including me. Let's sign him for the rest of the tour."

"Uh, uh," replied his manager. "Too undependable."

Tubb remembered Hank, and when he got back to Nashville he recommended him for a shot on the Grand Ole Opry. According to one story, Hank soon thereafter

was called to Nashville, where he auditioned for the
Opry and was rejected. That is highly doubtful. Hank
had a number of people pushing for him in Nashville,
but it is virtually certain that the first time he ever went
there he went unasked and got nowhere near the Opry.
He made contact, instead, with songwriter-publisher
Fred Rose—the most important contact of his life, leading to the Opry and beyond.

It was in the fall of 1946. The Drifting Cowboys
were making a go of the band business, and Hank was
making a modest name for himself as a songwriter. The
trouble was, he had never had a song published or recorded. In a backwater city like Montgomery in those
days, you couldn't do either without a lot of difficulty or
luck, or both. There were no Southern-based record companies. The only recording of country musicians was
done by a handful of men who took annual trips
through the South, hunting recordable, and salable,
talent; somehow, they had overlooked Hank Williams.
With one exception, the newly formed Acuff-Rose company in Nashville, there were no Southern-based music
publishers, and a writer's only chance was to send his
song North, where it was given a perfunctory and im-
personal hearing.

Hank rightly figured his best chance was with Acuff-
Rose, a young, aggressive outfit dealing in nothing but
country music. So he and Audrey traveled to Nashville.
They found Acuff-Rose president Fred Rose and his
son Wesley playing their regular noon game of ping-
pong at Nashville's WSM radio studio. "We were on
about our last game," recalls Wesley, who was then
general manager of Acuff-Rose and is now president,
"when a tall, skinny, sharp-featured kid came in with
a blond-haired woman. They looked like average country folks. The woman said, 'My husband would like to
sing you some songs.'

"It isn't normally done that way. I mean, you don't
just walk in cold and say, 'Let me sing you a song.'
My father turned to me and said, 'Have we got time?'

I said, 'Sure, why not.' It's lucky we had nothing more important to do than go to lunch.

"So we all went into one of the radio station's studios. Hank sang about six songs, all things he'd written. I don't remember for certain what they were, but I think 'When God Comes and Gathers His Jewels,' 'Six More Miles to the Graveyard,' and 'My Love for You [Has Turned to Hate]' were among them."

There is a story, widely told, that Fred Rose tested Hank's songwriting ability that fall day in Nashville by making him compose something on the spot. "The songs are good," the story has Rose telling Hank, "but how do I know you wrote them? Here, take this situation. There's a girl who marries a rich boy instead of the poor boy who lives in a cabin. Go in the room there and see if you can make a song out of that." Where-upon, Hank supposedly labored in solitude for a half hour and emerged with the song "A Mansion on the Hill," later one of his big hits.

A nice story, but not true. Rose needed no test to tell him Hank was a genuine songwriter, and a most promising one. He led Hank to his office and signed him to a contract as an Acuff-Rose writer. He also bought the half dozen songs Hank had sung at the impromptu audition. There was no thought at the time of Hank's recording them. Rose was looking for material for an established singer, Molly O'Day, and the songs were taken with her in mind.

So Hank was on his way, not as a singer but as a writer. It was a perfect way to start. He could not have found a better publisher, one more able to channel, refine, and market his rapidly developing talent. Acuff-Rose, in turn, could not have found a more valuable property. Now one of the largest music publishing houses in the world, it has yet to handle a more acclaimed or more profitable songwriter than Hank Williams.

Fred Rose was a small, slender man who went from pop songwriter to country publisher without a hitch. Several of the songs he wrote have become pop standards: "Red Hot Mama," the old Sophie Tucker special; "Honest and Truly"; " 'Deed I Do." But it was as a country music publisher that Rose, who died in 1954, left his brightest mark.

Born in Evansville, Indiana, Rose quickly demonstrated his musical talent. He taught himself piano at the age of seven and was playing the instrument professionally at the age of ten. He started writing songs in his mid-teens, soon moved to Chicago as a writer and performer. He worked with Elmo Tanner, who made a hit whistling "Heartaches" in the forties, with Fibber McGee and Molly, and with Paul Whiteman. On a radio show called "Fred Rose's Song Shop," he composed songs spontaneously around titles suggested by listeners.

When the Depression reached him, Rose was part of a trio called the Vagabonds. They took to the road as barnstormers. One rainy night, headed for Rose's hometown of Evansville, they literally took the wrong turn and wound up in Nashville. WSM, it happened, was looking for two acts, a single and a duet. Fred Rose became the single, and from then on his life was country music.

Rose left Nashville briefly to write songs for Gene Autry, turning out such all-time Autry favorites as "Be Honest with Me," "Tears on My Pillow," and "Yesterday's Roses." In 1942, he teamed up with Roy Acuff, already a top star on the Opry, to form Nashville's first publishing company. It was a bold venture, a challenge to an industry traditionally controlled in the North. Acuff and Rose made a success of it from the start. Rose wrote several hits for Acuff, including "Pins and Needles" and "Home in San Antonio," and Acuff wrote several hits for himself. They began publishing the songs of other country writers, and Acuff-Rose was on the way.

When Hank Williams joined Acuff-Rose in 1946, the company had a stable of country music writers. They included Pee Wee King and Redd Stewart, who combined to write "Tennessee Waltz," Jenny Lou

("Jealous Heart") Carson, Paul Howard, Clyde ("Shenandoah Waltz") Moody, and Mel Foree. Hank received the standard songwriting contract: three cents a copy on sheet music sold, fifty per cent of royalties from phonograph records, and the usual "writer's portion" of money received from the use of his songs on radio and in live performances. It was the same contract Hank was to work under during his biggest years as a writer. He never asked for a more lucrative deal. The only concession he received, and it was not an unusual one, was a fifty-dollar-a-month drawing account, which Acuff-Rose advanced against future royalties.

Hank and Audrey returned to Nashville, with Hank as happy as a child at Christmas. He had a contract with the number-one country music publisher, he had sold a half dozen songs, and a couple of them were going to be recorded by a name artist.

That was Hank's first break as a songwriter. Six months later he got his first break as a performer. Again Fred Rose was responsible.

Rose got a phone call from a small New York company, Sterling Records. Sterling was looking for two commodities, a Western singer and a country singer. (The two seem the same to the average listener, but the music industry at that time made a clear distinction between them.) Could Fred Rose find them?

"We picked up the Oklahoma Wranglers for the Western act," says Fred's son, Wesley, "but getting a country singer was a problem. Most of our good country acts were already placed, and Sterling wanted this done pretty quick."

Wesley Rose said to his father, "Hey, how about that skinny kid who came in with the songs. I liked his singing." "Okay," said Fred Rose. "Let's call him."

Hank made the Sterling recordings at Nashville's WSM studios. The studios were in the home offices of the National Life & Accident Insurance Company, which has sponsored the Grand Ole Opry for decades. Actually, Hank was among the first country artists to record in Nashville, for the city, despite its musical vitality, had become no more organized in recording than in publishing.

The first record cut in Nashville, according to the best estimates, was a Red Foley disk, in the spring of 1945. Before that, country artists either were recorded "in the field," that is, in their own locales, by traveling representatives of major record companies, or in the home studios of these companies. Each company, in the twenties and thirties, had its traveling specialist in country music: David Kapp at Decca, Ralph Peer at Okeh, Art Satherly at Columbia.

Peer is credited with starting the field recording movement, back in 1921, but Satherly was an equally influential figure in it. An Englishman with very uncountrified forms of speech and dress, Satherly "discovered" Gene Autry in Oklahoma in 1930 and Roy Acuff in Nashville in 1938. In a typical year, he traveled seventy thousand miles through "country" country and made four hundred recordings.

The engineers who recorded Hank Williams' first session for Sterling, Aaron Shelton and Carl Jenkins, pioneered in the Nashville recording industry. They worked full time for WSM and experimented with record making on the side. "Before the war," chuckles Jenkins, "we used old wax disks, the kind you had to bake. Our technical director, George Reynolds, forgot to take one out of his oven at home one day, and it almost ruined his kitchen."

Hank's first session was in Studio D, which was considered by the experts rather dead (that is, without much reverberation of sound) but quite modern in terms of equipment. Not that there was a choice of location; Studio D was the only professional recording studio in town. Hank stood around, awed and nervous, while the "Western act," the Oklahoma Wranglers, cut the first session. When it came time for his session, Fred Rose enlisted the Wranglers to back up Hank; the Drifting Cowboys had been left at home while the leader went to the big city.

The session went smoothly. Hank cut four sides:

"Calling You"; "Never Again"; "Wealth Won't Save Your Soul"; and "When God Comes and Gathers His Jewels." All were part of the package of songs he had sold to Acuff-Rose when he was signed to a contract.

"You could immediately recognize Hank had talent," says Carl Jenkins. "He had what we called the country touch." Adds Aaron Shelton, "When he sang one of those sad songs you knew he *was* sad, or had been mighty recently."

The four sides sold surprisingly well, so well that within a few weeks the owner of the company was after Fred Rose to line up another session with the Williams kid. Hank again left the Drifting Cowboys in Montgomery, with Rose engaging a group of local pickers to provide the backup for his singing. He recorded four more songs: two of those he'd sold to Acuff-Rose earlier, "My Love for You [Has Turned to Hate]" and "I Don't Care [If Tomorrow Never Comes]," plus two new ones, "Honky Tonkin' " and "Pan American."

"Honky Tonkin' " was a songwriting departure for Hank. There was nothing spiritual or lovelorn about it. It was a bouncy, frankly suggestive tune about "steppin' out" to the honky-tonks with "sweet mama"; all she had to do was "bring along some dough," and the action would be guaranteed. Hank sang the song in a grainy, hard-edged voice. He repeated the theme and the vocal treatment a few years later with "Hey, Good Lookin'," and it became a smash hit.

If "Honky Tonkin' " was well away from Hank's norm in one direction, "Pan American" was well away from it in another. It was the most popular of a handful of train songs Hank wrote.

The *Pan-American* (Hank, never concerned about grammar, ignored the hyphen) was the Louisville & Nashville's crack train during Hank's childhood years in south Alabama. It roared through Greenville and Georgiana twice daily, blowing its shrill whistle at the crossings. The passage of the *Pan* through those towns was one of the premier events of any day, and young

Hank was fascinated by the train. Sometimes he would get up around four in the morning, sneak down to the tracks and lie in the bushes, deliciously frightened, as the northbound section thundered past.

Another feature of the *Pan*, which Hank must have heard on the radio, was WSM's picking up the sound of the whistle as the southbound section came through Nashville each afternoon about five. He incorporated that into the chorus. The melody of "Pan American" bears a definite resemblance to Roy Acuff's "Wabash Cannonball," but there is no evidence that Hank consciously cribbed it from the Acuff classic.

Hank was paid a flat fee of 250 dollars for each of the two Sterling sessions. An artist usually makes a royalty arrangement on the records he cuts, but Hank needed the cash. More than that, he needed the exposure, so he probably would have cut them for nothing.

The Roses were highly impressed with the sessions, particularly the second one. "When he did 'Honky Tonkin',' it was like magic," says Wesley Rose. "He sang out of the groove. We decided we'd negotiate a record contract for him—with a big label."

Fred Rose went to New York and contacted Frank Walker. Walker, a pioneer in the record business, had been president of Columbia and then RCA Victor. He was starting a new label for Metro-Goldwyn-Mayer, and Rose saw that as a golden opportunity. The M-G-M label, with Metro's backing, obviously would be big and successful. Frank Walker was a seasoned professional, with years of experience making unknown artists into stars. He was also a fan of country music. It looked like an ideal place to "put" Hank Williams.

Walker liked what he heard on the Sterling records. He came down to Nashville and signed Hank to a contract. Record contracts usually specify a payment of three per cent per disk for the artist, but Hank balked at that.

"I don't understand per cents," he told Walker.

Walker shrugged. "Well, let's make it three cents a record then."

"That I understand," Hank said with a grin. (Later he went up to five per cent, the top figure for a popular music recording artist.)

So Hank joined M-G-M's small group of artists: Blue Barron; Art Lund, who had just recorded the popular ballad, "Mam'selle"; Art Mooney, who had made a hit out of a ditty called "I'm Looking Over a Four-leaf Clover." Hank was not the first country artist on the label—Carson Robison can claim that distinction—but he soon became its biggest artist, country or otherwise.

With the signing of the M-G-M contract, Fred Rose assumed a role in Hank's career and life that was to last until Hank's death. It was a combination business manager-father role, and Hank badly needed the services of both. M-G-M, for instance, agreed that Rose would do all Hank's recording in Nashville, without supervision from the company. He would send the records to New York with instructions on what to release and when to release it. M-G-M would do the promotion and merchandising. It was a sensible plan, and it worked beautifully.

"No song was ever recorded by us without Mr. Rose's approval," Walker said several years ago. "Also, no record session was ever held without either Fred Rose or Wesley Rose being present at the entire recording, and in most instances both were present. Many times Hank would call to ask approval for recording a song. It was my policy always to tell him to take the song to Fred Rose, who would look at it most carefully . . . and then submit it to me."

Both Rose and Walker soon realized how important it was to make Hank a recording star as well as a writer. One complimented the other beautifully, particularly since Hank now had plenty of his own songs to sing.

The trust Hank had in Fred Rose quickly became apparent. Before making the deal with M-G-M, Rose showed Hank's Sterling sides to an executive of another major record company. The executive said he wasn't interested. Then, when Rose left, he called Hank long distance and said he'd like to sign him to a contract.

"Get hold of Fred Rose," Hank said.

"I'm not interested in Rose," the executive snapped. "He's just out for himself. Besides, *he* can't do anything for you."

"He got you to call me, didn't he?" Hank asked angrily, and hung up.

Hank's first record for M-G-M turned out to be a hit. It was "Move It On Over," a delightful bit of country whimsy about being locked out of the house by an angry wife and having to move in with the dog. Hank set the words to a fast-paced, bluesy tune. Fred Rose added a few finishing touches, and M-G-M, realizing it had a prospective hit record on its hands, pushed it hard. The result was several hundred thousand records sold (all singles in those pre-LP days) and a place on "the charts," the weekly record sales listings compiled by such trade publications as *Billboard* and *Cash Box*.

Back in Montgomery, Hank again made the rounds of the honky-tonks with the Drifting Cowboys. But his mind was on other things—writing for Acuff-Rose, recording for M-G-M.

One night, during the band's regular appearance at the Journey's Inn in Camden, he told owner H. B. Hawthorne, "Henry, you and I are both poor boys trying to get a start, but someday I expect to have some real money rolling in. I've just signed a contract to make records in Nashville. It won't amount to much at first. But after a year or so, I'm really gonna be in the money."

7

One thing remained to establish Hank solidly in the country music field. He had to become a name in-person performer. Songwriter would be little help there; a man could write hit songs for years and be practically unknown to the public. Recording would be a help, all right, but more so in popular than in country music. In the country field, the consuming public places great reliance on personal contact. Indeed, the backbone of "country" is the personal appearance tours the performers, no matter how big they are, relentlessly make. The more "personals" an artist makes, the more interest he creates in himself and his records. This is still the working theory behind the Grand Ole Opry, where artists work for peanuts just to get the exposure the Opry affords.

Montgomery's WSFA and the honky-tonks of South Alabama were hardly the setting needed to make Hank a name in the personal appearance side of the business. He needed a spot on one of the stage-and-radio shows, like the Opry, the Barn Dance in Chicago, the Louisiana Hayride in Shreveport.

"In a case like Hank's," says Wesley Rose, "you know you have a successful artist started. But you also know that there's a big entertainment factor involved; some artists with a number-one record can't entertain at all. You can't tell about that in a man's home town. For one thing, everybody knows the guy and takes him for granted. For another, the audience is not big enough to be a reliable barometer."

Where should Hank go? The Opry was out of the

question at that point. Hank was simply not big enough to get a spot there. But there were other possibilities. As with the choice of a record company, he left the choice of a show up to Fred Rose. Rose consulted top management at Nashville's WSM, whose approval Hank would need if he were ever to make the Grand Ole Opry.

"My father and I sat in our office, one room at the time, and talked about Hank in every shape and form," says Wesley. "After 'Move It On Over' was obviously a success, my father decided to put him on KWKH in Shreveport." KWKH ran the Louisiana Hayride, just as WSM ran the Opry in Nashville. Along with the Barn Dance and Wheeling, West Virginia's, WWVA Jamboree, the Hayride was, after the Opry, the biggest country music show in the U.S.

Fred Rose picked Shreveport for Hank because the Hayride was more like the Opry than the other shows were. That is, it was strictly country. "The Barn Dance, for instance, had some pop singers on it," says Wesley. "A kid like Hank might have listeners in Chicago saying, 'Boy, he's awful.' We didn't really care what they thought, because we were trying to make Hank the number-one country artist. My father knew he'd get a straight reaction on Hank in Shreveport. The people there are real *country* fans."

Furthermore, the Hayride, like the Opry, had an artists' service bureau that lined up out-of-town show dates for its performers. Thus Hank would no longer have to scramble, with his mother's and wife's assistance, for dates.

There was nothing unusual in this procedure. Acuff-Rose had "placed" at least two other country acts, the Bailes Brothers, and Johnny and Jack, with the Hayride. Fred Rose simply called Henry Clay, the general manager of KWKH, and told him, "Henry, we've got a young guy we want to put on your show. His records are selling good, and we think he can be a great artist."

Clay said fine, and Rose said, "We'll send him down

for a Saturday-night guest shot. Then you let us know
if he's a regular."

The day after the guest shot, Clay called Rose and
said, "He's a regular all right."

When Hank and Audrey moved to Shreveport, the
Drifting Cowboys drifted—Sammy Pruett to WAPI in
Birmingham, the others to band jobs in other Southern
towns. Only Lum York, the bass player and baggy
pants comedian, went to Shreveport. Hank wanted Don
Helms, the steel guitarist, to go too, but Helms had
already caught on with another group. "It was a cooperative deal," says Helms. "I had twenty-five per cent
of the action, and it was goin' good. So I turned him
down.

" 'Okay,' he told me, 'I'll let you off this time. But
one of these days I'm goin' to the Opry, and I want
you to go with me.' I laughed and said, 'Okay, it's a
deal.' "

The people at WSM were not so sure Hank would
ever make the Opry. They knew he had the talent, but
they were afraid his drinking would ruin him before he
ever hit it big. That had been their fear of Hank all
along, and they saw nothing to make them change their
minds.

When WSM general manager Harry Stone and artists'
service director Jim Denny went to Montgomery to talk
to Hank about Shreveport, they couldn't find him.
Neither could station WSFA, where he was still working. "We extended our stay," says Stone, "and the
station manager sent people out trying to find him.
He'd been out getting drunk, but he sobered up by the
time he saw us. Anyway, I was used to hillbilly artists
being a problem. It seemed like they were drinking
most of the time."

Stone says the WSFA station manager told him then:
"If I were in your place I wouldn't consider hiring
Hank Williams a minute. You're going to be running
after him all the time trying to get him to perform on
your station." Well, Stone figured, that would be Shreveport's problem for the time being.

Stone also says Hank had "never ev/
Shreveport" when he and Denny broache
That is unlikely. J. C. McNeil, Hank'
that during his Montgomery days "Hank ᴜ.
times to get to Shreveport" to give his musical cᴀ.
boost. "He'd get as far as Pensacola usually. Then he ↘
call Aunt Alice, my mother, and tell her to send us kids
over to get him. One time he went with my brother.
They got as far as New Orleans and ran out of money.
Hank got drunk and called Mama for money. She sent
some, then she met the two of 'em in Mobile and
somehow got Hank back to Montgomery."

Hank's setup in Shreveport was standard. He got a
spot on the Louisiana Hayride, which meant appearing
on weekend shows. He got bookings through the Hayride's artist service, and he got a radio program of his
own on KWKH.

The Hayride bookings took him around east Texas
and the western part of Louisiana, where the folks
would get used to his name and songs on KWKH. He
put together another group of Drifting Cowboys: Lum
York; a guitar player from Missouri, and a couple of
local boys. York says that the band members each
received a straight salary of sixty dollars a week and
that Hank had a hard time meeting the payroll. He
even disbanded the group for a while. "He just wasn't
makin' it," says York.

Compared to the old south Alabama circuit, the
towns were larger—Lake Charles, Texarkana, Baton
Rouge—and the shows were longer and more polished.
Hank and the band often appeared with other Hayride
acts in what the trade calls "double-headers." There
was no more coming back to Mama's boardinghouse
each night. Trips lasted several days, usually one night
in each place and never more than two. At the Grand
Ole Opry, performers are required to come back to
Nashville each Saturday night they are scheduled to appear on the show. There was no such requirement at the
Hayride, but Hank made it a point to be there on

Saturday night. He wanted to send his voice and songs
into all those living rooms.

Not long after he got to Shreveport, Hank bought a
1949 Packard limousine. He loved big cars. For one
thing, they made the band's constant trips more bearable. For another, Hank wanted the world to know he
was somebody and to take notice when he rode by. In
this, he was following a custom in country music,
where stars often announce they have made it by buying the longest, widest, flashiest motor vehicle they can
find. Hank was to have a number of these in his time.
Most of them, of course, were Cadillacs, for when he
found out that Cadillac was a synonym for success, he
would have nothing else.

Several months later Hank also bought a trailer,
which he hauled along behind the Packard limousine to
carry show uniforms, instruments, and what not. Never
much on driving, Hank usually turned the wheel over
to one of the boys in the band. He scrunched his long
frame down in the back seat and passed the time staring
out the window, horsing around, and composing songs.

Several of Hank's best songs were composed in the
back seats of automobiles. His well-known hymn, "I
Saw the Light," for instance, was not only written
during but inspired by a trip in the car. That was back
in the Montgomery days, when Hank and the band
used to drive home after each show date. One time, in
the small hours of the morning, Hank was dozing in
the car as they approached Montgomery. His mother
spotted the airport lights and, realizing they were getting
close to home, exclaimed, "Thank God! I saw the
lights!"

Hank awoke with a start and asked, "What did you
say, Mama?" She repeated the words, and Hank
nodded. Then he settled back in his seat and mulled
them over. By the time they reached the boardinghouse,
Hank had the idea and many of the words worked out
for "I Saw the Light." It is probably the best of his
many fine "sacred songs."

New members of the band quickly learned when to

be quiet in the car when Hank was thinking out a song. He sometimes asked for suggestions on lyrics, and he often enlisted aid in setting down the words; he didn't like to be bothered with such details when he was creating. Nobody wrote down the music. Hank didn't know a note of it, and neither did most of the other Drifting Cowboys. He carried the tunes in his head.

Police around Shreveport began to keep an eye out for the Williams caravan, particularly when Hank added the trailer. One time they pulled the group over just after it had embarked on a tour and told Hank he couldn't go over thirty-five miles an hour pulling a trailer. "Hell," growled Hank when they got back on the road, "we'll never get anywhere driving like that." A minute or so later, Hank told the driver, rhythm guitarist Clint Holmes, to step it up. Holmes went back to his customary speeds of eighty to ninety on the straight, flat west Louisiana roads.

The demand for Hank and the band increased as more people in the hinterlands began listening to his radio show. His big show was an early morning, fifteen-minute program for Johnny Fair syrup. "The Old Syrup Sopper," he called himself. For a good while, Hank and his guitar were the whole show. Then he brought on the band as well. Hank sold syrup, all right. "When Johnny Fair started out advertising on that program," recalls a KWKH executive, "they were in bad trouble. Within six months they were selling more syrup in summer, which is usually the bad season, than they'd been selling in winter."

Hank's main interest, of course, was the Louisiana Hayride itself. This was his showcase, his ticket to Nashville and the Grand Ole Opry. Well before Hank got there, the Hayride was functioning as a sort of farm club for the Opry. "We've started more country stars than anyplace else," says Frank Page, then program director of the Hayride. "We've had a knack of finding people on their way up. The Opry never liked us much, but we gave 'em a lot of their stars, people like Webb Pierce, Jim Reeves, Red Sovine, and of course Hank Williams."

Elvis Presley got his start on the Hayride too, but that is a source of some embarrassment to show officials. "He wanted somebody on the Hayride to manage him," says Page ruefully, "but nobody would take him. Nobody thought he'd make it." So Elvis went on to Colonel Tom Parker and Hollywood and a fabulous career.

Presley did make one lasting impression on the Hayride. He introduced drums to its stage. Before he arrived, drums were forbidden on the Hayride (as they were on the Opry for decades). "That changed when Presley came," says Page. "You couldn't have him without drums." That started a trend that resulted, a few years ago, in Ray Price singing on the Hayride stage to the accompaniment of a fifteen-piece orchestra, including violins and a vibraphone.

It was on the Hayride that Hank developed much of his appeal as a stage performer. Part of the appeal was physical: his long, gaunt face, now getting the shadows and lines of maturity; his slender frame, curled over and around the microphone; his eyes, bearing hotly and steadily on the audience, usually on the first couple of rows, which he held spellbound. Part of the appeal also was his manner: relaxed, offhand, friendly. Then there was his voice, a wonderful, natural instrument that could rasp out a honky-tonk tune or sob out a sad one.

"He was just electrifying on stage," says Frank Page. "He had the people in the palm of his hands from the moment he walked out there. They were with him, whatever he wanted to do." This was a quality Hank never lost, not even in the last, shattered months of his life.

Curiously, Hank's Hayride performances appealed to black people, who normally are indifferent to white country music. Blacks around Shreveport flocked to the auditorium when he was on the show. The reasons were Hank's bluesy style plus a black oriented recitation or two he liked to do. One of the recitations, called "The Funeral," was a tear jerker about a funeral for a little

black boy at a rundown Southern church. It contained
a couple of somewhat slighting references to black
people, but they do not seem to have been offended.

Hank always liked to sing his hymns to Hayride
audiences, and the management obliged by making the
presentations as dramatic as possible. The house lights
would dim, the spots would come on, and Hank's intense, throbbing voice would fill the hall. Often, particularly on the road, he called the whole cast onstage
to help him do a religious number. That was the high
point of any show, and Hank loved it. The other performers liked his songs too. They sang them for fun on
long bus trips.

Lum York, the bass player-comedian, remembers
Hank as "one of the most professionalist guys on stage"
in his Shreveport days. "He could talk to people as well
as sing, and they'd listen. He could tell a joke or get
serious or do anything." York makes a comparison that
many others have made: "Him and Roy Acuff was
more alike, as stage performers, than any two I've ever
known."

It was also on the Hayride that people, especially
others in the country music business, began to notice
that Hank Williams was a different man off stage than
on. Off stage he was cool, quiet, aloof. He did not like
anyone asking about his personal affairs, which he
rarely discussed. He was not close to any of the Drifting Cowboys. They got used to his off stage manner,
but many other people never did.

"A lot of people didn't like Hank as a person," says
York. "You had to be around him to understand him."

One reason for that was Hank's lack of tact. He was
always plain-spoken. Bob McNett, a Northern boy who
became the band's lead guitarist a few months before
Hank left Shreveport, found Hank to be "quite abrupt,"
even in dealing with his friends. "I remember the first
time I worked with him on stage," says McNett. "We
came off, and he told me in no uncertain terms what I
was doing wrong." McNett was of course working for
Hank, so Hank had a right to tell him what to do. But

McNett also was a professional musician, and that was his first day on the job. Such nuances of person to person communication were lost on Hank.

Hank had many redeeming characteristics as far as the members of his band were concerned. He was generous with time, with money, and with opportunity for the other members to display their talents on stage. The Drifting Cowboys, under Hank, were not faceless assistants but individuals with professional identities of their own.

Under the show format Hank developed in Shreveport, the emceeing was often left to another member of the band. This was not wholly a matter of generosity, for Hank figured he would come on as more of a star if someone gave *him* the introductory build-up, rather than the other way around. This worked particularly effectively after he made his first big hit, "Lovesick Blues."

A typical show went like this. The Drifting Cowboys, minus Hank, would open with a couple of instrumental numbers. Then the emcee, Bob McNett after he joined the band, would introduce Hank with appropriate fanfare. Hank would come on, sing a song without saying anything, then introduce each of the band members. He always got some humor into his introductions, and the boys in the band led the audience in yukking it up over his jokes. One of his favorites, which he used in introducing McNett, a farm boy from northeastern Pennsylvania, was to tell how "We had to roll peanuts off the mountain to get him to go with us."

The body of the show was Hank's singing. He sang all of his own songs, and, since there weren't enough of those then to make a show, a number of others too. The band provided the accompaniment, with intermittent instrumental solos, and a bit of vocal work on the choruses. The arrangements were not left to improvisation. They were fixed, not by Hank himself, who would have had a terrible time doing it, but through repeated playing and practicing. In the case of songs Hank had already recorded, they were fixed by the recording itself. The record provided the "official" arrangement of a Hank Williams song, and the band was obliged to stick to it.

Although he couldn't arrange a piece of music himself, Hank knew precisely what he wanted to hear when the band played the piece. "He got the musicians to work behind him just as he wanted," says McNett. "Nothing complicated, just plain and simple. He was a nut about his rhythm. It had to be right and kept right." Although never much more than a strummer with the guitar, Hank had an unerring sense of rhythm, and his guitar work, while not impressive to the listener, had a great deal to do with the smooth sound of the Drifting Cowboys.

"If one of us got a little hot on the instrument," says McNett, "he was quick to tell us to cut it out. He wanted the stuff played straight. He liked it that way, and he was convinced the public did too. People still tell me, 'You had the best band I ever heard,' so he must have known what he was doing."

Although the arrangements were set, Hank made sure his musicians didn't go stale playing them. One way he did this was to push them into improving their own specialties. One night he told McNett, his lead guitarist, that if he didn't play his instrumental piece well enough to get applause in the middle of it, he'd be fired. " 'You haven't been doing as well as you should on that piece,' he told me," McNett says, "and he was serious. I played the thing—'Fingers on Fire,' it was called—faster and more furiously than I'd ever done before. And I did get applause in the middle of it. That indicated to me that Hank really wanted the rest of us to shine, not just himself."

Hank could be as serious about his comedy as he was about his songs. Once when he and Lum York were engaging in some on-stage repartee, the other band members broke out laughing. Hank was so angry he told them to leave the stage, covering up the incident by saying he had a song he wanted to do alone.

Generally, however, he was relaxed on stage. The

Drifting Cowboys respected him for his obvious talents and for what McNett describes as his "very fertile mind . . . quite receptive, quick to pick up things that might be good for the show."

Next to the development of his music, the most significant thing about Hank's stay in Shreveport was the drop off in his drinking. None of his friends there remembers him as a problem drinker. He got drunk a number of times, but seldom to a point where it affected his work. He didn't have to dry out for days and miss show dates.

The apparent reason for this reform was Hank's determination to make the best of the Shreveport opportunity. He knew he couldn't perform at his best when under the influence. Further, he was aware of the reputation he had developed in Montgomery, and he knew it would, it left unchanged, seriously hinder his chances of making the big time.

The only Shreveport drinking antic Hank's associates recall was more comical than anything. He showed up half drunk for an engagement in Lake Charles and proceeded to pull the curtain on one of the other acts, the Bailes Brothers. They laughed it off, and so did the audience. Wobbly when he himself took the stage, Hank managed to get through his segment of the show. The audience accepted his condition, as other audiences were to do many times later, without a complaint. "As long as Hank could talk or sing a little bit, they were pleased," says Lum York. "He was that kind of guy."

When Hank wasn't performing, he was usually writing. He had very few outside interests. His idea of relaxing was to sit around thinking up lyrics and tunes to go with them. Many of these, scribbled on odd scraps of paper, were lost or discarded, but Hank didn't really care. The important thing was to keep writing them. He liked to titillate his friends with the song fragments and to receive their praise.

"He used to tantalize me with new songs," says Frank Page. "He'd say, in that crazy drawl, 'Frank, come on in,' and there he'd be, sprawled out in a corner, his bony legs sticking out, his arms wrapped around a guitar. One of his favorite games was to play a song he'd already written, one I knew, and then weave in a new thought and new lyrics. My eyes would light up when I heard the new stuff, and he'd grin with delight."

Hank may have been spending too much time at such musical doodling and not enough at serious writing. He wasn't turning out any hits. After "Move It On Over" became a hit, Hank ran into a long dry spell as a writer. Acuff-Rose, of course, was not about to cut him loose during that spell. They were willing to wait until the songs started flowing again. Anyway, they were counting on Hank to be a performer as well as a songwriter, and he was doing fine on that score in Shreveport.

Hank was recording off and on, under the personal supervision of Fred Rose. The sessions were held in Nashville, at a new location, the venerable (and now demolished) Tulane Hotel. Carl Jenkins and Aaron Shelton, the WSM engineers who made Studio D Nashville's first recording operation, had set up the Castle Studio in the hotel. They took the name from WSM, which called itself the "Air Castle of the South."

Jenkins and Shelton worked hard to make Castle the best recording studio in the region. They bought, at a cost of over four thousand dollars, the first Scully master cutting lathe used in the Southeast; they also obtained, at the urging of Decca Records, an Ampex tape machine, which was then the only thing of its kind. "With those two pieces," says Jenkins, "we were really in business in a professional way. We'd walk into the studio and see them and immediately feel ourselves gain in stature."

Everyone tends to overlook another significant event that occurred in the Shreveport period: the birth of Hank's only child, a boy. Although Audrey's daughter by her previous marriage, Lycrecia, lived with the Williamses, he never legally adopted her. The boy was born May 26, 1949. Hank named him Randall Hank, in the style of his own name, Hiram Hank.

Hank Junior, as he was soon called, has a twofold importance in his father's story. One, he himself has fashioned a highly successful country music career, partly out of his own talent, partly out of his father's fame. Two, he became, during the years when Hank Senior was racing down the road to self-ruin, a symbol of the good and simple things his father saw slipping away. Hank was always devoted to his son, and never more than in his last, desperate months.

8

It is ironic that the song that started Hank Williams to the top of the country music world was written by someone else. The song was "Lovesick Blues," by an old-time pop tune composer named Cliff Friend.

It is also ironic that "Lovesick Blues" is far from a typical piece of Hank Williams material. The songs Hank sang, his own and those written by others, were almost invariably simple, musically unsophisticated pieces that followed the classic country music patterns: a verse followed by the chorus; a melodic line that is often the same for both verse and chorus; a chord progression that seldom ventures beyond the stock 1-4-5 (e.g., G-C-D), with a "passing chord" (e.g., A) occasionally thrown in; a rhythm that does not vary from one part of the song to the next.

"Lovesick Blues" breaks all these patterns. Wesley Rose calls it a "Broadway-type tune," and in a way it is. There is a good deal of Broadway-type razzamatazz:

for instance, leading into a verse with the line, "This is all I can say . . ."

But the song is more than that. It is a slick, city-style blues, with verses and chorus so smoothly integrated the listener can hardly tell where one starts and the other begins. The chord progressions must have impressed Hank, who was devoted to the G-C-D or G-C-A-D pattern. The chorus (if the song is played in C) goes from F to C to A7 to D7 before resolving in the standard country music fashion—to the dominant G and back to the tonic C.

Further, the middle section features repeating E-A minor progressions, seldom heard in Nashville music, before returning to the D-G pattern. Hank, like a lot of other country singers and writers, was uncomfortable with minor chords and used them sparingly.

Written around 1920, "Lovesick Blues" had been recorded by other artists but had never been a hit. Just how and why Hank got hold of it is uncertain. Ed Linn, in "The Short Life of Hank Williams," says Fred Rose was opposed to Hank's recording "Lovesick Blues."

"When he finally did let him record it," wrote Linn, "it was only because they needed an extra number to fill out a recording session. Even then, he thought so little of the song that he didn't bother to stay in the studio to supervise the recording."

Wesley Rose says that is not true: his father did not oppose Hank's recording the song, and he personally set up and supervised the session at which the record was cut. Wesley says he himself went to Shreveport to hear Hank sing the song for the first time. "He'd done it a couple of times before that, and he told us it was going over good. We set up a session in Cincinnati specifically to cut that song."

It hardly makes sense that a man with Fred Rose's musical savvy would have tried to keep Hank Williams from "Lovesick Blues," because the piece is so obviously suited to him. Hank was a great white blues singer (some musicologists balk at distinguishing between "white" and "black" blues, but there certainly is a distinction), and that song showed off his blues singing abilities as no other one ever did.

"Lovesick Blues" is a difficult song to sing well, and it is hard to see how Hank's rendition of it could be improved. His timing and phrasing, always two of his greatest assets as a singer, were perfect. He put a "tear" in his voice—as country singers call the little sobbing warble they inject into sad songs—at just the right places, particularly in the breaks that end a number of lines. Most important, he struck the perfect mood for the song, sorrowful yet swingy. It is a fine song, and Hank gave it a virtuoso performance.

Hank knew he had a hit with "Lovesick Blues," far more than with "Move It On Over," and he rode it for all it was worth. Even before he recorded the song he was singing it on all his shows in and around Shreveport. When he hit with it nationally, it became his musical signature. He always closed a show with "Lovesick Blues," usually encored it two or three times, and sometimes opened with it and sang it in the middle as well. Unaware of the advertising maxims about product identification and the value of repetition, Hank nonetheless knew a winner when he had one.

Hank's recording of "Lovesick Blues" took off like a rocket. It went to the top of both the *Billboard* and *Cash Box* popularity charts, and it stayed there for months. When that record hit, other songs Hank had recorded and done only moderately well with got onto the charts too.

By the end of 1949, Hank's name was prominent in the list of annual award winners. His version of "Lovesick Blues" was voted "Best Hillbilly Record" of the year in the *Cash Box* poll of music machine (jukebox) operators. It was voted number one in *Billboard*'s listing of the top country and Western records; in the same listing, Hank's recording of "Wedding Bells" ranked number five and "Mind Your Own Business" number twenty-four. In addition, *Billboard* made Hank runner-up to Eddy Arnold as the "Year's Top-selling Folk Artist."

Officials at WSM and the Grand Ole Opry didn't need to wait for these year-end honors to know how Hank was doing. The sales "Lovesick Blues" was racking up and the plays it was getting on radio and in jukeboxes told the story. Hank obviously was ready for a guest shot on the Opry.

"We wanted him to be an Opry regular," says Wesley Rose, "but the Opry people wouldn't buy that at that point. So we turned to the guest shot as our secret weapon. We knew what he could do. We knew that if he sang that one song it would produce a reaction that would take care of any problem about getting him a regular spot on the show."

Securing a guest shot for Hank was not easy, but WSM's Harry Stone arranged it. "When 'Lovesick Blues' got into the top five on the charts, the Opry people were convinced," says Wesley Rose. Hank came up from Shreveport in June, and he appeared on the Opry's Saturday night show. What happened is legend in Nashville: the standing ovation when the audience recognized the song and then the singer; the half dozen encores, unparalleled in Opry history.

Even with that kickoff, there remained some hesitation at the Opry about making Hank a regular member of the show. One reason was obvious. Although Hank had kept out of trouble with liquor for about a year, the stories of his earlier antics were still fresh in the memories of promoters and other business types in the country music field. Could he be counted on to honor his commitments, in sober fashion?

There may have been a less obvious reason too. The Grand Ole Opry was built on an image of clean, wholesome fun, which has meant no boozing or hell raising. Some long-time observers of the Nashville music scene think Opry officials stayed away from Hank as long as possible for fear of endangering the show's image.

There is testimony on both sides of this question. Wesley Rose calls Hank's drinking reputation, at the time he came to the Opry, a "misconception. . . .

People had told us Hank was quite a drinker," says Rose, "but I don't remember him drinking anything during that period, and for a long time afterward. The reason it was so hard to get him on the Opry is the plain fact that the Opry was a collection of great country artists, and it was hard for anybody to crack it."

Perhaps, but the Opry officials certainly knew of Hank's reputation, whether it was justified or not. What happened is that they decided to take Hank and the risk that came with him. With Hank holding the number-one spot in the charts and bringing down the house during his guest shot, they could hardly do otherwise. "I'd risked it with a number of others," says Harry Stone, who had the final word in matters of this sort, "so Hank's drinking problem really didn't worry me. Anyway, I can hardly remember an artist *without* a drinking habit in those days."

So Hank left the farm team, the Hayride, and joined the parent club, the Grand Ole Opry. Like any rookie, he was automatically overshadowed in his new environment. He was the biggest name on the Hayride, but Roy Acuff, Red Foley, Eddy Arnold, Ernest Tubb, in fact any of the top Opry stars, were infinitely better known on a national and international scale. He had a long way to go to catch them. The amazing thing is that he did it so swiftly.

The show Hank joined, in the summer of 1949, was an institution of twenty-five years standing. The Opry was, and still is, the oldest continuous show in the history of radio—as New York *Times* critic Robert Shelton has called it, "the grand old dinosaur of American radio."

Everyone has a gut reaction to the name Grand Ole Opry. To those unfamiliar with country music (a steadily shrinking group) or for one reason or another repelled by it, the name means an unbearably corny show, featuring terrible music and worse humor and attended by droves of over-clad farmers. To those who love country music and those who at least appreciate it, the name means by and large the best that type of music has to offer. The Opry does not have all the star artists and seldom has had them. But over the decades it has presented an unparalleled procession of great country music names.

As for the quality of the music and humor the Opry presents, it must be judged in terms of the largely rural, unsophisticated milieu from which it has sprung and from which it still draws most of its support. The Opry speaks to milions of Americans unmoved by Perry Como or the Beatles or Ray Charles. It also speaks, and this is what its detractors do not realize, to millions of other Americans who like popular music but like country music too. The two types of music are becoming increasingly interwined, largely because the pop people now understand the broad ranging appeal—and therefore salability—of country.

Beyond that, the Opry has always been star oriented. Frank Sinatra and the Beatles have never meant more to their fans than Roy Acuff or Eddy Arnold or Hank Williams has meant to his. Country music fans are simply quieter in their devotional exercises. All they do is buy millions of records, travel thousands of miles, wait hours in auditorium lines (without screaming or rioting), and sing their favorite songs over and over again. Moreover, they remain loyal for what seems like eternity. They do not die for the Beatles one year, the Rolling Stones the next, and T. Rex the year after that. An Acuff fan is an Acuff fan forever. Hank Williams' popularity has not been dimmed by death, although he died twenty-one years ago; indeed, the Williams legend is as vibrant today as it ever was.

One reason personalities are so important on the Opry is that the millions of people who see or hear the show on an average Saturday night really identify with the performers. It is important to these people that Ernest Tubb is from Crisp, Texas, that Johnny Cash came from a poor family in the Arkansas delta, that the Carter Family was native to the Clinch Mountain area of Virginia. The country music enthusiast is a good deal more conscious of background, particularly geographical, than his pop music counterpart. No pop fan really cares that Perry Como is from a small town in Pennsylvania; that is a curiosity, nothing more. What Como does, not where he is from, is the important thing. In country music, both origin and performance are important. In fact, they are often inseparable.

These distinctions between pop and country music, between the television special and the Opry, are blurring nowadays. But when Hank Williams broke into the Opry, just before the advent of mass television, the distinctions were clear cut. Again taking the matter of background, the Opry thrived on producing the American success story, in endless variations. Every country star from Jimmie Rodgers on down, it seemed, had fought his way up from poverty and, thanks to his great talent and to God's blessing, gone on to success. Those who didn't fit naturally into that pattern, finishing-school graduate Minnie Pearl, for instance, wriggled into it somehow. They had to, because it was what the fans wanted.

Hank Williams, of course, did not have to wriggle into this American success pattern. He was the archetype of it, the semi-educated, good-natured boy from a poor family in the heart of the South. He had scratched his way up the ladder by his own talent and hard work, and, yes, he'd done wrong a few times along the way. A little wrongdoing was perfectly all right. It titillated the fans and demonstrated that Hank was a regular guy, not one of those manufactured stars from Hollywood and Broadway.

Today the country has gone out of a lot of country music artists. It is not stylish to be a hillbilly, on stage or off. With the younger stars especially, the fashion is to be country slick, rather than plain country; that is, to have your hair carefully styled rather than casually cut, to speak in the artificially resonant tones of the radio announcer, to glad-hand disk jockeys and reporters and anyone else who is commercially valuable. All the while, the artist tries to maintain a basically country image. He usually does a rotten job of it, but the fans don't seem to mind. Why should they? They themselves are doing the same things, following the same fashions, as country yields inexorably to city.

It was not that way in Hank's day, luckily for him. He probably could not have adapted to the new style. He was plain country, not country slick. He was natural, on stage and off, and would have little stomach for these modern aspects of the country music business.

The Grand Ole Opry made its first radio broadcast in 1925, less than two months after WSM, the station that has always run it, went on the air. Its founder was a Memphis newspaperman, George D. Hay, who got the idea for a country music show while covering a funeral one day in west Tennessee. Attending a hoedown that night, which lasted "till the crack o' dawn," Hay was struck by the sheer enjoyment the musicians got from their music.

As he wrote twenty years later, "it [country music] is as fundamental as sunshine and rain, snow and wind and the light of the moon peeping through the trees. Some folks like it and some dislike it very much, but it'll be there long after you and I have passed out of this picture for the next one."

Hay turned to radio announcing, specializing in country music, and he was hired by WSM when it went on the air in October of 1925. Legend has it that the Opry itself started one night with the impromptu, and endless, playing of an old Texas fiddler named Uncle Jimmy Thompson. He appeared on George Hay's show, and after an hour of fiddling, Hay, perhaps in desperation, suggested the old man might be tired. "Heck no," snorted Uncle Jimmy, "I'm only gettin' started." He sawed away for hours, and the response was phenomenal. Cards and telegrams flooded WSM, welcoming the mammoth dose of Uncle Jimmy and demanding more of the same.

The show continued in haphazard fashion for the next couple of years. It took the name WSM Barn Dance, which was probably an imitation of Chicago's already established WLS Barn Dance. Its mainstays were fiddlers like Uncle Jimmy and old-time string bands with such picturesque names as the Fruit Jar Drinkers, the Gully Jumpers, and the Possum Hunters.

The show became known as the Grand Ole Opry through the glib repartee of Hay himself. WSM carried a network classical music program called "The Music Appreciation Hour," directed by Dr. Walter Damrosch, just prior to Hay's show. One night in December 1927, with Damrosch's sign-off still echoing in the ears of listeners, Hay introduced his Barn Dance as follows:

"Friends, the program which just came to a close was devoted to the classics. Dr. Damrosch told us that it was generally agreed that there is no place in the classics for realism. . . . However, from here on out for the next three hours we will present nothing but realism. . . . It will be down to earth for the earthy."

Hay there upon called forth harmonica player Deford Bailey, who incidentally was the first and only black man to be a regular on the Opry, to perform "Pan American Blues." When Bailey finished, Hay said: "For the past hour we have been listening to music taken largely from grand opera, but from now on we will present 'grand ole opry.' "

It was a throw-away line as far as Hay was concerned, but the name stuck. So did Hay, who became better known by the title, "the Solemn Old Judge." He ran the Opry with a firm hand for years afterward, turning away such threats as drums and electric guitars with the admonition, "Keep it down to earth, boys."

The Opry's first star was Uncle Dave Macon, a jolly, portly banjo player with a mouthful of gold teeth and a satchelful of Jack Daniels sour mash whisky. Uncle Dave, a farmer from Smart Station, Tennessee, did not become a professional musician until he was forty-six years old. He was a consummate showman, with foot stomping and high leg kicking his specialty, as well as a master of the frailing style of banjo playing. (Frailing is a traditional style utilizing the back of the fingernail for melody and the thumb, hitting the fifth or drone string of the banjo, for rhythm. It has largely given way, in this modern era, to the syncopated, three-finger style popularized by Earl Scruggs and bluegrass groups.)

Except for the times it yielded to President Franklin D. Roosevelt and his Fireside Chats, the Opry has been broadcast over WSM each Saturday night since 1925. Part of the show is aired regionally, part nationally over a network hookup. The weekly radio audience is estimated at ten million. For in-person shows (three or four each weekend), the house is invariably packed—3,500 people jammed into old wooden church pews, with hundreds more waiting outside. The shows are sold out weeks in advance, and, on a big weekend, cars from more than thirty states are parked in the Grand Ole Opry House parking lot. The typical Opry visitor has been to the show three or four times, and it is not unusual for him to drive five hundred miles to get there each time.

The setting and format of the Opry are striking. The stage is bare except for folding chairs, microphones, and a backdrop of large, garishly colored advertisements for products sponsoring that particular segment of the show. (A sample: the Stephens clothing company, whose motto is "work clothes a little bigger . . . sport clothes a little better," displays a comic book-style mural of various pieces of apparel hanging on a line.)

The back half of the stage is a jumble of instruments, artists, side men (those performing in the band behind an artist), and visitors. Included in the last group are friends of the performers, visiting celebrities, children, anybody able to get by the guards at the stage door. Everyone mills around, talks and laughs, and nobody worries about it. Backstage is just as crowded, with hordes of people in the corridors and rehearsal rooms.

There is method to all the madness. Despite the vast informality, the show proceeds on a strict schedule; encores are generally frowned upon. The master of ceremonies keeps the show moving and performs another important task: when a less-than-great artist finishes his song, the M.C. exhorts the audience to applaud with "come to me" waves of the hand. The audience never fails to respond. It is happy, and it wants the performers to be happy too. The Opry is that kind of place.

Still, the overall impression is one of astounding casualness. "New York advertising people just don't believe it when they see it," said Opry general manager Ott Devine a few years ago. "They just don't understand the informality. But when we start producing the show, we kill it."

Nonetheless, informality may give way to production when the Opry moves into a modern, Disneyworld-style setting in early 1974. The show's new home will be Opryland, a 328-acre, multi-million-dollar park located in a Nashville suburb. The Opry will have its own building, standing amid a welter of other activities, and it remains to be seen whether the show can and will retain its distinctive homey air.

Although the Grand Ole Opry is Nashville's most widely known institution, it is not always a source of pride to the city's social and educational elite. The elite in the past has down-graded the show to the point of wishing it would go away. The feeling is that in the "Athens of the South," as the city pretentiously calls itself, no person of taste and breeding should take pride in a country music show.

A writer named Alfred Leland Crabb expressed that view in *Nashville: Personality of a City,* which was published in 1960. "Nashville, as a whole, is not as willing to pay for its classical music as it is for its country music," complained Crabb. "It has spent more money for 'Sourwood Mountain' than it has for Schubert's 'Unfinished.' Eddy Arnold has far greater box office appeal than does Brahms. 'The Tennessee Waltz' has more economic standing here than 'Aïda.' The income of the Grand Ole Opry is at least three times that of the Nashville Symphony Orchestra and the Community Concerts Series combined."

Crabb's crabbiness may be understandable, but it is shortsighted. No one could seriously argue that Arnold

deserves a larger audience than Brahms. But that
is no reason to denigrate Arnold and the Opry too.
The Opry is an international resource, an important
center of popular culture, and Nashville is fortunate
to have it. The Opry and the associated industries of
recording, publishing and what not bring almost 200
million dollars a year into the city. Further, they bring
it a recognition its symphony orchestra and concert
series never could have provided. These facts, plus an
ever-widening acceptance of country music, are making
the Opry increasingly welcome in Nashville.

Actually, downgrading the Opry strenuously is passé
in Nashville these days. The city's elite treats it with
a tolerant sniff, and the political leaders—visions of
dollar signs dancing in their heads—act downright
friendly. Chamber of Commerce types are merchandising the country music image. "Music City U.S.A." is
now a far more common nickname for Nashville than
"Athens of the South." Ryman Auditorium has been
renamed the Grand Ole Opry House and the stretch of
Fifth Avenue it sits on, Opry Place. Sixteenth Avenue
South has long been called Record Row because of the
recording studios, music publishing houses, and talent
agencies that line both sides of it.

Local politicians have been surprisingly slow in getting aboard the Opry bandwagon. But every Tennessee
governor for many years has paid some form of obei-
sance to country music in general and the Opry in
particular. Last year, for example, Governor Buford
Ellington headed the list of well-wishers who showed
up at the Opry House to congratulate Roy Acuff on his
twenty-fifth anniversary on the program. Governor Gordon Browning, back in Hank Williams' day, not only
appeared at the Opry, he performed on it as well, singing the old country warhorse, "Tennessee Waltz." Next
to the Tennessee Valley Authority, country music and
the Opry may well be the biggest sacred cows in the
state's politics.

That brings up the question of why Opry stars have
not become political leaders in Tennessee. Several have

thought about it, and at least one, Roy Acuff, has tried. Back in 1944, Acuff let his name be entered in the Democratic gubernatorial primary before he came to his senses and pulled out. Four years later, however, under pressure from friends in his home territory of East Tennessee, he entered the Republican primary. Without even campaigning, he trounced his primary rival by an eight to one margin. Acuff then revved up a showman-like campaign, featuring entertainment by his Smoky Mountain Boys. He drews big crowds, but no Republican was about to be elected governor in the South in 1948. As someone later remarked, Acuff's crowds listened Republican but voted Democratic. Acuff lost to Gordon Browning and consoled himself by saying: "As governor, I would have been just another politician. As a singer, I can be Roy Acuff." Few country music fans would doubt that being Acuff is a lot more important.

One country star who did make good as a politician is Jimmie Davis, the singer-songwriter who become two-time governor of Louisiana. Davis, however, did not try to enter politics at the top, as Acuff did. He worked his way up the ladder, starting at age thirty-six, serving first as a public service commissioner, then as a criminal court clerk. Davis also has a decent background for politics. He had an M.A. from Louisiana State University and for a time taught history and social science at a small college in Louisiana.

Yet no one doubts that Davis' singing and song-writing propelled him along the political path. He recorded for RCA Victor and later for Decca, and he wrote such hit songs as "Nobody's Darlin' But Mine," "Sweethearts or Strangers," and the enduring "You Are My Sunshine."

(Davis, who couldn't read music, liked to play up the homey side of country songwriting. "When I have thought up a song," he used to say, "I run through it with my wife, who's a graduate in piano from Centenary College. If she doesn't like it, it's going to be a smash hit.")

Country music has of course been part of Southern politicking for many decades. Rare is the touring candidate who does not warm up his audience with a few numbers by a hired country band or singing group. They may be slicked up and electrified, but they are carrying on the grand tradition of mixing music with campaigning. Mississippi's John Bell Williams won the governorship in 1967 with the aid of a gospel singing group. On the national level, such politically distinct candidates as George Wallace and Glen Taylor have made use of country music. Taylor, Progressive Party vice-presidential candidate in 1948, strummed a guitar during campaign appearances, while Wallace employed a country-rock band to belt out his theme song, "Are You for Wallace?" during his presidential bid in 1968.

The growth of the Grand Ole Opry has been paralleled by the growth of the only sponsor it has ever had, the National Life & Accident Insurance Company. Ever since National Life began putting on the Opry, back in 1925, criticism from anti-country music circles has kept its officials wondering if they were doing the right thing. The balance sheets have kept them convinced they are.

Contrary to common belief, said Edwin Craig, the late board chairman of National Life, the Opry image has helped the company in the cities as well as in the country. "We operate fundamentally in a blue collar market," said Craig, "and we found a lot of customers in the cities who had moved in from the country. This was the music they'd known and loved, and they brought it with them to the cities.

"For years, thanks to the Opry, National Life was the fastest-growing life insurance company, in percentage growth, in the nation. Our insurance was all sold door to door. Our man would knock on a door in Wichita and say, 'I represent the Grand Ole Opry,' not 'I represent National Life.' 'Sure, come on in,' the prospect would say. Then our man would pitch insurance. We still use that approach."

9

Nowadays few Opry stars have their own bands; they simply pick up side men, all thoroughly experienced professionals, as they need them. When Hank arrived in Nashville, however, forming one's own band was still very much the thing to do, so Hank set about the task without delay.

Lead guitarist Bob McNett, alone among the Shreveport group, had come to Nashville with him. He summoned steel man Don Helms, and Helms, recalling his pledge to join Hank when he hit the Opry, quit his job and did just that. For the other two band members, Hank found a couple of young Nashville-area men, bass player Hillous Butrum and fiddler Jerry Rivers.

Hillous Butrum, then twenty-one, had already been playing as a side man on the Opry since he was sixteen. A farm boy from Lafayette, Tennessee, he moved to Nashville as a teenager and got his first break in show business by convincing a band leader he was a bass player. He really wasn't, but he quickly became one, complete with baggy pants and all the standard comedy gear.

Jerry Rivers, then nineteen, short and stocky with blond hair, was doggedly pursuing a country music career. Rivers had been leading the sort of double life typical of many young country artists trying to get a start in the business. In addition to his regular, eight-hour-a-day job as an electronic parts salesman, Rivers was doing a radio show at five each morning, another show at five-thirty each afternoon, playing a couple of schoolhouse dances each week and playing a four-hour square dance each Saturday night.

Ironically, although Rivers was to become a permanent fixture with the Drifting Cowboys and one of Hank's best friends, he passed up two opportunities to work for Hank. The first came in 1948, when Hank was still in Shreveport and Rivers was passing through that city on the way home from a job in Dallas. Hank needed a fiddle player at the time, but homesickness got the best of young Jerry; he continued on to Nashville without applying for the spot. Soon afterward, Hank called Rivers and invited him to Shreveport to join the current version of the Drifting Cowboys. Rivers was hot for a job on the Opry, however, and turned him down. Then "Lovesick Blues" hit the charts, Hank hit Nashville, and Jerry Rivers thought he'd blown his chances.

Not so. A friend tipped off Rivers that Hank was still looking for a fiddler for the band that would work with him on the Opry, and Jerry hustled over to audition for the job. "I saw Hank Williams for the first time sitting on a stool at WSM radio studios while Clifford shined his sharp-toed boots," Rivers has written in *Hank Williams: From Life to Legend.* "I guess Clifford, a WSM porter, has shined the shoes and cowboy boots of every artist and musician whose shadow darkened the stage of the Grand Ole Opry."

Hank was at WSM on that occasion to perform on the Opry's Friday night broadcast, one of his first Nashville radio appearances. Rivers stood, fiddle in hand, waiting for Hank to finish his shoeshine, "hoping that the parts I had memorized from his early records would stay with me." When Rivers opened his fiddle case, Hank surprised him by taking the instrument and sawing out the old fiddle tune, "Sally Goodin'."

"It was pretty ragged," Rivers recalls now, but naturally he complimented the boss on it. Hank asked Rivers if he could play that tune, and of course he could, many times better than Hank. When Rivers finished, Hank said promptly, "Anybody that can play 'Sally Goodin' better than me is a darn good fiddler. You're hired."

So Hank had himself another bunch of Drifting Cowboys. He went out and bought them all stage uniforms —black and white shirts and dark, tight-fitting pants, both in the Western style, and ten-gallon hats and cowboy boots. The next night the band appeared on the Grand Ole Opry, with Hank again stopping the show with "Lovesick Blues." Rivers and Helms, in their first appearance on the Opry, were awed. Says Rivers: "I believe the roaring applause continued for at least five minutes after we finally returned to the dressing room."

Right after the show the Drifting Cowboys left for a tour through the Midwest, the first of dozens of trips they would make during the next three years, playing virtually every major city in the country. Along the way, Hank arranged a visit with Nelson King of Cincinnati's WCKY, then the nation's most popular country music disk jockey. Courting disk jockeys is a task no recording artist can ignore, for the D.J.s hold the key to success or failure for a record. If a record gets a lot of "air time" (plays on the radio), it almost always will sell a lot in the shops and bring in a lot of dimes in the jukeboxes. That, in turn, will lead to high standings on the charts, the popularity listings compiled by the trade publications, and thereby to more sales and more jukebox plays. A great many country music performers think the charts are "hyped," artificially controlled to boost certain records, but none disregards them or the disk jockeys who can help place a record on them.

Visiting Nelson King, Hank got his first listen to "high fidelity" music. King played some of Hank's records on a "hi fi" phonograph and also told the boys of the impact the new 45-rpm records, just about to hit the market, would have on the recording industry.

The first show date on that road trip was at a fair in Springfield, Ohio. The trip was supposed to last only a week, but Hank and the boys were such a success it was extended by several days. That was fine except for one thing: each man had only the one uniform Hank had bought him before they left Nashville, and it got progressively more gamey as the week wore on.

Hank was an instant hit. Audiences reacted the way that one had his first night on the Opry: they were unsure of the name, Hank Williams, but they damned well knew the song, "Lovesick Blues." Country music fans all over America were humming it.

"Hank was drawing crowds above some of the old, established artists who were playing the same places," recalls Don Helms. "The reason was that song."

"It was like Presley later on," says Hillous Butrum. "The artist had to get as big as his records. Why, people in the audience would be asking before the show who the tall, skinny feller was. After we were on for a couple minutes, they *knew* who the hell he was."

Anybody who liked the way Hank sang "Lovesick Blues," of course, wanted to hear him sing other songs. So a number of the songs Hank had been singing without acclaim now became, literally, music to the public ear. Audiences began applauding when Hank announced "Wedding Bells" or "Mind Your Own Business" as his next selection.

"Mind Your Own Business" is a bouncy little number, simple in melody and lyrics, that is most notable as a bit of marital commentary. It was apparently one of the first in what was to become a long line of Williams songs about the joys and trials of life with Audrey. This one was aimed at people who were even then beginning to comment on, and ask questions about, the relationship between Hank and his wife. The song told them off bluntly: ". . . me and that sweet woman's got a license to fight."

"Wedding Bells" is not a Hank Williams song. It was written by Claude Boone and contains most of the clichés about marriage ceremonies that songwriters, pop as well as country, rely on: the chapel, the little band of gold, the walk down the aisle, the bells that ring for somebody else, the little cottage in the valley. It is a corny, unimaginative piece of music, but the fans found the combinations of clichés, phrased in Hank's doleful tones, irresistible.

Despite their youth and inexperience in the big time, Hank's new band of Drifting Cowboys had no trouble becoming a cohesive unit. Not a man in the group, other than the leader, was over twenty-one, and none save Hillous Butrum had played the Opry. Why did Hank, on the threshold of real stardom, chose such a group?

One reason is that when the Opry beckoned, he had to get a band in a hurry; the Opry was band conscious in those days, and no star performer was complete without one. Another reason was that Hank was still more comfortable with musicians of his own age and background. Most important, perhaps, he wanted a band he could tailor to his own musical tastes and requirements. As the men who played with him in Shreveport point out, Hank had very definite ideas about song arrangements. He did not want people so set in their musical ways they could not carry out these ideas.

The Nashville version of the Drifting Cowboys was the best band Hank ever put together. It had ties with the former bands, to be sure—Helms, McNett, and Sammy Pruett, who rejoined the group in 1950. But it developed a smoother, more polished style that reflected Hank's increased maturity as a leader as well as the members' increased abilities as musicians.

The Drifting Cowboys retain, even today, a quiet confidence that they comprised as good a country music band as there was in those days, and they are probably right. Hillous Butrum, who has seen scores of bands come and go, says the Drifting Cowboys were the equal of the best country ensembles of their day, which he lists as the Jimmy Dickens and Cowboy Copas bands, the Oklahoma Cowboys, and Ernest Tubb and his Texas Troubadours. The Oklahoma Cowboys, according to Robert Shelton in *The Country Music Story*, were "both a prototype and a pioneer" among Western-style bands. The Cowboys, who traveled in a caravan of custom-built cars and employed publicity men, featured a left-handed banjo picker and a wide repertory of folksy and sentimental Western songs: "Sucking Cider Through a Straw," "The Old Maid and the Burglar," "The Song of the Dying Cowboy," and so forth.

Tubb and his Texas Troubadours are still headliners today, more than a quarter-century after he joined the Opry. Tubb is credited with helping develop the "honky-tonk style" of country music, which Hank Williams carried to perfection, and also with being among the first to make the electric guitar a regular instrument in the band. The electric guitar had a tough time getting accepted on the Opry, but Tubb took to it in the early 1940s without a qualm. The reason, as described by country music historian Bill C. Malone, was partly economics:

". . . as the jukebox became a firm fixture in road-side taverns, some of the honky-tonk operators complained to Decca that it was difficult to hear the Ernest Tubb records after business picked up at night," Malone has written.

"Prior to this time, the Tubb instrumentation had consisted of two unamplified guitars. At his next recording session, he was accompanied by an electric guitar played by Fay (Smitty) Smith, the staff guitarist at KGKO in Fort Worth. Tubb then instructed his regular guitarist, Jimmie Short, to attach an electric pickup to his conventional Martin guitar."

Bob McNett, as lead guitarist for the Drifting Cowboys, played an electrified instrument in both Shreveport and Nashville. Hank Williams was no purist when it came to country music. The electric guitar gave him the kind of bluesy, commanding sound he wanted on some of his songs, so he was happy to use it.

The distinctive instrument in the Drifting Cowboys band, however, was not the electric guitar but the steel guitar, as played by Don Helms. The origins of the steel guitar are obscure, but it has roots in the Dobro and, going further back, the Hawaiian guitar. It is an unattractive, severely functional-looking instrument, essentially a rectangular metal box with anywhere from six to twelve steel strings stretched lengthwise along the top. It can either be held on the lap, like a dulcimer, or supported by four legs and played in a standing or sitting position.

The steel guitar is the perfect example of what electricity has meant to popular music. Without electricity, it would produce nothing but dull, thumpy sounds. With electricity it becomes a weird and sometimes wonderful instrument, capable of all sorts of compelling musical effects. Helms was drawn to the steel guitar at an early age. One of his idols was Leon McAuliffe, one of the all-time great steel players, who played with numerous Western bands and wrote "Steel Guitar Rag," now a country music standard.

Helms, as a Drifting Cowboy, was not quite Leon McAuliffe, but he was very good. Hank Williams knew that full well, and he gave Helms unusual latitude to improvise on the steel guitar. The results, in the midst of the rather regimented Williams arrangements, were often gratifying.

"The lonesome sound of Don's steel guitar fit right in with the lonesome sound of Hank's singing," explains Butrum. "Don gave the Drifting Cowboys their sound, their style, like Roy Wiggins did when he played steel for Eddy Arnold."

When Hank arrived in Nashville, he landed a program on radio station WSM. That was more or less part of the package deal for an artist joining the Opry. WSM controlled the Opry, as KWKH controlled the Hayride in Shreveport, so appearances on both the station and the show were routine.

Hank and the band appeared on several WSM shows during his years as a Nashville star. Most notable among them was a program on five days a week at 7:15 A.M., for Mother's Best Flour. (Shows were known by the names of their sponsors in those days.) It operated with a relaxed, Opry-type format: a couple of songs, some jokes and folksy chatter, and relentless plugs for "enriched" and "phosphated" Mother's Best, delivered by Hank or by the program's announcer, "Cousin Louie" Buck.

Hank and the band were also regulars on the various Opry "warm-up" shows that preceded Opry broadcasts on Friday and Saturday afternoons and evenings. One was for Jefferson Island salt, another for Royal Crown Cola, a third—the best remembered—for Duckhead work clothes. This type of country music show, although not so popular as it once was, still survives in the South on television as well as radio. In sophisticated Atlanta, late Saturday afternoon TV offers an abundance of country music fare: Buck Owens, Porter Waggoner, and "That Good Ole Nashville Music." All keep the format simple and homey. For years, the best of the Saturday shows was Flatt and Scruggs. Lester Flatt sang bluegrass vocals (some of the best in the business) and pitched Martha White's Self Rising Flour, while Earl Scruggs, poker-faced and barely audible on the vocal sections, picked banjo in the syncopated, three-finger style he made popular. Each Flatt and Scruggs show included a couple of banjo showpieces, some lighthearted country banter, and "our sacred song," the latter reverently introduced by Flatt. The show went off the air when the two stars split up to form their own groups.

The WSM shows, like the Opry itself, paid poorly. Hank and his boys got union scale, no more, and Harry Stone says, "If Hank made as much as hundred bucks a week out of that morning show, I'd be very surprised." When the band was on the road, of course, it could not play the radio shows "live," so before leaving on tour the boys would pre-record enough programs to last until they returned to Nashville.

As with the Opry, money in the form of direct payment was not the radio performer's prime consideration. Exposure, leading to big money later on, was the thing. With the Opry, the big money came from personal appearance tours, song publishing, and record contracts.

With Nashville stations WSM and WLAC, it came
from on-the-air merchandising, by relative nobodies
more than by name performers.

These two stations developed a group of "studio
stars," radio entertainers whose following consisted entirely of members of the listening audience; many of
them, in fact, were unknown outside that sphere. They
had a common approach. They strummed and sang
country songs, told a few funnies, and merchandised the
hell out of all kinds of products.

"They sold books, pictures, everything, all by mail
order," recalls Jerry Rivers, who played in a studio
star's band before joining the Drifting Cowboys. "Those
letters with fifty cents enclosed would come pouring in,
from all over the Southeast. Why, they'd rack up fifty,
a hundred, a hundred-fifty dollars a day just pushing
these products. For a while there, before Hank came
with WSM, a guy who got on a 50,000 watt station in
the early morning really had it made. You didn't need
any pay from the station, just the air time. Your area
coverage would be so great you'd make a big name for
yourself and sell a ton of stuff too."

The studio stars have their spiritual descendants in
the homey hucksters who gull listeners into sending a
dollar for "an auto-graphed pho-to of Je-sus Christ," but
the breed seems to be dying out. Certainly it does not
now flourish as it did in Nashville twenty years ago. "I
know people who've retired to Florida in luxury, who
nobody more than three hundred miles from Nashville
ever heard of," says Rivers. "They got on the radio with
a harmonica or a guitar and made a pile."

One of the breed was Mac O'Dell, who used to make
this kind of pitch: "Friends, I got a little souvenir hymn
book here that contains that there hymn I jest sang. I
got a nice autographed picture of m'self too. Now, you
jest send ol' Mac fifty cents an' he'll send you both the
hymn book *an'* the autographed picture." The song-
books often contained material donated by struggling
songwriters happy to see it in print anywhere.

Then there was Big Jeff, a studio star on WLAC. Jeff

took more or less the same approach, but he had another function as well. He provided a sort of training ground for aspiring young musicians just in from the sticks. A lot of boys who later made the big time got their start in Big Jeff's studio band, among them Rivers and top guitarist Grady Martin.

"They're all gone now, the studio stars," says Rivers, a little sadly. Why? " 'Cause the little old gal in the gingham dress who used to listen to 'em so faithfully is now watching Andy Williams on T.V. The gullible, bright-light-struck hillbilly is a thing of the past."

For a performer who struggled so hard to get established, Hank Williams now moved with remarkable speed. Almost simultaneously, he secured the M-G-M record contract, the Acuff-Rose publishing contract, the WSM radio performing contract, the Grand Ole Opry stage performing contract. This package inevitably meant headaches as well as rewards, and Hank, lacking in both intelligence and background, badly needed advice. Fred Rose became his number-one counselor, in many matters other than songwriting; "He was like a father to Hank," says Wesley Rose. Two other men who functioned as advisers, one official and one unofficial, were Sam Hunt and Jim Denny.

Sam Hunt was an executive with Nashville's Third National Bank. A lean, gruff-voiced but amiable man, he handled Hank's finances during the latter's short but spectacular stay in Nashville. Hunt handled the finances for many country artists, and some of them involved fairly intricate investment deals. Hank was no investor, however. He was a cash man, and Hunt's services to him consisted mostly of watching over his bank account and doling out living expenses to him.

While Sam Hunt's advice to Hank was mostly financial, Jim Denny's, like Fred Rose's, covered a multitude of subjects. Some people today claim Denny was even closer to Hank and had a greater influence on his career than Rose. That is very doubtful, but certainly Denny was an important figure in Hank's life. As general manager of the Opry and head of its now-defunct artist's service, he would hardly have been otherwise. But Denny's relationship with Hank went beyond bookings and other business affairs.

Denny, who died in 1963, was a patient, thoughtful man who came up the hard way. As a boy, he sold newspapers in front of the building that later housed "his" radio station, WSM. He got his start in the country music business working in the mail room at National Life, later worked as an usher at the Opry. Those were the days when National Life's door-to-door agents gave free Opry tickets to their policyholders. An old friend of Denny's recalls the two of them collecting the free tickets from households that weren't going to use them and selling them outside the jam-packed Opry the night of the show. Business was generally good enough to bring them double the pittance they were earning from their regular jobs.

Denny shared more than a disadvantaged childhood with Hank. He also shared a certain bitterness about, as magazine writer Ed Linn put it, "the inequalities of life," which he had overcome through the counsel of an older friend. Denny tried to provide that kind of counsel for Hank, but he was never convinced he succeeded.

"I never knew anybody I liked better than Hank," Denny told Linn in 1957, "but I don't think I ever really got close to him. I don't know if anyone really could. He was so bitter. . . . He thought everybody, in the final analysis, had some sort of an angle on him. I suppose that's why everybody has misinterpreted him. Because despite it all, he was very kind and generous and very determined to be the top man in his profession."

10

"I remember one day," says Jimmy Rule, a veteran Nashville songwriter, "Hank was scribbling a song on a piece of paper. He looked up, kind of in despair, and asked me, 'D'you think people will understand what I'm tryin' to say?' "

Rule looked at the paper and read what is probably Hank's best-known single verse:

> Did you ever see a robin weep
> When leaves began to die.
> That means he's lost the will to live
> I'm so lonesome I could cry.

"Don't worry," Rule told Hank. "They'll understand."

They did, too. "I'm So Lonesome I Could Cry" became one of the greatest country songs ever written, and Hank Williams became one of the greatest American songwriters. The keys to his greatness as a writer were simplicity and sincerity. Everybody understands what a Hank Williams song means, and almost everybody senses the simple, straightforward emotion—be it joy or anguish—from which it springs.

His audiences and colleagues felt this in different ways. Most have trouble articulating it, but they all know it was there. "It was just something in him that made him see the real, down to earth thing and made you feel it," says Jimmy Rule. "He was a genius in that way."

"He had the ability to write lyrics that the average

person could emotionally relate to," says Capitol Records' Ken Nelson, a seasoned and perceptive observer of all forms of popular music. "He had the ability to write music that the average unmusical person could understand and yet was not trite. His songs were accepted in the pop field because they were realistic, and they were melodically and lyrically understandable to everyone."

Mitch Miller, who ranks Williams with Stephen Foster, says, "He had a way of reaching your guts and your head at the same time. No matter who you were, a country person or a sophisticate, the language hit home. Nobody I know could use basic English so effectively. Every song socks you in the gut.

"Take his song, 'Cold, Cold Heart.' 'Why can't I free your doubtful mind and melt your cold, cold heart.' This is the complaint of every lover, and that country boy didn't even know he was turning us all on."

Vic McAlpin, another veteran songwriter, who occasionally collaborated with Hank, says Hank's simplicity was largely calculated. "He knew," says McAlpin, "that the man with a dollar ain't gonna buy your song if it's got over three chords. Simplicity, in melody and lyrics, sells–99 and 99/100 of the songs every year. You got a good song if the public, whether it's kids at Vanderbilt or a farmer plowing a field in Murfreesboro, hear it three times and go 'round humming it."

Beyond that, admits McAlpin, who is grudging with praise, Hank "did have an artistic touch. Look at 'Your Cheatin' Heart' and 'Cold, Cold Heart.' Tremendous lyrics. They're bound to touch the average guy, because they describe situations that most people over twenty have been involved in."

The point is not that those songs describe common situations, in this case infidelity and suspicion. Thousands of country songs have done that, but they haven't "touched the average guy" as "Your Cheatin' Heart" and "Cold, Cold Heart" have done. That is where talent comes in.

Hank himself often said his songs "just come bustin'

out," which was a colorful but not too informative way of putting it. Once, in an interview with a writer for *Nation's Business* (of all publications), he became a good deal more explicit. He was talking about country music in general, but certainly what he said applied to his own writing and singing.

The success of country music, Hank said, "can be explained in just one word: sincerity. When a hillbilly sings a crazy song, he feels crazy. When he sings, 'I Laid My Mother Away,' he sees her a-laying right there in the coffin.

"He sings more sincere than most entertainers because the hillbilly was raised rougher than most entertainers. You got to know a lot about hard work. You got to have smelt a lot of mule manure before you can sing like a hillbilly. The people who has been raised something like the way the hillbilly has knows what he is singing about and appreciates it. . . . what he is singing is the hopes and prayers and dreams of what some call the common people."

One of the common people himself, Hank never tried to be anything else. Not even when he had the money to do so. This became a source of friction between him and his wife, Audrey, but Hank was resolute. He was a country boy, and throughout his life he harbored a strong suspicion of people who were "better," or thought they were.

Sincerity alone, of course, is not a guarantee of a good song or a successful song. Many Tin Pan Alley writers, and a fair number of Nashville writers, are not "sincere" in the sense of living their song or putting their soul into it or whatever other metaphor one cares to use. They write as disinterested craftsmen, bent on turning out the most pleasing, most salable song possible. A lot of fine songs have been written this way. Talent and technique are at least as important as sincerity.

Hank Williams obviously had the talent. He wasn't overloaded with technique, but he had enough to get by, and Fred Rose was there to provide what he lacked.

As for sincerity, that had to be tempered by technique. Sincerity alone can produce hackneyed, wooden lyrics of the "roses are red, violets are blue" variety. Hank turned out some that are, at least to the sophisticated ear, of that variety. Writing in the country music genre, that was inevitable. The remarkable thing is that he turned out so many lyrics that deserve to be called poetry.

Songwriters get their ideas from all sorts of places: signs, dreams, television, snatches of conversation. Vic McAlpin recalls how one of his hits, "How's My Ex Treatin' You," was conceived. He was sitting in Linebaugh's restaurant, a country music hangout in Nashville, when singer-composer Roger Miller walked in. After exchanging hellos, McAlpin asked jokingly, "How's my ex-girl friend treatin' you?"

"About like she's treatin' you," Miller replied.

"That really hit me," recalls McAlpin. "I jumped up, got a pencil, and wrote eight lines of a song based on that on a napkin. Then I turned the napkin over and wrote eight more. Jerry Lee Lewis recorded it, and it sold over a hundred thousand."

When inspiration strikes, most writers turn it into a song in a hurry. "The ones that are hits you write in five minutes," says McAlpin. "If you spend four or five days, they're usually not worth a shit. I don't write on a schedule, either, unless somebody has asked me for a song. The guys who write on schedule come out with a mechanical product.

"Hank was like this too. He'd start a song backstage, riding in a car, anywhere. And once he got the idea, he wrote fast." Hank often said, only partly in jest, that if he couldn't finish a song in a half hour he threw it away.

Don Helms remembers a night on the road when Hank wrote five songs in the back seat of the car. "It was somewhere in Arkansas or Missouri, raining like mad. The brakes were out on the car, and we were just crawling. I was playing the guitar on the jump seat, chording for him while he made up the melodies. I remember we laughed at some of the songs, and Hank said, 'Okay, laugh. I bet you every damned one of 'em is recorded within three weeks.' He wasn't too far wrong, either. But the best thing he wrote that night never was published." Appropriately, it began: "The night is dark and stormy. . . ."

One of those songs that became a hit was "Sing, Sing, Sing," a driving hand-clapping hymn that shouts joyfully about the good things waiting "when I get to Glory." This theme of getting to "glory" (heaven) doubtless sprang from the storm, the lack of brakes, and so forth. Hank was a fidgety passenger under the best of conditions, and on this occasion he probably figured he *was* headed for glory, rather than for his next show date.

The other Drifting Cowboys used to pass time on the long car trips by teasing Hank while he was thinking up songs, particularly while he was searching for a rhyming word to end a line. One time when Hank asked, "What's a good line to follow, 'One day I passed you on the street'?" Helms dead-panned, "And smelled your rotten feet." "This," says Jerry Rivers, "slowed progress on one of Hank's big hits."

Some songs were written in hospitals or sanitariums, while Hank was drying out from severe bouts with booze toward the end of his career. Montgomery writer Allen Rankin recalls visiting him in Montgomery's St. Jude Hospital: "Hank, melancholy, was complaining of troubles in general. A hulking Negro hospital attendant grinned. 'Mr. Hank,' he said, 'never trouble trouble till trouble troubles you.' "

"Hank grabbed his notebook and wrote the phrase down. In fifteen minutes he had made a new song of it."

A few songs were written on fishing trips with Vic McAlpin. They grew spontaneously out of what in today's parlance might be called musical brainstorming. "We'd start fooling with a song idea, half and half, in the boat," says McAlpin. "When we got something, he'd give me five hundred dollars for my half, and I'd stick the money in my pocket and forget it. He wanted the credit for everything himself."

On one of the "fishing" songs, "You Better Keep It on Your Mind," Hank shared the credit with McAlpin; their names appear as co-authors. It is not a bad song but it never became a hit. Two of the others, for which Hank paid off McAlpin, did a good deal better: "I've Been Down that Road Before" and "Long Gone Lonesome Blues." The latter, a whimsical blues of the old look-how-rotten-things-are school, has become a Hank Williams standard. It is a fine example of how songwriters draw their material from the situation at hand, for the first verse is about . . . that's right, fishing.

McAlpin has a vivid recollection of how the song was put together. "We left Nashville about three in the morning, to get to Kentucky Lake about five. We stopped for breakfast at a place near the lake, and when we got back into the car, Hank stretched out in the back and started talking about writing. He said, 'I gotta have me another blues to record, somethin' like "Lovesick Blues." '

"All of a sudden he started singing something like, 'She's gone along, gone along blues.' He hummed it over a couple of times, then he dropped it.

"Well, we got in the boat, and I threw my line out. He was fussin' with his bait. You could tell his mind wasn't on it. I said to him, 'You come here to fish or watch the fish swim by?'

" 'Hey, that's the first line,' he said.

" 'Huh?' I said.

"He said, 'Watch the fish swim by.' I got the idea and said, 'Okay, but why not say the river was dry?'

" 'Yeah, okay,' he said, so we put the song together." Hank used his idea for the first line of the first verse, McAlpin used his for the last line. They tossed ideas back and forth to fill out the rest of the song.

In writing "Long Gone Lonesome Blues" as well as other songs, McAlpin says, the emphasis was strongly on lyrics. "I was a lyrics man, and Hank was too. He didn't worry about melody. He knew that with ninety percent of all hits, country and pop too, the basic melody is familiar to the guy who hears it. Hell, if it wasn't familiar, nine out of ten people wouldn't buy it. At least that's my opinion after twenty-three years of writing songs.

"Three or four of Hank's songs, for instance, were taken from the same basic melody. The meter and tempo, and of course the lyrics, are different. You add three or four new notes, put things together a little different way and get an 'original' melody."

Somebody mentions Jimmie Rodgers, and McAlpin snorts derisively. "Every damn one of Rodgers' melodies are basically the same. All those 'Blue Yodels,' for instance, on up through number fourteen or fifteen. All they had was different words, and they were the biggest sellers of their time. Why, I remember working a day and a half as a kid, making fifty cents a day, just to buy one of his damn records." To anybody concerned with melody, McAlpin implies, that was a swindle.

The problem nowadays, says McAlpin, is how to vary the lyrics as well as vary the melody: "There's really nothin' more to say in songs. You just have to try to say it a different way."

Hank understood that, but he managed to say it simply while saying it differently. Once, when a fellow writer showed him some lyrics for his comments, Hank read them and remarked: "You write just like Shakespeare. If you don't watch out, you'll be buried in the same grave with him." No country music writer can risk that, and chances are that henceforth that writer heeded the Solemn Old Judge's admonition to "Keep it down to earth."

On another occasion, talking about song arrangements, Hank said, only half facetiously, that he wouldn't let his musicians play more than three chords. "I know a lot of good guitar players," he explained, "who've educated themselves right out of a job." Country music fans, he knew, do not want a tapestry of chords; or, if they do, they listen to a master guitarist like Chet Atkins. What they want from top artists and their bands are simple, solid, singable songs.

Frank Page, of the Louisiana Hayride, recalls Hank making the same point one day in Shreveport. Page, trying to learn to play the guitar, bought a cheap instrument and a book showing the chords. After a few self-taught lessons, Page went to Hank to learn some more exotic chords. "I've learned C, D, and G," Page said, apologetically. "Shoot," replied Hank, "that's all there is."

Hank had a habit of using other musicians as critics for songs he was whipping into shape. He would approach almost anybody, stranger as well as friend, and say, "Hey, I got a new song. Take a listen to it, would you?" Before he became a highly successful writer, he did this relentlessly and often took his listener's advice in changing this or that. This was flattering to some people, but, according to Drifting Cowboy Hillous Butrum, it made others "madder'n hell"; they did not like being made unpaid sounding boards for another Hank Williams hit.

When asked by reporters about his songwriting, Hank sometimes issued stirring statements about divine inspiration. "I just sit down for a few minutes, do a little thinking, and God writes the songs for me," he said of his hymns on one occasion. His mother followed suit with such statements as: "Hank's most serious songs were his hymns, and he meant them so much he would often shed tears while composing and recording them."

Hank was indeed serious about his hymns, and some probably were written under a special sort of inspiration. Most of them, however, as well as most of the rest of his songs, were products of his imagination and hard work. When he published a booklet on *How to Write Folk and Western Music to Sell,* the hand of God and the tears born of the creative process were not mentioned. The book dwelled instead on the common sense techniques of writing a song that would get published and, with a lot of luck, become a hit.

Hank co-authored the booklet with Jimmy Rule, another Acuff-Rose writer. Rule, a math teacher at one of Nashville's best private schools, pursued a lucrative moonlight career as a country songwriter, turning his knowledge of classical music into hits for the likes of Eddy Arnold ("I Have Other Fish to Fry" was the title of one distinctly non-classical number).

The booklet, published in Nashville, has had five printings and sold ten to twelve thousand copies, many of them from the racks of the Ernest Tubb Record Shop. In it, Hank offers tips on how to get a song idea, how to construct the song once you get it, how to sell it after that, and so forth. For gathering ideas, he recommends carrying a little note book at all times and studying the top tunes "to determine just what type of song is best received by the public," both common sense suggestions.

For constructing the song, he recommends starting with the chorus because that is "the part of the song that is sung most" and keeping the chorus "simple and easy flowing," without "a lot of trick phrases or impossible chords. . . . Always build a chorus that people will naturally want to hum after they have heard it."

The words of the title, Hank points out, "will usually start your chorus. . . . The title will then be used at least once more, preferably to close the song. Do not overlook the fact that your title MUST be used somewhere in your song and preferably at least twice. . . . it is necessary to select the right title for your song if you hope to gain attention. That is half the battle."

The lyrics must be kept within the bounds of good taste, as defined by the country music market: "Don't write any song which might offend a certain class of people. You should avoid especially the offending of any religious groups or races. . . . Avoid writing songs that have or could have double meanings or could be interpreted in any indecent manner." While these strictures are gradually softening, they are still widely heeded in the country music business.

As for pushing a newly completed song, Hank recommends sending it to a singer (preferably one in your home town) or to a music publisher. "Remember that you should have the song in complete form when it is presented to a publisher. Words without music or music without words will receive no consideration whatever." Hank excoriates "song sharks," the musical equivalent of vanity publishers, firms that lure songwriting neophytes into paying to get their songs published. "Bear in mind that NO reputable firm advertises for songs to be sent into them for consideration," which seems to put music publishers in an ethical league with doctors and lawyers. "Remember first, last, and always that NO reputable publisher will ask you to pay ANY amount of money for helping to defray the expense of publication of your song!"

The Williams-Rule book continues to sell because amateur songwriting continues to flourish, especially in Nashville. Country music sources estimate there are eight hundred more or less established songwriters in Nashville and thousands of dabblers. The dabblers can be anything from taxi drivers to beauticians to housewives to businessmen. They dabble in songwriting partly because it's an entertaining way to pass time, partly because they hope they can turn out one big, moneymaking hit.

The odds against a big hit by a rank amateur are very, very long. Indeed, the odds against his even getting a song published are long. But that doesn't stop him from trying. The largest Nashville music publishers receive an estimated three hundred unsolicited tapes a week, each bearing a new, and often pitifully bad, song, complete with words and music. The large publishers have staff men who function as "listeners"; their job is to listen to this volume of songs by dabblers and, perhaps, select a handful of them to be played before the head men of the company. The head men may pick one or two of the week's crop. If they do, they quite likely will turn it over to one of their staff songwriters for publishing or even rewriting, while at the same time giving the writer who sent it in a contract for that particular song.

Some of the biggest publishers do not even consider

the unrequested tapes. They return them unopened, for fear that a staff writer will turn out a similar tune and then be sued for plagiarism by the amateur whose tape had been played and rejected. Wesley Rose, head of Acuff-Rose publishers, told Nashville reporter Wayne Whitt not long ago that, the plagiarism problem aside, it is just not worth while for his company to examine tapes from amateurs: "Songwriting is a craft, and song publishing is a business. It is almost a fairy tale for a song by an amateur to become a hit. This is a highly competitive business, and a company must produce the best product."

Such harshly realistic words from a mogul of the publishing business should shatter forever the dreams of the songwriting dabblers, but of course they won't. The dabblers will go right on churning out country songs and sending them in with all the irrational hope of a man buying a cheap ticket in a national lottery.

Among Nashville's professional songwriters, there is a wide variety of writing techniques. Many rely, as did Hank Williams, on inspiration. For instance, the highly successful John D. Loudermilk ("Abilene," "Tobacco Road") occasionally flies down to the Gulf of Mexico in search of hurricanes, which he finds inspirational. The furious winds and churning clouds, he says, bring forth the country muse.

Other Nashville professionals make songwriting as much like a regular job as possible, sitting in an office, and matching the most commercially acceptable tunes with the most commercially acceptable lyrics. The country music fan these days doesn't worry about how a song was written, if indeed he ever did. What he cares about is whether the lyrics make sense and the tune is catchy; whether, in short, the song grabs him.

11

As promising a performer as Hank Williams was in his early days in Nashville, Fred Rose knew he was an even more promising songwriter. With proper management, Rose realized, Hank's songs could become as successful in popular music as in country music, a feat no country writer had ever accomplished on more than a one- or two-song basis. He gave this task—promoting Hank in the pop field—to his son Wesley, who had joined the publishing firm after working as an auditor for Standard Oil.

"My job," says Wesley Rose, "was to get Hank's songs placed with pop artists. Our theory was, 'If he is so big in the country field, what's to stop him in the pop field?' The war had led to the spread of country music, as country people came to the cities to work in defense plants and as they came into contact with city people in the military service. We thought there would be a real pop market for somebody like Hank."

Trying to spread a country song in a country artist's version wouldn't work, Rose figured. "Pop fans might think it beneath them to buy that kind of record. We had to do it a little fifth columnish."

To launch Hank's songs in the pop field, the Roses picked the recently written "Cold, Cold Heart." It was an ideal choice. "Cold, Cold Heart" is a soulful ballad about a man's trying to win over a sweetheart who is still carrying the torch from her last romance. The theme is universal, and, more important, the language used to develop it is a good deal less countryfied than in the typical Williams song. Its lines range from simple exposition to pop poetry, and the hand of a master pop songwriter—Fred Rose himself—is evident.

It is obvious in retrospect that "Cold, Cold Heart" had great pop possibilities; it eventually went to the top of the pop charts. At the time Wesley Rose was pushing it, however, the song's appeal was lost on the men who are supposed to know pop music.

"I beat on everybody's door with 'Cold, Cold Heart,'" recalls Rose, "and I got the same answer everywhere: 'That's a hillbilly song, and there's no use kidding yourself into thinking otherwise.'"

Finally Rose went to see Mitch Miller, the goateed, effervescent arranger-conductor who was a commanding figure in the pop field. At that time he was in charge of popular music at Columbia Records. Rose "placed" two country songs with Miller that day— "Bonaparte's Retreat," which was destined for top "chart position" (as the industry calls it) in a rendition by Kay Starr, and "I Love You Because." Miller agreed the two songs had pop possibilities and said he would find artists to record them.

Then Rose brought out the third song he'd carried to New York, "Cold, Cold Heart," which nobody in the pop field seemed to want. Miller listened to it and said, "What do you think?"

"I think it'll be a smash hit," replied Rose, a little desperately.

"Have you shown it to anybody?"

"I've shown it to *every*body."

"What'd they say?"

"That it was nothing but a hillbilly song."

Mitch Miller nodded and chuckled. "Well, we'll show 'em," he said.

Miller began shoping around, and before long he had placed the song with an aspiring young pop singer named Tony Bennett: Bennett's Columbia recording of "Cold, Cold Heart" sold over a million copies and became number one on the pop charts. It also launched the Bennett career.

Polly Bergen already had made a hit with a Williams

song, "Honky Tonkin'," but it was Bennett's record of
"Cold, Cold Heart" that finally established Hank as a
pop songwriter. That was in 1951. In the next few
years such titans of pop singing as Frankie Laine and
Jo Stafford recorded Williams' work. Bennett then made
a hit out of "There'll Be No Teardrops Tonight." That
launched a trend that still continues. For since his
death, Hank's songs have made their way into the
singles and albums of just about every leading pop
artist.

"Hank," says Wesley Rose, "earned two major distinctions as a songwriter. He was the first writer on a
regular basis to make country music national music.
And he was the first country songwriter accepted by
pop artists and pop A and R men." A and R, or Artists
and Repertory, men are a critical part of the recording
business. They direct the entire recording process and
sometimes help select the artist's material as well.

A number of country writers before Hank's time
broke the pop barrier with a song or two. Jimmie Davis
had "You Are My Sunshine"; Ernest Tubb had "Walking the Floor Over You"; Redd Stewart and Pee Wee
King had "Tennessee Waltz," which Patti Page turned
into a nearly two-million seller. But no country writer
broke the barrier over and over again, as Hank did.
Hank, in fact, put a permanent hole in it. Since he
showed the way, the distinctions between pop and
country have become more and more blurred.

The pop field has done most of the blurring, for its
own advantage. Pop artists of varying styles now record
in Nashville to get the modern, upbeat country sound
behind them. The list is long, full of big names, and
comprised of foreigners as well as Americans: Ray
Charles, Johnny Ray, Al Hirt, Burl Ives, Gogi Grant,
Pete Fountain, Johnny Halliday of France, Lonnie
Donegan of England, and many more.

Having pop music as a customer has given Nashville's country music industry a significant boost. The
bulk of it, of course, is publishing, recording, and
talent management. A recent survey turned up thirty-

five record company offices, four record-pressing plants, three performing rights societies (ASCAP, BMI, and SESAC), four major and eight independent recording studios, several dozen song publishers and eighteen talent agencies. Nashville, which was barely in the recording business when Hank Williams arrived there twenty years ago, is now second only to New York as a recording center.

One of the most important factors in this tremendous growth has been the ability of Nashville's musicians to produce, on demand, what has become known as the "Nashville Sound." Nobody has a perfectly clear idea of what Nashville Sound is, and it may be as much fancied as real, as much psychological as tangible. At the same time, nobody denies that it is something very important.

According to popular music people of all stripes, the Nashville Sound is the peculiar combination of tones, textures, and rhythms produced by the city's side men, musicians who back up the artists at recording sessions. The sound is smooth, uncluttered, and above all relaxed, a sort of honeyed country style that has become one of the most sought-after commodities in all of popular music.

If the Nashville Sound cannot be defined, it can at least be described. Chief among its hallmarks is lack of written musical arrangements. The musicians learn the song by ear and then, in the recording studio, improvise the accompaniment to it. Originality and spontaneous changes are encouraged. The technique, in the trade, is called "faking" or "using head arrangements," and only in Nashville is it so widespread in recording sessions. Owen Bradley, head of Decca in Nashville, calls it "sort of like a jam session, only with much smoother results." Bradley adds: "Perfection is not necessarily what you're looking for. You don't want to miss notes or louse up the rhythm, of course, but you do want to play free."

Another hallmark is a casual, friendly, cooperative atmosphere in the studio. "The musician doesn't just sit down in his chair and say, 'Get it up there and I'll play it,' " says George Cooper, long-time head of Nashville's American Federation of Musicians local 257. "He thinks about what he's playing and about how to improve it. He and the side men he's working with are interested in one thing—getting the record perfect. The boys in New York say, 'Okay, the three hours is up, let's go home.' Here they're more likely to stay till the record is the way they want." Musicians in Nashville are really little more charitable with their time than those in other cities, but they do seem to have a greater personal interest in the recording and a greater willingness to search for something different in order to improve it.

A Nashville recording session is a surprisingly casual scene. A session for singer Ray Price I watched in 1964 contained as much talk about fishing as about music. Group leader Grady Martin, who is one of the top music men in town, led the first two takes on a song while eating a sandwich, and steel guitarist Buddy Emmons swigged from a bottle of beer between solos. Martin and pianist Floyd Cramer, who is a recording artist as well as a first-rank side man, warmed up for the session with several games of ping-pong.

It is the side men, not the headliners, who produce the Nashville Sound. Although they get little recognition for it outside the music fraternity, their financial rewards are considerable. About fifty of them are "first call" side men, that is, in constant demand at the various recording studios; among this group, earnings of 50,000 dollars or more are not unusual (adding in publishing and songwriting profits, royalties from records on which they are the artists, and so forth, brings the total income for some into six figures). Side men who earn that much make it from work, not from higher prices, because they all belong to the AF of M and get union scale. The only exception is for the group leader on a given session, who gets double the regular rate of sixty-one dollars for a three-hour session.

The Nashville Sound, or at least the awareness of it, is a rather recent phenomenon. In Hank Williams' day, the Drifting Cowboys produced the then-standard country music sound by paying strict attention to the predetermined arrangements. They played, say, "I'm So Lonesome I Could Cry" on a recording session almost exactly the way they played it on show dates. The arrangements were treated more lightly when non-Drifting Cowboys worked the sessions as side men.

In turning Hank's songs into pop as well as country hits, Fred Rose had to be very careful not to undercut Hank as an artist. Rose realized that immediately, and he and Mitch Miller made an informal agreement. As Miller described it several years ago, the agreement was that, after Miller had decided which songs he wanted to place with pop artists, he would hold up until those songs were cut by Hank himself and getting a full run in the country field. Pop recordings of a Williams song, Miller said, "would be released only with Rose's permission, after Hank's record was out for a certain amount of time, so that we could take advantage of both fields." This arrangement, Miller pointed out, "protected Hank as an artist and, at the same time, it enhanced him as a writer."

Fred Rose, in pursuit of what was best for Hank Williams—and for Acuff-Rose—became by far the greatest influence on Hank's career. Not only did Rose decide what songs would be released when, what markets would be invaded and how, he polished and shaped and reshaped dozens of Hank's songs. He also, with the full approval of M-G-M, acted as overseer of the recording sessions themselves. In this capacity, he had more influence on the artist's recording techniques than anyone else. Fred Rose and Hank Williams, it must be acknowledged, formed one of the most successful artist-management combinations in all of show business.

Rose was among the most talented men ever to hit the country music field. According to an old story, he didn't even like the music when he first got to Nashville, fresh from writing and singing stuff in the pop vein. As a magazine writer told the story several years ago, Rose's first reaction to country music was astonishment: "Do they really let stuff like that go out on the air? People who sound like that ought to be in jail." But Rose was definitely impressed with the economics of country music, which permitted artists like Roy Acuff to make five thousand dollars a week while Rose himself was making thirty-five.

The explanation, Rose said later, "came to me one day while Acuff was singing, 'Don't Make Me Go to Bed and I'll Be Good.' Suddenly I said to myself, 'Are those tears splashing down that guy's shirt?' They were. And that's when I got it—the reason people like hillbilly tunes. 'Hell,' I said to myself, 'the guy *means* it.' "

Some country music people considered Rose abrupt, even unfriendly, at first meeting, but no one felt that way about him for long. For one thing, he was too generous with his time and talent. "He knew music more than anybody who's ever been in this town," says Jimmy Rule, the songwriter, "and he would go out of his way to help writers without claiming any credit for himself. You knew that if he completely rewrote your song, made a hit out of a dog, he wouldn't take anything for it."

The industry took note of this Rose quality when it elected him, in 1961, one of the first five members of the Country Music Hall of Fame, and the only one of the five not a performer. The Hall of Fame plaque begins with the words: "Fred Rose was always ready to lend a helping hand to a young artist or a new songwriter. His guidance helped many to stardom. . . ."

Two of Rose's most endearing characteristics were nearsightedness and tenaciousness. His poor vision was the butt of many a gentle joke. Jerry Rivers of the Drifting Cowboys recalls how "a recording session almost broke up once when Fred filled his cigarette lighter with Three-in-One oil." Country music people still chuckle over the story, probably apocryphal, about how Rose, riding in a car one particularly dark night, pointed to an object ahead and said, "Let's get a cup of coffee at that restaurant," whereupon his companion said, "Hell, Fred, that's no restaurant, that's a truck!"

Aaron Shelton and Carl Jenkins, Nashville's pioneer recording engineers, recall vividly how Rose suffered a heart attack one day during a Hank Williams session at the old Tulane Hotel. "He just went out to the lobby and sat down," says Shelton, still awed at the memory, "and a little while later he was back in the studio, sitting at the piano and working out arrangements. 'I'll be all right,' he said." Rose was a Christian Scientist, but everybody who saw that performance considered it Christian Science plus. He died of another heart attack several years later.

When Rose and Roy Acuff formed the Acuff-Rose publishing company, it was not an uncommon occurrence for a country music writer to get a raw deal. The publishers were up North, the writers, for the most part, down South, and there could be many a slip between writing a song and getting paid for it. "In the early days," says Jimmy Rule, "the publishers would take you for a sucker if you let 'em do it. I remember one time a songwriter friend of mine placed a song he'd written with a certain company in Hollywood. They told him to record the song on a demo [demonstration record] and they'd send him an advance of a thousand dollars. Well, he recorded it, and they didn't send him a check for any amount. Then they told him to sign the contracts, and they'd send the money. He signed them, and still no money. When he called them to see what was going on, they denied promising him anything.

" 'You're a bunch of damned liars,' he told them. 'You got me, all right, but I'm gonna tell every writer in this town about this deal, so you'll never get anybody else.' Two days later, he got his check for a thousand dollars."

Perhaps because it was a home-town firm, perhaps because it was run by a couple of honest, considerate men, Acuff-Rose eschewed the shady deal from the start. It treated its writers as people, not as victims. "They didn't pay better than the other publishers," says

Rule, "but they always paid. Whatever your song made, you got your share."

Fred Rose was well known as a soft touch for song- writers. Not for deadbeats, but for productive, bona fide writers, and not so much for charity as for an investment. When he first recorded Hank Williams, he went out and bought Hank a new stage uniform, largely to give him a psychological boost. Rose gave Hank ad- vances against royalties many times during their associ- ation. Sometimes he gave other Acuff-Rose writers, and perhaps Hank as well, advances out of his own pocket. More often than not, his confidence in them paid off in profits for Acuff-Rose.

While Fred Rose helped and to some extent man- aged most of Acuff-Rose's songwriters, he devoted more time to Hank Williams than to any of the others. For one thing, Rose felt a certain sympathy for and rapport with Hank. More important, he saw quickly that Hank had the makings of a great writer and recording artist.

There were carefully laid plans for marketing Hank Williams' talent. "One of the secrets of Hank's success as a recording artist," says Wesley Rose, "was that my father never came back to the market with the same kind of song. He went from a blues to a ballad to some- thing else in bringing out Hank's records."

But the Roses realized that there were two markets for Hank's songs—country and pop. Despite several great successes in the pop market, Hank could not go "across the board" on most of his songs. That is, his own recordings could not generally be expected to sell to pop fans primarily because of his country singing style, particularly the "tear," or break, in his voice. "We knew Hank could sell a half million records to one market," says Wesley Rose, "then Rosemary Clooney or somebody else could sell another half million to the other market. That is the great thing about Hank's songs. A lot of country stuff is *only* country. But Hank's songs can be done successfully by colored singers, by Japanese singers, by any type."

While Fred Rose was varying Hank's records, Wesley

was visiting the offices of pop music people trying to get Hank's songs recorded by pop artists. It was a two-front war, records and songs, and the Roses fought it relentlessly. Hank's great success on both fronts was due substantially to their efforts.

Under the arrangement between Acuff-Rose and M-G-M Records, Fred Rose supervised all of Hank's recording sessions. Rose was not an A and R man, and he was not being paid by M-G-M; he did it because he had a vital interest in the finished product. "We'd do all the recording, ship the masters up to M-G-M, and tell them what to release and when," says Wesley Rose. "Their job was to do the promotion and sell the records."

Nashville's recording facilities, in those days, had no echo chambers, no sophisticated techniques for making a full sound out of a thin one or a good sound out of a poor one. Hank's backup in recording sessions normally consisted of a steel guitar, a rhythm guitar, an electric guitar, a fiddle, and a bass. Hank always played his own guitar as well, meaning there were often two rhythm guitars in the group. He played despite Rose's urging that he stick to singing and let the side men handle the backup work.

When Rose suggested he put aside his guitar, a fine, steel-stringed Martin "dreadnought," Hank replied, "I paid good money for this old box, and I ain't goin' to lay it down now."

His insistence on playing as part of the session made good sense. As Jerry Rivers has written, "He could feel the tune better when he accompanied himself, and he also knew that the simple 'long chord' rhythm suited his singing style and added to the finished record." This same long chord style, the steady strumming of the basic chords of the song without embellishments, remains a staple of Nashville recording sessions.

Fred Rose occasionally played piano as part of the backup group, quite an innovation in those days. The piano added fullness and smoothed out the rough, chunky sound of the string band.

Hank liked his side men to get a little solo recognition, but Rose shunned that for himself, preferring to keep his piano work soft and undistinguishable. So one day Hank trapped him. He told the other musicians to stop playing and singing a few notes from the end of the song. They all did, together, and Rose, faithfully following the arrangement, played on alone. "I just wanted to have you on records," drawled Hank. He insisted the record be issued that way, and it was, with Rose's mini-solo preserved for posterity.

Many of Hank's songs required some kind of group singing of the chorus. There were no polished groups like today's Jordanaires, so the Drifting Cowboys or whoever else was backing up the session did the singing. It didn't matter that they were principally instrumentalists, not singers. Other people in the studio often joined in on the choruses. "We'd sing—or holler—right along," recalls Wesley Rose. "I can still pick out my voice on one of Hank's records."

Fred Rose also used the boys-in-the-band approach to provide rhythmic responses in a number of Hank's songs. "Move It On Over" is a good example. The boys half sing, half chant "move it on over" as their contribution to the chorus.

Rose also introduced what is known as the "dead string" technique of rhythm to Hank's recording sessions. He turned the amplifier for the electric guitar way down to make the sound of the guitar a thump. This dead string sound took the place of a drum, which was taboo in country music at that time.

Few of the backup musicians read music, so Rose either played the song they were going to record on the piano or played an acetate disk of it. The acetates were cut in the attic of Rose's house, on Rainbow Trail in Nashville. Rose had fashioned a record cutter out of an old Majestic radio and assorted spare parts, hauled in a piano, and turned the attic into a workable studio. Whenever a session was imminent, he and Hank would get together in this attic studio to go over the music that would be recorded.

"Hank would bring in a shoe box full of lyrics," says Wesley Rose. "Some of them were complete sets of lyrics, others were just snatches of songs or ideas for them. My father would go through them and give back all but a half dozen or so. 'Work on the rest,' he'd tell Hank. 'They're not ready.' He and Hank would finish up the half dozen, get them ready to record. Then they'd put them on acetate, usually with my father playing the piano and Hank singing."

The most important function of the acetate disk was not to demonstrate the song to the side men but to give Rose something to work with in polishing it. He would change a little here, a little there, and still go back to the original song whenever he wanted to.

The sessions in the attic studio were usually private, but on one occasion Rose brought his partner Roy Acuff along. "Roy and Hank spent the whole time singing each other's songs," recalls Wesley Rose. "Hank would cry when he sang one of Roy's, and vice versa. When I drove Roy back to town he told me, 'That's a good boy, Wes. You watch out for him.' "

Wesley Rose minimizes the differences between his father and Hank over what songs would be recorded, but inevitably there were some. They stemmed, it seems, from the vast differences in the backgrounds, musical and non-musical, of the two men. One of the regulars on Hank's recording sessions recalls Fred Rose's angry reaction to the song, "My Bucket's Got a Hole in It," a whimsical ditty about losing beer through a hole in the bucket. "Fred said, 'That's not music, you go ahead and cut it if you want to,' and he walked out of the studio. He was smart enough to realize that if Hank wanted to cut it, it probably should be cut, but he couldn't bring himself to be part of it." Hank did record the song, and it became a hit.

Rose also had a hand in the marketing of Hank's "Luke the Drifter" records. Luke the Drifter was a pseudonym Hank applied to a number of recitations he performed and recorded. The recitations generally were doleful pronouncements packing rather commonplace maxims, such as, don't criticize other people unless your own house is in order. There are a few noteworthy exceptions, however. A number called "Too Many Parties and Too Many Pals" blames men and society in general for prostitution by means of a little courtroom scene in which the judge admits to the jury that the shady lady on trial is his own daughter. "The Funeral," in which Hank happens upon a shabby black funeral service, is a sympathetic portrait of "the wisdom and ignorance of a crushed, undying race."

In all, the recitations form an interesting picture of Hank's own simple philosophy, with its emphasis on humility, compassion, love of God and mother, and frequent flashes of humor. They were usually set against a sweetly sad, three-quarter time background, with a steel guitar accenting the plaintive theme. Hank always loved the recitations, because of the showmanship they required and because they offered a vehicle for putting across some of his more serious thoughts.

Writer Allen Rankin recalls that one time after playing a recording of "Men with Broken Hearts," a recitation that sounds the don't-criticize-others theme, Hank exclaimed happily: "Isn't that the awfullest, morbidest song you ever heard in your life?" After another playing of the same song, he turned serious and told Rankin: "Don't know why I happened to of wrote that thing. Except somebody that's fell, he's the same man ain't he? So how can he be such a nice guy when he's got it and such a bad guy when he ain't got nothin'?"

Although Hank sometimes performed Luke the Drifter material onstage, the fact that he was Luke was supposed to be a secret—undoubtedly one of the worst-kept secrets in Nashville. The reason for the secret was that the people managing Hank's recording career didn't want the public to get Hank and Luke, and the different types of material they offered, mixed up. As Wesley Rose puts it, "Recitations are not built for the saloon trade. That's like preaching in a tavern." Hank agreed. He didn't like the idea of his more serious songs having to compete with the boozy noise found in such places.

Hank wrote most of the Luke the Drifter material himself. But Fred Rose wrote at least one of the pieces, and others, says Wesley, came from "stuff we sorta kicked around between us."

Fred Rose's most important contribution to Hank's success, even more important than guiding his recording career, was the way in which he shaped Hank's songs. Nashville people talk about how Rose "polished" the songs, but his influence went well beyond polishing. Songwriter Jimmy Rule, who knew and worked with both men, says that "Fred Rose added as much to those songs as Hank did. It took the two of them together to turn out material like that."

Rule is overstating the case, and Rose, a modest man, would spin in his grave at such praise. In truth, the Rose contribution varied widely from song to song, because the condition of the material varied widely. Hank's songs reached Rose in all sorts of stages, from complete lyrics and melody to half verses and a rough outline to a chorus and no melody to nothing but a theme or an idea. Rose, who was one of the slickest, most professional songwriters in the history of American popular music, took each song or germ of a song and did what had to be done.

Although it is difficult to point to specific examples, most of the songs Hank wrote after he joined Acuff-Rose bear the Fred Rose imprint in one way or another. Jimmy Rule, pondering the poetry of "I'm So Lonesome I Could Cry," says, "I can see Fred Rose in that song. It is expertly written, and I don't believe Hank could have done it all himself."

Rose's most frequent contributions was smoothing out Hank's lyrics, adding a word or a phrase that brought the song alive. But he effected basic changes as well. He is credited, for instance, with adding the twist that made "Kaw-liga," one of Hank's novelty songs, a big hit in 1952. "Kaw-liga," wrote Eli Waldron in a 1956 issue of *Coronet,* "began with Williams as the

usual dull and customary recital of unrequited love—
this time among the Cherokees of Alabama—and ended
with Rose as a lively little ditty about unrequited love
between a pair of wooden Indians."

Hank got the basic idea for "Kaw-liga" (pronounced
Kuh-lie-juh) from Lake Kowaliga, a vacation spot near
Montgomery where he had fished. He whipped off a
catchy, foot-tapping song with a ONE-two-three-four,
ONE-two-three-four beat. Rose added the wooden Indian theme, and the resulting song was twice as good
as Hank's original.

Rose took credit as co-author on "Kaw-liga" and on
five other pieces commonly known as Hank Williams'
songs: "If I Didn't Love You," "Minni-Ha-Cha" (a
follow-up to "Kaw-liga"—"Minni-Ha-Cha was the
name of the maid that was ol' Kaw-liga's gal"), "You're
Barkin' Up the Wrong Tree Now," "I'll Never Get Out
of This World Alive," and "Mansion on the Hill." The
last two became hits, which is ironic in both cases.
"Mansion" is the song that, according to false but persistent legend, Hank composed on the spot to prove to
Rose that he was really a songwriter. And "World,"
one of Hank's last songs was fulfilling the doleful
prophecy of its title at precisely the time it became a
hit—early in 1953, just after Hank died; in January
of that year, it ranked number three in the *Billboard*
country and Western chart.

Generally, however, Rose declined to put his name
on songs he helped Hank write. He gained his satisfaction, and made his money, by working in the background. "Rose was a hell of a touch-up man," says
songwriter Vic McAlpin. "When I saw a fancy word or
phrase in one of the songs, I'd tell Hank, 'Fred just
about wrote that song, didn't he?'" That was one
writer's way of needling another, and Hank, who had
only an average amount of vanity, didn't mind.

Rose was as strong on the nuts and bolts of songwriting as on the flourishes. McAlpin remembers a piece
of advice Rose gave him many years ago: "The first
song I ever wrote had no bridge—just one sixteen-bar

verse after another. Fred listened to it and told me, 'Don't ever write another song without a bridge. When you've got one, your song's got twice as much chance of appealing to people.' "

Bob McCluskey, an executive with Acuff-Rose, recalls, "Hank told me frankly that most of his songs couldn't have been commercially successful without the aid of Fred Rose." Hank was right about that; some of the songs could not have been nearly so successful without Rose. But neither could Rose's work on them have been nearly so effective without the great material Hank provided. That was the key to the Williams-Rose songwriting success. Many of Hank's songs were rough diamonds, which Rose polished to a high gloss. Hard as it is to apportion credit in such a partnership, it is clear that Rose's contribution was craftsmanship, while Williams' was genius.

12

While Hank's songs often took some polishing, his in-person performances did not. He was strictly a self-made talent on stage, combining natural showmanship with a keep appreciation of other performers. Roy Acuff and Ernest Tubb were two country artists who impressed Hank as a young man. He mixed a little of their styles with a lot of his own and emerged with a stage personality that has never been surpassed in the country music field.

From the time he joined the Grand Ole Opry until literally the day he died, Hank was a traveling performer, playing one-night stands in cities and towns throughout the United States and up into Canada. He liked that life, but following it was a matter of necessity, not of choice. That is the way the country music business works, even today in the era of lucrative television appearances, movie contracts, and strings of hit records. It is the way the country artist builds his market value and his image and, if he is a good one, his own spirit as well.

Hank followed the Grand Ole Opry pattern: work the Opry Friday and Saturday nights, hit the road to capitalize on your Opry name the rest of the week. Although Hank became a top artist almost as soon as he reached the Opry, it took him months to command top money on show dates. He and the Drifting Cowboys knocked down 250 dollars or a little better when they began working out of Nashville in the summer of 1949. One thousand dollars a night was the top wage in those days, and he didn't get that until late the following year.

Jack McFadden, now the personal manager for Buck Owens, the country star in Bakersfield, California, secured the first thousand-dollar payment for Hank. "Hank told me that the most money he had ever received for him and the band was six hundred dollars," says McFadden, who was just twenty-three years old and, by his own admission, "financially unstable" at the time. "I booked a tour from San Diego to Washington for him for a minimum of a thousand dollars a day against a percentage, whichever was greater. The way the tour turned out, he went into a percentage almost every date." In other words, he was drawing capacity crowds all along the way.

Once Hank reached the thousand-dollar-a-night level, he cut the price only for small towns. For big dates, he got the top wage. He knew he was worth the money, and he got it.

Hank paid each of the Drifting Cowboys the same amount of money, and it was always above union scale. When he assembled the group in Nashville, he paid fifteen dollars a performance; scale was ten. In his last few months, when scale was up to twenty-five dollars, he paid forty. During his big years, he paid each band member a salary rather than on a per-job basis. As a top artist, he could not take the risk of having one or more members off on another job when he needed them for a show or recording date. That would have meant scrounging around for last-minute replacements, an aggravating chore the top artists avoid wherever possible.

There was ample precedent for putting the band members on salary. Roy Acuff in his heyday, made his Smoky Mountain Boys and Girls an integral part of the Acuff empire. Acuff kept the group under yearly contract, and when its members were not performing they were working at his Dunbar Cave resort, near Clarksville, Tennessee, painting, feeding Roy's fancy fowl, and so forth. As Acuff once explained it, "We live together and we play together."

When Hank first began working out of Nashville, he did all his traveling by car. Later, he traveled by private plane while the band members hauled themselves and the instruments in the car. Later still, when he was often drunk and sick, he hired limousines to take him to show dates.

Hank brought his blue Packard and accompanying trailer when he came to Nashville from Shreveport. He bought a Cadillac convertible for his wife Audrey— the first of several Cadillacs he was to own—and kept the Packard-*cum*-trailer for his traveling car.

The trailer had no brakes of its own, and Hank reluctantly abandoned it after its momentum resulted in a couple of near-miss accidents. On one occasion, hauling the trailer, Jerry Rivers was whistling along a highway when a farm truck pulled out from a side road. "I put all my weight on the brake pedal for about a quarter of a mile," recalls Rivers in his booklet, *Hank Williams: From Life to Legend,* "before stopping just in time to avoid a collision. When we finally got stopped we smelled something burning and found both back wheels were red hot and both tires were on fire."

In 1950, Hank bought a green Cadillac, the then-new fish-tail style with all kinds of accessories and gadgets he and the boys had never seen before. The Cadillac, although outfitted with jump seats, was none too spacious a vehicle when forced to hold five men, their instruments, their suitcases, and assorted other gear.

"By today's standards, we were pretty crowded and uncomfortable," says Rivers, "especially since we often traveled all day long to get to that night's show date. But all the bands did the same thing, so we didn't think much about it. Nowadays, most of them have buses of some kind, and it's a lot easier traveling."

Indeed it is. Some of the buses are not only roomy, they are rather luxurious. David Houston and his band, the Persuaders (named for Houston's big hit, "Almost Persuaded"), travel in a bus that sleeps six and is equipped with an electric stove, built-in television set, wood-grain paneling, wall to wall carpeting on both floor and ceiling, and full closets. Houston bought it from a wealthy businessman who used it for weekend jaunts.

An investment in a comfortable vehicle is money well spent for a country music performer. Playing a series of one-nighters is at best a grueling business, and if he and his side men can relax a little along the way they will be that much fresher for their show dates. Hank and the Drifting Cowboys had to do their relaxing by jockeying for leg room, slouching into a semi-reclining position to catch a few winks, and joking among themselves to help the hours pass.

When Hank and the band were traveling, says Rivers, the only groups that had buses were the Western bands; they had more members, and a car simply wouldn't hold them all. The Drifting Cowboys, on long trips, seldom spent money on hotel rooms. They would grind straight through from one date to the next, catching what sleep they could in the car. Even trips from Nashville to California were pretty much non-stop except for meals, gas, and "piss calls."

"On those long trips," says Rivers, "we'd generally leave just enough time to get to the destination, by driving straight through. If everything went okay, we'd catch some sleep after we got there, before the first show."

Hank seldom did the driving (the prerogative of the man who owns the car), letting the band members split it among them. He was not an easy man to drive for. Except when he was composing a song, he was apt to be jittery and overly concerned with the road tactics of the man behind the wheel. He loved to listen to baseball games on the car radio. Any game would do—he had no favorite teams—and he drove everybody half crazy switching back and forth between games, trying to pick up the scores or find an exciting inning. For a while he carried a ball and some gloves in the car, so the boys could play catch during idle hours on tour.

One thing Hank's luxury limousines did not have was air conditioning, which was still in the developmental stage for automobiles. Summer travel was rugged, and Hank became determined, by gum, that he'd have some kind of "window water cooler," a gadget that was supposed to keep the inside of the car moderately cool by constant evaporation of water. The trouble was, it was meant for dry climates, not for the humid bayous.

One summer day, the temperature rose higher and higher inside the car, and Hank kept pulling the gadget's "saturation cord" to get more water to evaporate. Finally, when the temperature climbed over the hundred mark, recalls Jerry Rivers, "he gave the cord a violent, desperate pull, and the entire two-gallon water supply discharged into the side of his head and onto the front seat." Hank proceeded to stomp hell out of the cooler, and on the return trip, he left it on the doorstep of the place where he bought it.

When Hank became really big time, he abandoned the car in favor of an airplane, which cut travel time and left him less fatigued. He seldom flew commercially, preferring the charter services of Henry Cannon, a Nashville man who is the husband and manager of comedienne Minnie Pearl. Cannon flew a lot of Opry stars around in those days. "Hank didn't really like to fly," says Minnie Pearl, "and he got to the point where he didn't want to go up with anybody but Henry. Even though he could've gotten where he was going a lot faster in a bigger plane, he felt safer with Henry."

He felt relaxed enough with Cannon to write songs en route. According to Pearl, he wrote one of his biggest hits, "Jambalaya," in the rear seat of Cannon's plane. The band members, meanwhile, stuck to the road, hauling themselves and their equipment in Hank's car.

Like most country music artists, and many other people as well, when Hank hit it big, he had to have Cadillacs from then on. So the trusty Packard that had served him in Shreveport and through the first months in Nashville gave way to a series of Cadillac limousines. They came in a variety of colors, but all had jump seats, to accommodate the band members, and each one seemed longer and wider than the last.

When funny incidents cropped up along the tour routes, the limousines themselves frequently were involved. Jerry Rivers, in his booklet on Hank, recalls a couple of such incidents:

"I was driving Hank's new Cadillac into Tampa, Florida, when a buzzard flew up off the highway and right through the windshield to distribute himself about the inside of the car in various assorted pieces. I finally got the car stopped and frantically thought I was blind until I found my sunglasses were matted with feathers. Ken Marvin, who was riding with us, had to get out and be sick.

"Another time we were pulling a small 'bullet' utility trailer into Nashville from Little Rock. When we stopped at the Tennessee River for a catfish supper, we found nothing attached to the car but the coupling rod, axle, and wheels. The trailer body containing all our instruments and clothes was gone. About fifteen miles back down the highway the aluminum body had disengaged and slid along the highway for about a quarter-mile with a shower of sparks from the steel frame. We found two farmers with heavy sticks standing by to see what was going to get out."

Adds Rivers: "All of this was about the time George Morgan and his band were having rotten-egg fights in a hotel room, and Bill Monroe had to chase his bus twenty miles in a taxi after the band drove off and left him in a service station rest room." Those were the days.

Such "funnies," as the boys called them, eased the grind of traveling. So did stopping at occasional spots where friends and hospitality and diversions could be found. One of these spots was Biloxi, Mississippi, where a night club owner named Si Simon was always ready with a welcoming smile and plans for relaxation. "Regardless of where we were booked around Biloxi, in the auditorium, on the beach, or in the stadium," says Rivers, "Hank would always make a deal with Si to make a late appearance at his club, Si's Place." After the show, Si provided tubs of boiled shrimp, a cruise on his yacht, lemon fish or mackerel fishing in the gulf, and enough libations to keep everyone happy.

Hank was so fond of Simon and so grateful for his hospitality that he never failed to honor a date at Si's Place no matter what inconvenience it might entail. "On one occasion," recalls Rivers, "he took a taxi from Nashville to Biloxi to avoid missing a date there, and on another occasion he chartered a DC-3 with about twenty-four seats. The plane landed in Biloxi with Hank, the pilot, and co-pilot aboard." Hank was that kind of man. He craved friendship and kindness, and he returned them with interest. That is, he did so during his good years. Later, beset by drink and emotional problems, he could be rude, overbearing, and totally unresponsive to kind words or offers of friendship.

One trait Hank never lost was generosity with money. He handed it out in great gobs to the most unlikely people at the most unlikely times. For one thing, he thought this was the way a big country music star was supposed to act. For another, he was plain careless about money. But he was also truly generous in spirit. He enjoyed making people, especially little people, happy, and giving them money was an obvious and easy way of doing that.

One time he did display the human weakness for wealth, and he did so in a childlike manner. When Vic McAlpin, the songwriter, went to pick him up for fishing one morning, he led McAlpin into his den. "There were stacks of one-dollar bills all over the floor," says McAlpin, "probably four thousand dollars in all. He'd gone to the bank and drawn it all out."

While McAlpin stood there amazed, Hank scooped up handfuls of dollar bills and scattered them around the room. "I was so poor most of my life," he said as the bills fluttered to the floor, "I've always dreamed about being able to do this."

Except for that occasion, when he literally wallowed in money, Hank showed little concern for the stuff. He bought fancy clothes, a fancy house, fancy cars, because this was what a rich man did; besides, he hoped it would make him and Audrey happy. There is a story that Hank stashed money, payments for his show dates, in little banks all over the country, as the late W. C. Fields is said to have done. If he did, his closest friends didn't know about it. Anyway, that kind of fearful hoarding was not in line with Hank's personality. He was open and relaxed about money, and he was unconcerned, too much so, about people taking it away from him.

Hank habitually carried money around in wads of large denomination bills. When he had to buy something, he simply peeled off enough bills and stuck the wad back in his pocket. No one can recall him getting rolled, and if he never did, it is a small miracle.

On show dates, Hank often told the promoter to pay one of the members of the band. After all, somebody else—his mother—had gotten the money at the roadhouses back in south Alabama. Hank figured he'd get his share in the end, and he saw no need to keep track of it along the way. On one occasion he brought several fistfuls of bills into his Nashville bank and piled it up in front of the teller. How much was Mr. Williams depositing? the teller wanted to know. "How the hell do I know?" replied Hank. "My job is to make it. Your job is to count it."

Hank was a soft touch for country music people with hard luck stories and for anybody just starting out in the business. He was startlingly generous with waiters and bellhops and other service personnel. In Beaumont, Texas, he once gave a clerk a hundred-dollar bill for a bottle of whisky, and when the clerk offered him the change, he said, "Forget it. You need it more than I do." Tips of ten or twenty dollars were not uncommon. They were given casually, even carelessly, without concern for effusive thanks or anticipation of extra services in return.

Hank's generosity had a quiet, private side as well as a splashy, public one. After his death it was discovered that he had for some time been contributing four hundred dollars a month to a Catholic orphanage in Montgomery—and he, of course, was not a Catholic.

Comedienne Minnie Pearl, who has seen hundreds of country music performers come and go, considers Hank Williams something special. His magic, she agrees, did not stem from any single asset—not his voice, nor his appearance, nor his style. None of these was extraordinary. "We got boys who can sing three times as good as him, people used to tell me," says Pearl. "Sure, but they'd never get that great, cataclysmic reaction from the audience that Hank got. Look at me, I'm not funny, but I've built up the fact that I love to perform, and the people know I love it. That sort of thing is contagious, and it's more valuable than being able to sing or being funny or anything else. So you can't criticize the way an artist like Hank sings. You just swing with it and admit, 'Don't he kill an audience?' "

Pearl recalls the first show she played with Hank, in Great Bend, Kansas. "I was supposed to follow him on, and I never had such a time following anybody. He got a fantastic reaction from the audience. I couldn't get on stage, because they wouldn't let him off. My act was going well at the time, and it was downright embarrassing for me. I remember I told the promoter, and I was only half joking, 'I don't ever want to follow this man again.' There was no way for anybody to get near Hank when he was at his best."

"You could hear a pin drop when Hank was working," says Little Jimmy Dickens, who shared many a stage with him. "He just seemed to hypnotize those people." Why? "You couldn't put your finger on it. Simplicity, I guess. He brought the people with him, put himself on their level."

"Hank didn't have much personality except when he was singing," says Allen Rankin. "That's when his real personality came out. He'd come slopping and slouching out on stage, limp as a dishrag. But when he picked up the guitar and started to sing, it was like a charge of electricity had gone through him. He became three feet taller."

To Ott Devine, former general manager of the Grand Ole Opry, Hank was "a genius" as a performer. "He has to have been the top artist during his time," said Devine not long ago. "I'd stand on stage and watch our audiences when Hank was working. They were plain spellbound." Asked if Williams has any peers in today's ranks of country music performers, Devine named a couple of current stars, then said, "but I wouldn't want to put them in a class with Hank."

When *Downbeat* magazine took a poll the year after Hank's death, he was voted the most popular country and Western performer of all time—ahead of such giants as Jimmie Rodgers, Roy Acuff, Red Foley, and Ernest Tubb.

It is worth examining Hank the performer in detail, for the insights it offers into country music as a whole as well as for an understanding of Williams as an artist. First, his voice. It was a good voice, but not a great one. Certainly it was not a pretty voice; it had no crooning qualities, highly prized by many of today's country artists. Hank's voice, no matter what the song, had a cutting edge. The edge gave his songs much of their emotional impact, in pieces ranging from "I Saw the Light" to "Your Cheatin' Heart" to "Lovesick Blues."

Allen Rankin caught the essence of it in the booklet *Our Hank Williams,* which he wrote for Hank's mother: "He had a voice that went through you like electricity, sent shivers up your spine, and made the hair rise on the back of your neck with the thrill. With a voice like that he could make you laugh or cry." Talk of shivering spines and rising hair are not mere hyperbole. Hank at his best could produce these reactions.

Aside from the quality of Hank's voice, several other things made it distinctive. One was his range. He had good range, including the ability to sustain high notes at the right volume and with the right vibrato. Another was his phrasing, which was natural and distinct, and a third was his timing. He could slide easily from one note or one tempo into another, and he handled demanding songs such as "Lovesick Blues" without difficulty.

Finally, and most important, his voice had heart—or soul, as it's now called. Just as he tried to write it like it was, so did he try to sing it like it was. In so doing he was much more in the lineage of Ray Charles and Aretha Franklin than of the average run of country artist. Among the country types, Roy Acuff had this quality, and Johnny Cash has it today. Hank had it to a greater degree than either of them.

The comparison with soul music is not idle. Although there are obvious differences between it and country music, they have at least one basic feature in common. As the manager of the late Otis Redding, one of soul's biggest stars, expressed it: "Country and soul are the music of the have-nots of both races."

Hank often said his own style was a conscious cross between those of Acuff and Tubb. He took, he said, a little from each—the wailing, bluesy sound of Acuff and the phrasing of Tubb—added his own talents, and came up with a unique style.

Like all fine country singers (and this can be said of

soul singers too), Hank performed best on material he really liked. In his case that meant, almost invariably, songs he'd written himself. You can count on the fingers of one hand the songs Hank made great that were written by somebody else. Few country music stars ever have stuck so closely and so successfully to their own compositions. (Few stars in other fields of popular music have even tried; in pop, for instance, the writers traditionally have been writers, and the artists have been artists, with almost no overlapping.)

Wesley Rose, Hank's publisher, put it this way some years ago: "A lot of people misunderstood Hank. He was a blunt speaking man. He had the habit of saying exactly what he meant, and he didn't have the sophistication to flower it up. His best work was done on material that he actually lived and felt. He couldn't sing very good on just words and music. In a recording session, he was telling a story with every song." On stage, he was doing the same thing.

Considering voice alone, it is interesting to ponder a self-deprecating remark made by Ernest Tubb, quoted in the Nashville *Tennessean* in 1967. Tubb said he owed his fame "to a single, strange thing. I've never been able to hold one note longer than one beat, and then it sort of trails off. So all over the country there are guys sitting in bars getting soused and trying to impress their girl. Then my voice comes on the jukebox and they say, 'I can sing better than that guy.' And in about ninety per cent of the cases, they're right."

It is hard to believe Tubb is serious. But if he is, his remark would hardly apply to Hank Williams. Hank knew he didn't have the world's greatest voice, but he knew he had a good one, a voice that was perfect for country music.

There is a great deal of showmanship in country music, more than in jazz and folk and most forms of pop. Hank had the peculiar blend of staginess and naturalness the country audience demands. The general public tends to think of country music in terms of flashy uniforms, corny jokes, and sobbing songs, but the ability to appear as one of the folks is as important to success as all of these. After Hank died, an old friend from Suttles, Alabama, Allen Dunkin, captured the man's folksy ability in one sentence. "I guess one reason people liked him so well when he was playing hillbilly music," Dunkin wrote to a Montgomery paper, "was he talked and acted just like an old country boy, and that is what we all were."

Hank had the easy smile, the homey good looks, and the howdy-friends-and-neighbors approach that country music audiences have always sought. He cut a commanding figure, with his six-foot, 140-pound frame draped in an impeccably tailored stage uniform. Hank wore the fancy costumes favored by country music performers. Like most aspects of country music, they have been slicked up and modernized in recent years. The "in" thing now is the Continental cut. But in Hank's day it was all pseudo-Western, with rhinestones and embroidery and fringe, the more outlandish the better.

Hank's stage uniforms were made by Nudie's Rodeo Tailors, in Hollywood, which has outfitted top country and Western artists for many years. Hank bought dozens of uniforms from Nudie, all custom made, at prices ranging up to 300 dollars, those he bought for the band cost 150 dollars apiece. Hank had no color preferences, but he was partial to decorations of piping and of embroidered music notes and musical instruments. For a rush order, Nudie would fly to wherever Hank was playing, take the measurements and decorative details, and rustle up a suit in no time.

(Although Hank is dead, Nudie marches on with the Williams legend. He made the suit Hank was buried in and the suit (same style as the burial outfit) worn by George Hamilton when he played Hank in the movie, *Your Cheatin' Heart*. He also makes the stage uniforms used by Hank Williams, Jr.)

Until drink took its toll, Hank's face was one of his chief show business assets. It was a long, angular face, with the piercing brown eyes, prominent cheekbones, and square jaw of a movie cowboy—an image accented by the Western hat he habitually wore. Pleasant when composed, his face was downright handsome when he smiled. His smile was his best single feature: warm and ingenuous, it was an irresistible opening wedge into the hearts of his listeners.

Actually, Hank's hat did more than accent the Western look. It hid a head that was sparsely endowed with hair. Hank was very sensitive to his balding condition, and although he had a toupee, he' seldom wore it. "I put that thing on last night, and when I woke up this morning I looked like Mo of the Three Stooges," he once told Don Helms. "The damn thing had gone crosswise on my head."

The toupee's last stand, recalls a fellow songwriter, came early one morning when the writer came by to take Hank fishing. The damn thing had gone crosswise again, prompting the writer to crack, "Boy, Audrey really socked you one last night. She turned your head halfway around." Hank rushed to the mirror, tore off the offending hairpiece, and never put it on again. The hat became his sole protection, and it was seldom off his head in public.

On stage, Hank had a little store of folksy sayings, which are always much appreciated by country music audiences. In his time, a couple of them became as well known as Minnie Pearl's famous introduction to her act —"How-DEEEEE!" They were the closing promise to see the folks again "if the good Lord's willin' and the creeks don't rise" and the chuckle-producing bromide, "Don't worry about nothin', cause it ain't gonna be all right nohow." To the "good Lord's willin'" line he often added an enthusiastic, "I'm comin', Bocephus!" Bocephus was his nickname for Hank, Jr. who sometimes listened to his daddy on the radio, and this meant the show was over and Daddy was on his way home.

"I was so proud to be on stage with him," says Minnie Pearl. "He had a real animal magnetism. He destroyed the women in the audience. They just had to have his autograph and get close enough to touch him.

It wasn't sex per se, like with some artists. He appealed to their maternal instincts a lot."

Pearl is being overly protective. Hank had plenty of sex appeal, and there was nothing maternal about it. On stage, he enhanced it with the body movements he made while singing a song. He hunched forward toward the microphone, buckling his knees and swaying with the music. "He'd close his eyes and swing one of those big long legs, and the place would go wild," says Don Helms.

Even today there is a minor debate in country music circles over Hank's stage movements. Some say they were unconscious, others say they were contrived. Some say that, contrived or not, they were the forerunner of Elvis Presley's pelvic gyrations. In any case, they contributed to the makeup of a great stage personality. With his genial folksiness, his compelling voice, his movements, and his ability to put over a song ("He wasn't a singer," says one Nashville musician, "but he could really sing"), Hank made his own songs sound even better than they were.

When Hank put together the Nashville version of the Drifting Cowboys, he made a few changes in the Shreveport format. The pattern was firmly established for all country bands, and he was not interested in changing it. At a typical show, the other Drifting Cowboys would go on stage alone at the outset, do a couple of instrumentals and perhaps sing a couple of songs together. Then one of the boys would introduce Hank, and he'd sing three or four songs with the band occasionally adding vocal as well as instrumental support. Among them, invariably, would be Hank's hottest song of the moment plus one of his religious numbers.

Then Hank would take center stage to deliver a monologue: a Luke the Drifter piece, a bit of light repartee, or some gentle barbs at the Drifting Cowboys. He had nicknames for everybody in the band—"Shag" for wavy-haired Don Helms; "Burrhead" for crew-cut Jerry Rivers; "Mule" for Hillous Butrum, to rhyme with his middle name of Buel—and he managed to work them into his monologue. "Now, Mule here . . ." he'd say. (The boys struck back by calling him "Old Harm," countrifying his give name, Hiram.)

While Hank was doing his bit, the bass player would slip off stage and don baggy pants, loud shirt, and the rest of his comic uniform. The average country music bass player in those days had to be a slapstick comedian too. Hank had always had one in the Drifting Cowboys, and he adhered to the tradition when he reformed the band in Nashville. Again, he did not think such a thing through; he did it automatically.

Hillous Butrum was the band's first bassist-comedian after Hank hit Nashville. Before long he gave way to a tall, goofy guy named Howard Watts. For some reason, Watts took the stage name Cedric Rainwater. Apparently he thought it was funny. Even if it wasn't, Ced himself was good for laughs. All gussied up in the usual silly suit, telling corny stories, and serving as the butt of the other boys' jokes, he quickly became a favorite with Hank's audiences.

Cedric could be funny off stage too. Jerry Rivers recalls a time in Mobile when Hank took the band into a fancy restaurant for dinner. When the waiter touted lobster, Hank, feeling expansive, ordered it for everyone. "We'd never, none of us, had lobster before," recalls Rivers. "But Ced was even more of a hillbilly than the rest of us. When his lobster came, he grabbed a nutcracker, put it across the middle and squeezed like mad. The lobster flew in two, and butter and lobster and everything went all over Hank. He jumped up and started cursing Cedric for being a dumb hillbilly. All Ced could manage was to stammer out, 'Well, shucks Hank, Ah hain't never had me none a them before.' "

When Cedric replaced Butrum, in July of 1950, it marked the last change in Drifting Cowboys personnel. The four men who played behind Hank then—Rainwater, fiddler Rivers, guitarist Sammy Pruett, and steel guitarist Don Helms—were the same four who played behind him until he left Nashville. It was a talented group of musicians, and if their talents weren't more readily apparent that was because the country music conventions of the day dictated that they not be. Hank was the bright light, and they, in effect, were the reflectors.

The Cowboys never griped about their role. On stage, Hank's enthusiasm was so contagious they were swept up in the general desire to make the best damned music possible. Hank, like Notre Dame's Knute Rockne, delighted in getting his boys up for the tough situation. "When we were going on after a particularly good act," says Hillous Butrum, "Hank would always say, 'Let's hit 'em hard, boys.' You knew then he was aimin' to tear that place up and we'd better be ready for encores."

When Hank wanted encores, he got them, just by singing his heart out. At a show in Atlanta one night, when "Cold, Cold Heart" had just hit the top of the charts, he encored that song a half-dozen times or more. The audience kept clapping and howling, and Hank kept singing. Had life required only that he sing to loving crowds of people, he'd be singing to them still.

13

In his travels as a Grand Ole Opry star, Hank performed in every section of the United States. Most of his show dates were in the South and Southwest, but he made many appearances—including several high-paying ones—in the Midwest. America's heartland is a surprisingly fertile field for country musicians. Midwesterners like the country sound almost as much as do Southerners, for country music is at least as much rural as it is Southern.

Everywhere he went during his two prime years,

Hank drew large and enthusiastic audiences. In the towns and smaller cities, he often was treated like visiting royalty. Jack Cardwell recalls that when Hank hit Mobile, he put up at the best hotel in town, the Admiral Semmes, and drew admirers by the score:

"He came across the street to station WALA," says Cardwell "and everybody followed him. They thought he was gonna go on the air and sing, but he wasn't. He remembered when he'd been in Mobile before, as a kid working in the shipyards. He hadn't been able to get on the station then, and he hadn't forgotten. He walked into the boss's office and told him, right in front of all of us, 'When I was in Mobile before, I tried to get on this station. I wasn't good enough then. Well, I reckon I still ain't good enough.' And he turned around and went over to the other station and went on the air there."

Later, Cardwell recalls, Hank appeared on stage in Mobile. "When he walked on that stage, he just gripped 'em. I mean, anything he did was great. He could've sung off key and it wouldn't't've made any difference— it was Hank Williams. It was like he was saying to those people: 'You've listened to the rest, now listen to the greatest.' "

In the big cities, Hank was not so self-assured. Still a country boy, he was awed by the tall buildings and the bright lights and the fast pace. Sol Handwerger, the veteran publicity director at M-G-M Records, remembers Hank as shy and introverted when he was in New York City. "He didn't seem to trust people," says Handwerger. "I know it took him a while to accept me, and I was all on his side. But when he loosened up he was a very warm, friendly individual. We'd philosophize and talk about the simple things. He was a down to earth guy."

This, his friends agree, was the real Hank Williams off stage: shy and standoffish, but basically kind and warm and wanting to like and be liked.

Oddly, in all his travels, Hank went out of the continental United States only three times. Two of the times were trips to Canada, where he played before throngs of eager listeners; Hank Snow, a Nova Scotian, had stirred Canadian interest in country music when he became a star on the Opry. The third time was a trip to Germany, in 1949. He went there as part of an Opry troupe touring U.S. military bases. It was a high-powered cast: Acuff, Pearl, Little Jimmy Dickens. But Hank, though new to the Opry, more than held his own.

"With 'Lovesick Blues' alone he practically destroyed those people in the military," says Dickens. "They screamed and hollered for him," recalls Minnie Pearl. "The women especially. When he'd start singing, they'd give out a long, drawn-out sigh."

Pearl remembers Hank as being "very happy" on the trip to Germany. "We all took our wives and husbands, so Hank took Audrey. She was beautiful then—real pretty hair and skin."

Although all the concerts were staged on American military bases, the Opry troupe could profitably have played for the natives as well. Germany at that time was in the throes of a boom in American country music. A group of U. S. Army personnel was performing every Saturday night at the Frankfurt Palmgarden and breaking all Palmgarden attendance records, including those established by stateside stars Bob Hope and Horace Heidt. Native bands were taking on such names as Hank Schmitz and his Goober Growlers, and Red Schmucker and his Mountain Boys. A group of Nashville tourists, seeing a band come onto a café stage in Tyrolean hats and leather pants, was astonished to hear the master of ceremonies introduce Eric (Grandpappy) Ritter and his Alpine Hillbilly Briar Hoppers, "who will now perform 'How Many Biscuits Kin You Eat This Mawnin'?' followed by 'Git Them Cold Feet Over on the Other Side.'"

Hank saw nothing strange about this trans-Atlantic cultural togetherness. "There ain't nothing at all queer about them Europeans likin' our kind of singing," he told a *Nation's Business* writer. "It's liable to teach them more about what everyday Americans are really like than anything else."

One of the highlights of Hank's career was his tour, in 1951, with the now-legendary Hadacol Caravan. The caravan was the spectacular last fling of super salesman Dudley J. LeBlanc, the inventor of Hadacol, the largest-selling patent medicine of all time. It brought together some of the brightest stars in all of show business, and Hank, who started the tour as one of the lesser acts, wound up as a top attraction.

Dudley LeBlanc and Hadacol comprise one of the great stories of American salesmanship. LeBlanc, a colorful, fast-talking Cajun from Lafayette, Louisiana, was a politician in salesman's clothing. A state senator off and on since 1924, he wanted nothing so much as to be governor of Louisiana. His one outright attempt at the governorship, in 1932, ended in failure when a Huey Long-backed candidate rolled over him. LeBlanc never abandoned his dream, but he did get down to the business of making lots of money.

He began turning out, down in Lafayette, a potion that contained twelve per cent ethyl alcohol as a preservative. In the South, which was much drier then than it is now, a legal, readily available 24-proof drink was something to be cherished—and purchased wherever possible. LeBlanc made it possible everywhere, at $1.25 for the eight-ounce bottle, $3.50 for the twenty-four-ounce family jug.

He named the stuff Hadacol, and he described it on the carton as a "dietary supplement . . . formulated as an aid to Nature in rebuilding the Pep, Strength, and Energy of Buoyant Health when the System is deficient in the Vitamins and Minerals found in this Tonic. . . ." *Time* magazine, somewhat less lyrically, described it as "a murky brown liquid that tastes something like bilge water, and smells worse."

LeBlanc himself seldom tasted his product: "I doubt if I drank four bottles altogether." But it was an instant success with the aches and pains public as well as with folks who simply needed a bracer. LeBlanc insisted that nobody could get drunk on the stuff; it tasted too bad, he cheerfully admitted. Hadacol sales, stimulated by such promotions as three-dimensional display ads in New York's Grand Central Station, were phenomenal. By May of 1950, LeBlanc was selling over two million bottles of Hadacol a month.

Satisfied users were attributing all sorts of wondrous things to Hadacol. A sixty-eight-year-old Mississippi man wrote the company: "I was disable to get over a fence, disable to get up out of a chair without help, but after I took eight bottles of Hadacol I can . . . tie up my own shoes and feel like I can jump over a six-foot fence and am very sassy." Legal and medical authorities were getting sassy too, and they began pressuring Le-Blanc to tone down his exuberant promotions for Hadacol. Fearful that might curtail sales, he dreamed up a big new promotion: a star-studded, whirlwind traveling stage show, which would lure thousands of ailing and thirsty customers. The admission price would be only a box top from a Hadacol carton.

LeBlanc dubbed the show the Hadacol Caravan. He ran one caravan in 1950, and it was a success. For 1951, he made it bigger and better. He hired a special seventeen-car train and filled it with hawkers and drummers and the flashiest collection of show bizzies money could buy. There was Bob Hope and Milton Berle, Jack Benny and Jimmy Durante, Jack Dempsey and Candy Candido ("The Man of 1,000 Voices"), Dick Haymes and the Tony Martin orchestra, Carmen Miranda, Minnie Pearl, and Sharkey Bonano and his Kings of Dixieland. There were sideshow acts too: Ted Evans, "tallest man in the world" at nine feet, three and one-half inches; Emile Parra, "The Man Who Skates on His Head." And there was Hank Williams and his Drifting Cowboys.

LeBlanc selected Hank because of the success he and the band had met on a recent show date in Lafayette. "They played for a dollar and a quarter apiece," Le-Blanc recalled a few years ago, "and they overflowed the house. I said to myself, 'I'm tryin' to draw people. This fella obviously can do it.'"

Hank and the senator took an instant liking to each other. Hank paid the Hadacol man a major compliment by working him into a song inspired by his travels through Louisiana. The song, of course, was "Jambalaya," one of Hank's biggest hits. A sort of love song *cum* culinary guide, it is laced with references to the Cajun country: crawfish pie, fillet gumbo, the pirogue boat. It also, with questionable results, attempts to Nashvillize the local dialect: "my ma cher a mio," for instance. (Local references aside, the song contains a notable one-sentence summation of Hank's recipe for happiness: "Pick guitar, fill fruit jar, and be gay-o.")

There are two sides to the question of how "Jambalaya" was received by the natives of south Louisiana. One story has it that Hank was hooted and scoffed at when he appeared in Cajun country, with local folks shouting derisive references to the ersatz patois in the song. The way Hank told it, however, the natives were ecstatic over this "tribute" to them and their land. "Those Cajuns'd throw twenty-dollar bills on the stage when they heard me sing 'Jambalaya,'" he told his cousin, Taft Skipper.

The caravan spent the late summer of 1951 touring the South and Midwest in a series of one-nighters. The crowds were tremendous: fifteen to twenty thousand was not unusual. Headliners like Hope and Benny moved in and out of the show, but Hank and his band were part of the regular cast. Hank drew a thousand dollars a week plus room and meals and occasional Saturday night air fare back to Nashville to fill obligations at the Grand Ole Opry.

At the outset, Hank was given a routine spot in the show, up around the top. The audiences were his kind of people, however; they liked country music and they loved him, and the ovations he received were so long and loud that after a few nights he was switched to the end of the bill, the section reserved for the biggest attractions.

When the show hit Louisville, Hank upstaged one of the top men in the business, Bob Hope. An overflow crowd of some thirty thousand packed the local ball park that night to see Hope and the caravan. Hope, as the star, was to close the show, and Hank was scheduled to go on just before him. Hank ambled up to the microphone, which was perched on the pitcher's mound, went through a couple of numbers and then swung into "Lovesick Blues." When he hit the last note, recalls Jerry Rivers, "the packed stadium seemed to explode, the ovation was so great." The M.C. tried to introduce Hope, but his words were drowned in a sea of cheers.

As Rivers relates it in *Hank Williams: From Life to Legend,* "I never heard Hope's name called on the microphone. . . . they just brought him on anyway and he stood there in front of the microphone for several minutes while the applauding gradually died down. When the roar was down to a point where his voice could be heard over the sound system, Bob pulled a big ragged cowboy hat down on his ears and said, 'Hello, folks, this is Hank Hope. . . .' The roar went up again, and Bob Hope shared in some of Hank Williams' glory."

One story has it that after this happened another time or two, Hope went to Dudley LeBlanc and suggested Hank close the show. LeBlanc passed the suggestion on to Hank. "I'll be durned if I'll close. Hope's closing," Hank replied. "You're paying him fifteen thousand dollars for fifteen minutes. Pay me a thousand dollars a minute and I'll close it for you."

Despite this competitive situation, Hank got along fine with Hope and with all the other Hadacol stars save one—Milton Berle. Berle, like Hope, was an occasional member of the Hadacol troupe. He was booked for the Kansas City stop, and on that occasion he volunteered to M.C. the show as well as to close it with his own routine. The trouble was, Berle interpreted his M.C. role as a license to ham it up during other acts. When Dick Haymes sang a tear-jerking version of "Old Man River," the effect was reduced by Berle's clowning;

as children in the audience giggled, he stood on one side of the stage, a red bandana around his head, and pantomimed the old Jolson standard, "Mammy."

When Hank saw this, he was infuriated. He said a few angry words to "Big Bill" Lister, who was playing rhythm guitar for the Drifting Cowboys on the tour, and Lister walked over to Berle's manager. "Tell Milton," Lister told the manager, "that if he sets foot on the stage while we're out there, I'm gonna bust this big guitar over his head." Thereafter, Berle saved his funny stuff for his own part of the show.

For Hank and his band, who had never experienced big-time show business outside of country music, the caravan was great fun. But Rivers sensed a certain unhappiness in Hank, particularly when he went back to Nashville to fill Saturday night Opry commitments. "When Hank would return from these trips to Nashville, he seemed upset," says Rivers, "and I learned that things at home were not as they had been and Hank was experiencing a breach with his family"—a rather quaint way of saying Hank and Audrey were having major problems. In less than a year, they would be divorced.

Meanwhile, the Hadacol Caravan was rolling to a halt. Stories circulated at the time saying the shows simply weren't producing enough sales. LeBlanc denied that. In a sense, the caravan was too successful, for an obscure, tax-free medical research foundation offered him 8.2 million dollars for the Hadacol name, formula, and production facilities. "A country boy like me," reminisced LeBlanc, "why, I was glad to take that kind of money. Now, if television had been as big then as it is today, I'd never've sold. I'd've put a dead woman on the ground, poured a bottle of Hadacol in her, and had her spring to life, all as an ad on T.V."

The foundation did not envision these great facilities, and it not only told LeBlanc his services were no longer needed, it decided to do away with the caravan. The news caught the show in Dallas, as it began its final couple of weeks. Hank, the Drifting Cowboys, and everybody else packed up and headed for home, bringing an abrupt and unsentimental end to America's last great medicine show.

Most people assume Dudley LeBlanc raked in that eight million dollars and lived a life of ease ever after. LeBlanc said no. "I never got anything but a 500,000-dollar down payment," he said. That was enough to pay the milkman, of course, and LeBlanc remained active. Almost until the time of his death last year, LeBlanc represented his area in the state senate and worried over several hundred prize magnolia bushes in his yard at Abbeville, near Lafayette. He also promoted two new patent medicines: a tonic called "Kary On" and "KP," a product that, according to LeBlanc, cured prostate gland trouble. "If I was as young as I was when I had Hadacol," he said three years before his death, "I could make that KP as big as Hadacol was." Alas, the Senator thought it too late for another big promotion, and an aching world was the loser.

14

The tour with the Hadacol Caravan, in the summer of 1951, was the high water mark of Hank Williams' career. He was at the top of the country music business. His records were selling in the pop as well as the country field; his songs were being successfully recorded by pop as well as country artists. He was outperforming and outdrawing many of the biggest names in American show business.

Further, Hank was at the peak of his creative powers, turning out some of his greatest songs. "Hey, Good Lookin'" and "Cold, Cold Heart" both were written around that time, and both wound up at or near the top of the charts. "Cold, Cold Heart," according to *Billboard,* was the biggest country and Western seller of 1951. "Hey, Good Lookin' " is a rollicking tune that catches the flavor of a big night in a small town, with the hod rod Ford, two-dollar bill, and "little spot right over the hill."

New doors began opening for Hank. He made appearances on major network television shows, including Kate Smith's and Perry Como's. He had an offer of a part in a Hollywood movie and the prospect of more offers to follow. One of the movie offers came from producer Joe Pasternak, who wanted him to play a sheriff in *Small Town Girl,* with Janie Powell and Farley Granger. Hank seemed agreeable to the idea and went away with a script, but when the time came to film the picture Pasternak's people could not find him; by that time he had fallen off the wagon, and there was no hope of his making a movie.

M-G-M also considered using Hank to play the lead in a movie of his own life. M-G-M officials had a meeting or two with Hank—again complicated by his return to the bottle—and the meetings proved unsatisfactory. According to one story, a session in the office of M-G-M's Dore Schary ended rather abruptly when Hank insisted on limiting his replies to a series of grunts and sneers.

Since Hank was now a full-fledged celebrity, the word of his budding film career spread quickly. Nashville newspapers and press agents began talking of his rumored five-thousand-dollar-a-week contract with M-G-M; one press agent had the contract extending for four years, which would have meant a cool million dollars from the movies alone. M-G-M now says, and so does Joe Pasternak, that Hank never had a film contract.

Even without the movies, Hank was making lots and lots of money. His three main sources were records, song publishing royalties, and show dates. All were going strong through most of 1950 and 1951, and his income during that period is estimated at several hundred thousand dollars a year.

In 1950 alone, according to one source, M-G-M sold over a million Hank Williams records, with Hank getting his cut from every one. Throughout his best years, his releases sold an average of a half-million records each. The big hits—"Cold, Cold Heart," Lovesick Blues," "Why Don't You Love Me," "Jambalaya"—sold well above that. "Your Cheatin' Heart," the biggest of all, sold way over a million.

Had he been working in the heyday of television, and had he followed through on one or more of the movie opportunities, there is no telling how much money Hank could have made in these prime years. As it was, he was probably earning more than any artist in Nashville —after having been almost broke a couple of years earlier.

Hank let Sam Hunt, the Nashville banker who served as his financial counselor, handle his money, but he couldn't resist making a few purchases befitting his status as a member of the nouveau riche. He bought a couple of Cadillacs to go with the couple he already had. He started a Western-style clothing store in downtown Nashville, which he called "Hank and Audrey's Corral." He and Audrey built a flashy forty-thousand-dollar home on Nashville's Franklin Road, not far from the Acuff-Rose offices. Then they bought a big farm in Franklin, outside Nashville.

Everything had to be done on the grand scale—cars, houses, farms. Everything had to be magnificently equipped, down to the last detail. This is not unusual in the country music business, where rags to riches stories are routine. Hank and Audrey, at the outset in Nashville, were the perfect country music couple, making money as fast as they could and wearing their dollar signs on their sleeves.

The house on Franklin Road was one of Nashville's showplaces, and in fact it still is. It is on the regular itinerary for tourists visiting the city: the Parthenon, the Grand Ole Opry, Vanderbilt University, the Hank

Williams home. It is a low, rambling structure set on a plot sloping away from the road. Audrey has added to and glamorized the place considerably since Hank's death (it is now said to be worth a quarter-million dollars), but it was something special when he lived there too. He called it, aptly, "the house music built for me," and he decorated the wrought-iron fence enclosing the patio with notes of the song that did much of the building, "Lovesick Blues." Inside, Audrey went for Oriental decor. Hank's personal room was the den, which he did Western style, with heavy leather furniture, guns on the wall, and so forth. He stocked the den with a tape recorder, a console phonograph, and a collection of pop recordings of his songs.

The wrought-iron work alone cost more money than Hank had ever seen until a couple of years earlier, but he was vain enough, and simple enough, to enjoy that tasteless little extravagance. He shrugged off tactful suggestions from friends that he might be laying it on a little thick. After all, this was the Nashville way.

Buying a farm was also consistent with the country music life style. A number of Nashville stars, once they made their pile, have bought 'em a spread in the country. While part of this is pure show, part of it also is a desire to have a place away from it all, the kind of place they may have wished they'd had as kids. When Hank bought his farm in Franklin, he was also looking for a tax shelter; he was now making more money than he could spend, and this seemed a reasonable way to invest it.

Hank paid about forty thousand dollars for the farm, which consisted of 507 acres of good but undeveloped land and a rundown, ante-bellum-style house. He used the place mostly for hunting and riding, two of his favorite pastimes. He had a vague intention of fixing up the house and making it the family home, but that never went beyond a few repairs on the roof to keep it from falling down. The whole place was sold, at little or no loss, around the time of his death.

So Hank lived the life of the Nashville star. But he

was not the flashiest or the fanciest. Other stars have outdone him in all the categories used to measure success in Nashville. Webb Pierce, for example, sports a guitar-shaped swimming pool and used to drive one of the world's gaudiest cars—a convertible with silver-dollar-studded upholstery, a bullet-studded steering wheel, and real six-shooters mounted on the dashboard, doors, and seat backs.

One of the clichés of country music is that its stars are simple homebodies who love God, family, and song above all else. Although the evidence is often to the contrary, the average fan readily accepts—indeed relishes—the disparity. One reason is that the Grand Ole Opry itself has promoted the wholesome image. This is an interesting contrast to pop music, where a reputation for unwholesomeness can be a real asset. The country code pretty well rules out sexy and drug-related material, and only in recent years have subjects like infidelity been dealt with directly. The code has loosened considerably now, but the All-American image is still zealously guarded.

The Opry, for instance, had a rule forbidding the mention of alcoholic beverages on its stage. Hank Williams came up against the rule one time with the song "My Bucket's Got a Hole in It." According to the song, what came out of the hole was beer. The Opry, after some fussing, agreed to let him sing the song providing he cleaned up the offending lyric. Since almost every line ended with a word rhyming with beer, everyone figured he'd have to do the song over completely. Instead, Hank sang the song as written—except that every time he reached the word "beer" he shouted "milk." The Opry audience, which is not nearly so square as the image makers think, laughed itself silly.

While Hank eventually shattered the Opry star mold with his drinking, he shook it all along with other nonconforming habits. One of the most interesting was his disinterest in formal religion. Ever since boyhood, he had attended church only sparingly. Perhaps this was a reaction against the Sundays spent squirming alongside his mother as she played the church organ; more likely, it was a personal feeling that organized religion had little to offer him.

Nonetheless, Hank was in a sense religious. He had convictions, and he enjoyed talking about them. "He felt something personal inside," says Jerry Rivers. "It came out in his music, for most of his serious songs are religious songs."

On one occasion, recalls a songwriter friend, Hank and the late Red Foley sat in a drugstore booth between shows at the Opry and "discussed nothing but religion. Hank had some pretty deep thoughts on it, and so did Foley, though both of them drank like fish. I remember Hank saying that he knew what he was doing—drinking and what not—wasn't in keeping with his religious beliefs but that he believed them just the same."

In spite of Hank's independent approach, these beliefs appear to have been emotional, almost fundamentalist. Foley recounted a time when Hank had heard Foley sing his classic "Peace in the Valley," not in person, just on the radio. "He was in a coffee shop, he told me, and he started crying when the song came on. He got so embarrassed he had to get up and walk out of the place. I remember he said to me, after he told me that story, 'If I go before you, would you sing that song at my funeral?'" Foley said sure, and less than two years later he found himself honoring the pledge.

A curious offshoot of Hank's religious streak was his strong antipathy toward taking the Lord's name in vain. The general run of swearing, including all the crispest four-letter words, was perfectly all right. But if someone said, "God damn," Hank bristled. He waged periodic crusades against cursing among the Drifting Cowboys. One time he cut a slit in the top of a cigar box and announced, "Anybody who uses the Lord's name in vain gotta put a quarter in the box." Hank himself wound up stuffing the box on that occasion, parting with $2.75 before the road tour was finished. He kept a sense of humor about it, however: when he used two "in vains" in one sentence, he put a dollar bill into the box with the comment, "Okay, I got two curses comin' free."

While Lilly Williams would not have approved of it, Hank's religious independence was in a good country tradition. The great majority of country folks do attend church regularly, but a stubborn minority has always resisted the blandishments of preachers and the scowls of neighbors, preferring to "get religion," if at all, in its own way.

In non-religious matters, Hank was firmly in the mainstream of south Alabama thought and attitudes.

He doused everything with ketchup and was resolutely unadventurous when it came to eating. He was just as resolute about books and ideas; that is, he had little use for them. His reading consisted almost entirely of comic books and an occasional cheap murder mystery. He had no strong feelings about the race problem, but he knew blacks ought to stay in their places.

Considering his passion for songwriting, Hank might have had at least a passing interest in other kinds of music. But he had none. Country music was the whole thing as far as he was concerned.

Also considering that passion, he might have had some interest in the use of words. Again, he had none. He had a very limited vocabulary, the product of what today would be called a culturally deprived home and of too little attention paid in too many poor schools. His spelling was shaky: "How to you spell 'sigh'?" he once asked a fellow songwriter. His pronunciation was unadorned country. A musician says that once, when Audrey scolded him about saying "pitcher," he told her, "Listen, that word's got you a lot of nice things." He had a ready supply of malapropisms: asked by a disk jockey why the words to his songs were so sad, he replied, "Well, Cottonseed, I guess I always have been a sadist."

Hank's songwriting genius cut through these handicaps. He was blessed with insight and the talent for expressing it, and the formalities of language can never stand in the way of that.

Hank's pastimes best displayed the country boy in him. Hunting, fishing, and riding were what he loved. He never tried to upgrade his leisure life: no golf; no tennis, boating, or bridge. When he did take on another pastime, it was one shunned by the upper classes—bowling. Once he took a liking to something, he pursued it zealously. Bowling was no exception. When Hank "discovered" bowling, he and Audrey and the boys in the band made regular trips to Nashville's Melrose Bowling Center. "Hank was just a fair bowler," says Jerry Rivers, "but he was really enthusiastic. Anything he enjoyed, he would go at like killing rattlesnakes."

During his affluent years, Hank kept a small stable of horses. His favorite mount was "Hi-Life," and Hank often rode him over the pasture land on his Franklin farm. He couldn't do much rough riding because of the back injury he'd sustained as a boy.

His hunting was confined mostly to squirrels and other small game. He had a pack of beagles at one time. He also had a favorite mongrel hunting dog named Skip, acquired from a farm girl at a steep price. Skip, says Rivers, was "the finest squirrel dog I've ever seen, before or since. When he barked up a tree, you could count on a squirrel being there . . . he never lied. Hank made up his mind he had to have that dog regardless of cost. . . ."

Skip belonged to the daughter of the farmer on whose place Hank hunted, and the farmer said Hank could have him for whatever small contribution he cared to make toward a watch the girl was saving to buy. Hank promptly pulled his own diamond-studded watch from his wrist and swapped it for the dog.

For a long time Hank and the band had a 5 A.M. radio show on Nashville's WSM, the Opry station, and when it was over he would often head for either the woods or the water. The getaways were always swift, recalls Rivers. "There was almost nobody around at that hour. You could be stark nekkid if you wanted. We'd stack our shotguns or fishing poles in the corner, do the show in boots and overalls, and take off as soon as the last note was played."

Hank's favorite fishing spot was Kentucky Lake, about sixty miles from the city, where there were crappie in abundance. Once on the water, he was tenacious to a fault. The boys in the band, says Rivers, "were accustomed to leaving early in the morning, fishing from daylight till the sun got high around ten, then coming back home with whatever the catch might be. But not Hank. He would buy two or three hundred minnows, which he would sink around the boat in several large minnow buckets so they would live all day, and then he would anchor the boat on a good crappie hole and fish from daylight till dark. I have gone out with Hank many times when we had to use a searchlight to find our fishing hole in the morning, then have to use the light to find the boat dock that night.

"Hank was a nigger fisherman. He'd put out maybe ten poles and go back and forth from one to the other all day long. It's the only thing I ever saw him do where he showed any patience. He was completely relaxed, like he could sit there forever. After six hours or so without a bite, I'd say, 'Don't you think we ought to move?' and he'd say, 'Why move now? They're just about to start biting.' "

Hank's love of outdoor life was on a par with his love for guns. He was wild about old guns, particularly pistols, and when he hit a new city during his travels he would poke through pawn shops, junk shops, and the like in hopes of adding to his collection. Often he enlisted the help of local policemen; a vice squad captain in El Paso, Texas, was one of his best gun locators. People would give him pistols, even matched sets, and he'd carry them home in his luggage, happy as a kid with a new toy.

Much as he loved guns, Hank was careless about them, and sometimes with them. Rivers recalls that, during the Drifting Cowboys' first trip to the West Coast, Hank got a tip on a matched pair of Colt .45s. "He spent a couple of days locating them and reaching a purchase price, which I'm sure was very high. Hank would sit in the hotel for hours admiring the twin chrome-plated Colts. Don Helms picked up the guns; while examining them he chanced to fit a dime into one barrel; then he was surprised to find the dime wouldn't go into the second barrel. One pistol was a .45 and the other was a .44, otherwise perfectly matched!" Hank had never checked the "pair" thoroughly. By the time the discrepancy was pointed out to him, he was too attached to the guns to take them back.

Although he never actually packed a gun, Hank sometimes carried one or two just for effect—effect on himself as much as on others. A Nashville secretary recalls Hank showing up at a party one night wearing a pair of pistols, making her and several other guests quite nervous. When he went on the rocks later, his gun handling, under the influence of alcohol, made people plain scared.

Hank used the police as a source for another kind of information—on girls. His long, thin face and his easy-going ways appealed to women, and, like many a traveling entertainer, he sometimes sought their companionship. Although he kept a sharp eye out on show dates, he relied on the local cops for accurate information on who would and who wouldn't. He'd cozy up to an officer, ask him a few questions about his pistol, and then say casually, "Know any goin' women around here?" More often than not the cop did know some, right on the premises, and Hank would be fixed up for an after-the-show engagement.

He was as immature in sexual matters as in other areas of his personality. A friend recalls with a laugh a traumatic experience Hank had with a female acquaintance in California. The band was playing in a rough joint, a "blood bucket," as the boys called them, and Hank spied a likely looking waitress. A policeman on duty at the joint fixed Hank up with her, and the two of them slipped off to a nearby motel. The rest of the band drove up a while later and, per instructions, sat quietly outside waiting for the leader.

"All of a sudden," says the friend, "the door flies open and Hank comes out, hoppin' along with one leg in his trousers. He jumps in the car all excited and says, 'Come on, come on, let's get outta here!' The guy driving figured it was somethin' good, so he dawdled with the keys. Hank gets even more agitated and shouts. 'Hurry up, durn it!'

" 'What'sa matter, Harm?' we asked him. Well, he wouldn't say at first. But it turns out that after he'd gotten his, he dozed off, and when he woke up her pussy was right in his face, like she was expectin' somethin'. That was too much for an old country boy like Hank. He got the hell out of there."

(Entertainers have an unfailing appeal for legions of frustrated females. Politicians, oddly, have much the same appeal. At least they attract the same sort of camp followers. A veteran Alabama political reporter recalls that, during the governor's race of 1958, a very attractive young woman kept showing up at the rallies of one of the candidates. She said nothing, took no part in the program, just stood on the edge of the crowd. Finally the reporter asked her why she kept following the candidate around. "Because he's hung like a horse," she replied.)

Songwriter Jimmy Rule remembers that, after their book on writing country music was published, Hank received dozens of letters from women. The most notable letter, actually a series of them, came from a lady rancher out West. "Please come live with me," she wrote. "I can love you twenty-four hours a day and stand up to it." So far as Rule knows, Hank never took her up on the offer, but he got a kick out of reading the letters.

Hank's away-from-home dalliances may or may not have crippled his home life. He wasn't worried about that enough to abandon them. But he did worry about the effect they might have on Audrey and her actions. In the last weeks before their breakup, friends recall, the subject would flash through his mind, and he would hurry to a phone booth to call home.

Sex aside, Hank and Audrey had a ragged, sometimes tempestuous relationship. Each was headstrong and, in his own distinct way, talented. Each had personality traits that rubbed the other the wrong way. Hank was tense inside but easygoing on the surface; except in moments of self-pitying bitterness, he was not aggressive, and he was not really ambitious in the materialistic sense.

He was never comfortable with all the money and lavish surroundings. It seemed to him a betrayal of his south Alabama heritage, of the people and the poverty from which he had come. He was not particularly proud of having risen from obscurity to fame, from Georgiana to Nashville, except insofar as it was a recognition of his musical talents. Aside from recognition, he had little concern for anything his talents might "get" him.

These traits inevitably brought Hank into conflict with Audrey, who was at least normally acquisitive and interested in moving up the ladder. The conflict was aggravated by Hank's lack of fully developed maleness, which was his legacy from childhood, and by the alcoholism this eventually produced. A marriage burdened with these problems could hardly be expected to survive.

What apparently happened was that Hank's weakness and abdication of responsibility led Audrey to assume the dominant role in their relationship. It was Lilly and Lon all over again: dominant female, passive male; "strong" woman directing and taking care of "sick" man. The critical difference between Lon and Hank was that Hank possessed creative genius, and it burst through the wall of emotional problems. Some psychiatrists would say that simply by marrying a strong woman like Audrey, Hank was subconsciously but compulsively repeating the pattern set by his own parents.

Although Audrey's own musical talents were barely marketable, she contributed substantially to her husband's success. She was the flint against which he struck his musical genius. Without Audrey and the problems he felt she caused him, many of Hank's best songs would not have been written. Few people doubt that his greatest laments—"Your Cheatin' Heart," "Cold, Cold Heart," "I'm So Lonesome I Could Cry"—were composed with his marriage uppermost in his mind.

Some interpreters of the Williams marriage have played to the hilt Audrey's role as a catalyst in the creation of Hank's songs. There are stories about how Hank retired in solitary anguish to write this or that masterpiece after squabbling with Audrey on this or that occasion. "I'm So Lonesome I Could Cry," according to one of these stories, was written after she had spurned his entreaties, backed by candy and flowers, to make up after a fight.

It is easy to overemphasize the part personal unhappiness played in Hank's songs. People like to think it literally created them, but it did not. The songs were the product of his genius, which would have been present had he been the happiest man in the world. Neurotic conflict of the type that afflicted Hank can enhance and concretize creativity, but the creativity is not a product of the conflict.

Few of Hank's friends found anything strange in his relationship with Audrey. The relentless round of loving and quarreling often was routine in their own lives. Tears of hatred turn to tears of love and back again, in an emotional ebb and flow that never seems to end. This is the nature of life and marriage in much of America, and Hank and Audrey's mercurial relationship was not so much different in kind as in the publicity it got.

"Hank couldn't live with her, and he couldn't live without her," is the way one old friend sums it up. Others agree, and they understand the predicament perfectly. Indeed, that sounds like the theme, maybe even the title, of a typical Nashville ballad.

Audrey's own musical career was a source of friction between her and Hank. As soon as they got married, she began appearing with Hank and the band on show dates around Alabama. Hank didn't mind at all. She was his fine new wife; he was young and not fully developed as a talent. Besides, she was useful. She sold tickets, helped manage the band affairs, sang a bit, filled in on a rhythm instrument when the occasion demanded. Old acquaintances from those days remember Audrey as a sweet, talented young girl. One even remembers her as having a sort of social conscience: "She was always embarrassed when Hank and the band put on a Negro act."

Audrey came to fancy herself as quite a singer. Actually, she was not, and as Hank's talent matured, that fact became obvious. Still, she tried to establish her own artistic career. Even when Hank reached Nashville and a position at the top of the country music business, Audrey tried to share the limelight, by singing with him and recording on her own.

Hank did cut a number of records with Audrey, and some of them are not bad. One of them was a duet on Hank's "Dear Brother," a rather maudlin song about a mother's death:

> Dear Brother, Mama left us this morning
> For the city where there is no pain.

He also sang with her from time to time on his various radio shows on Nashville's WSM. According to WSM personnel, he kept her from singing with him a number of other times; the result, they say, was often an unpleasant scene right in the studios with Hank sometimes winning the argument with the help of physical persuasion.

Station officials were embarrassed, to say the least, by these scenes, but they put up with them nonetheless. They sympathized with Hank and regarded Audrey as a glory seeker who should be staying out of his way. "Hank wasn't jealous of *her*," says a WSM official of that time. "It was the other way around. His not letting her on the air was simply his way of protecting her."

The station knew about Hank's domestic problems, and it had a stake in keeping them under control. "He'd tell us, 'I have to use Audrey tonight,' and we'd put them on together," says the WSM official. "You know, good wives are important in this business. Eddy Arnold was as wild as any buck you ever saw when he was young, but Sally kept him on even keel after they were married. Roy Acuff is wealthy today partly because of his wife and the way she kept the finances straight and things generally in balance." Hank, the implication is, wasn't so lucky.

Occasionally, Hank made a crack about Audrey's compulsion to perform. In Washington, D.C., one night, he remarked to a couple of musicians: "It's bad enough to have a wife who wants to sing, but it's worse to have one who wants to sing and *can't.*" Another time he said to bass player Hillous Butrum, "Mule, I'm gonna get you on records. You sing pretty good. You want a contract?" Butrum just laughed, but Hank said, "You know, if I can get Audrey a contract I can get you one too."

Audrey did have a recording contract, obtained for her, country music people say, largely at Hank's behest. The contract was with Decca Records, and she cut a few sides that resulted in modest sales. Nashville firms published a few of her own composition, including "Living It Up and Having a Ball" and "Ain't Nothin' Gonna Be All Right No How." Again, the sales, as well as the trade recognition, were modest.

Except for the scenes at WSM, Hank and Audrey kept their difficulties pretty much to themselves. Hank had few confidantes, and he did not burden them with his domestic problems. He kept those problems, like that of his drinking, bottled up inside him, letting them out only in song.

The Drifting Cowboys, though well aware that, as they put it, "Hank was having trouble at home," knew few of the details. They did not offer their assistance, and Hank did not request it. Hank was not that sort of person, and the band members, who after all were his employees, avoided anything that might seem like prying. All that surfaced, on Hank's side of the struggle, was an occasional remark or display of emotion.

So while there was a constant undercurrent of rumor about the Williams' troubles, the public image of their marriage was good. One reason is that what the public saw most were the lavish gifts Hank kept giving Audrey. The house on Franklin Road was the most lavish, but it was hardly the only one. There were a series of Cadillac automobiles, a fifteen-hundred-dollar platinum and diamond wristwatch, a three-thousand-dollar diamond ring. (Audrey, according to newspaper accounts, lost the watch a few months after Hank's death, and charged that the ring was stolen from her, several years later, by a young house guest who had visited her several times.)

In addition to gifts, Hank allowed Audrey to spend lavishly on her own. A magazine writer recalls that, during one of Hank's road tours, "when he made 75,000 dollars, she was at home spending 110,000 dollars—widening their big driveway, starting up their clothing store, and so on." The figures may be inflated, but there is no doubt that Audrey knew how to spend money.

Hank sometimes complained to friends that Audrey was not grateful for the gifts and the money. "He'd say something like, 'What d'ya think of a woman who'd take a mink coat and just throw it in the front yard?' " says one friend. "I don't think Hank did anything about it. But a guy with an income like me would just had to've backhanded her."

15

"When I went to work with him, Hank never touched a drop," says Jerry Rivers. "He didn't take a social drink or an anti-social drink or any other kind." That was in 1949. Hank was so careful about avoiding alcohol that when he toured U.S. bases in Germany that year he checked his glass at the meal table to make sure it contained water, not wine.

Yet, on the first day of 1953, he was dead. The cause of death can be traced to excessive consumption of alcohol.

Hank was of course no stranger to drinking when he came to Nashville, and everyone knew it. He had been drinking since his early teens, with spells of temperance punctuated by spells of flat-out drunkenness. His reputation around Montgomery was so bad it delayed his progress as a country music star. But Rivers, Fred Rose, Jim Denny, and everybody else with a stake in Hank's success hoped those days were behind him. There was reason to hope. During his two years in Shreveport, his springboard to Nashville and the big time, Hank had been relatively sober. And for months after he reached Nashville, he had drunk only moderately.

"Somebody had convinced Hank that drinking and work just didn't mix, if you wanted to be a success," says Rivers. Chances are Hank had convinced himself. He saw what a tough time he had had surmounting his reputation in Montgomery and, conversely, how smoothly things had gone for him after that, when he cut down on the booze.

Rivers recalls clearly the first time he saw Hank drunk. It was at Baltimore's Hippodrome theater, where Hank and the Drifting Cowboys were playing a one-week stand. They were part of a package show that played four times a day, between showings of the feature movie. "Early in the week, the second or third day, Hank failed to show for one of the matinee shows. We found him drunk, really gone, in the hotel room. I was flabbergasted to find him like that."

The Grand Ole Opry was alarmed. It was bad enough to have one of its stars default on a show date commitment, but to have one default because of drunkenness was worse. Opry general manager Jim Denny dispatched a detective to Baltimore to ensure Hank's sobriety. That worked for a day or so, and Hank performed as scheduled. Then, just before one performance, he suddenly became too drunk to go on for the show. It turned out he had bribed the stagehands and, quite ingeniously, had gotten them to stash miniature, airline-type bottles in the toilet tank in the men's room.

Denny finally had to get someone to ship Hank home, where Denny stuck him in a sanitarium to dry out. "It was a shock to all of us in the band," says Rivers, "because none of us had seen him drunk for a long while. I'd *never* seen him that way. But he was as bad that first time as I ever saw him later."

Word soon spread that Hank was back on the booze. At first the drunken periods were short and far between, but they got progressively longer and more frequent. Country music people might run into a drunken Hank almost anywhere—backstage, at a party or a bar, even on the floor of a public building. "The first time I saw Hank Williams, I literally stepped over him," recalls Bill Williams, the veteran *Billboard* correspondent in Nashville. "I got off an elevator at WSM, early in the morning, and there he was, lying on the floor."

It was a repeat of the Montgomery situation, only worse. Then, few people outside Montgomery knew, and those inside hardly cared. Now, with Hank a national name, it was no longer just a bit of local color;

a lot of people cared, particularly the officials of the Grand Ole Opry.

Although he had come a long way since Montgomery, Hank picked up his old drinking habits pretty much as he had left them. He did not have a constant craving for liquor; he could, and did, go a couple of weeks at a time without touching a drop.

Once Hank started drinking, however, he seldom stopped until he had either passed out or was so drunk he could no longer lift a glass. Neither condition took long to reach, for Hank still had a woefully small capacity for alcohol; a few drinks would usually make him dead drunk. He liked whisky best, because of its potency, but would gladly drink beer or anything else with a kick. He never developed strong preferences. And as a raw country drinker, he had no qualms about switching from one potion to another.

"Hank would start out on beer and wind up on whisky," recalls Sammy Pruett, the Drifting Cowboys' lead guitarist. "It didn't take much of either to put him totally out of commission. I've seen him drunk to where he couldn't even hold water on his stomach. He'd be foaming at the mouth like a goddamned mad dog."

"The way Hank went at it," says Rivers, "you'd hardly ever catch him in the getting-drunk stage. If you saw him drinking, you saw him drunk. He'd drink himself right down to the floor." Rivers considers Hank a "true alcoholic," in that, "if he abstained at all, it had to be total abstention."

Doctors specializing in problem drinking nowadays avoid trying to pin down just what an alcoholic is, and they would not classify Hank or any other individual as a "true alcoholic." As Dr. Vernelle Fox, former director of the renowned Georgian Clinic, says: "There is no one 'alcoholism.' There are a number of disabilities manifested by compulsive drinking. Sometimes the disability is physical, a defect of metabolism. Sometimes it's psychological or emotional, and sometimes it's a learned response to cultural and environmental situations."

The public has been slow to realize that drinking itself is seldom the problem, only the manifestation of the problem. "Society has always wanted to say, 'the whole problem is that he drinks.' " remarks Dr. Fox. "Certainly drinking compounds the problem, but in most cases it is not the whole problem. Some alcoholics would manifest worse problems if they *didn't* drink."

In modern medical parlance, Hank would be classified as a spree drinker, or compulsive drinker, a man who becomes compulsive once he tastes alcohol and proceeds to drink himself into oblivion. In many cases, this is "self-medication," the equivalent of taking a sedative to knock oneself out. The goal, for this kind of drinker, is to consume as much as he can before he is physically unable to consume any more.

Like many spree drinkers, Hank did not need company. He was perfectly content to hole up, alone with his bottles, in a hotel room.

A good many country music artists, including some of the biggest names, have been two-fisted drinkers, a fact they naturally try to hide from their public. Hank at his worst was a bigger lush than any of them, and he seldom bothered to hide it from anybody. His fans as well as his friends knew about it, and they loved him in spite of it. Hank, they believed, was the victim of a series of problems that he was essentially powerless to solve. While friends and fans were overly charitable toward him, they were fundamentally correct: Hank did have more than his share of problems, physical as well as emotional and psychological, and he seemed unable to do anything about them.

First, there was the strain of his marriage to Audrey, a woman so similar to himself in background but so dissimilar in temperament. It seemed rather romantic, all this squabbling between lovers, but actually it tore the hell out of Hank and upset his emotional stability.

Second, there was a latent bitterness from Hank's youth. He was resentful and somewhat ashamed of his background and the limitations it had imposed on him. All his success never succeeded in wiping the resentment and shame away. This was coupled with an in-bred suspicion of "better" people, people who had enjoyed advantages he had not. One time, when Hank, as a full-fledged star, returned to Montgomery to play a date, he received a phone call from a local banker. An entertainer who heard Hank talk to the man noticed his voice go cold before he hung up. What was wrong? he asked Hank.

"He invited me up to his house for dinner," Hank said grimly.

"Well what's the matter with that?"

"Look," said Hank. "I've known that guy most of my life. When I was starving in this town, the son of a bitch wouldn't buy me a hamburger. Now there's nothing too good for me. What's the matter, ain't I the same guy?"

A critical burden from Hank's younger days was his relationships, so totally different, with his father and mother: his mother was as omnipresent and domineering as his father was absent and uninvolved. Although Hank resented his mother and her influence, he never broke away from either her or the influence. They remained a major force in his life.

Third, there were Hank's physical problems. Drinking itself produced the most obvious of these: a run-down condition that bordered on chronic malnutrition. When Hank was on a binge, food was as good as forgotten. Members of the Drifting Cowboys recall his going three or four days without a bite to eat. None too robust to begin with, his body could not stand up under this kind of treatment forever. Then there was the bad back. It became increasingly painful during his Nashville years, and after he fell trying to jump across a gully on a squirrel hunt, he had to have an operation. The operation, performed at Vanderbilt University hospital a year before he died, was an attempt to correct two slipped disks. It may have been successful, but soon afterward he fell off a stage in Ontario, Canada. All this left Hank in such discomfort that he had to resort to a brace and to pain-killing drugs. Overuse of the drugs, in turn, aggravated his already run-down condition.

Fourth, there was the grind of the Opry life, the constant round of trips from Nashville to city after city and back to Nashville again in time to fulfill his Saturday night commitment. The routine seldom varied: travel all day long, play one or two shows at night, catch a few hours' sleep, and head for the next city. Faced with this prospect, many a country music star has turned to drink to ease the strain.

Lastly, there was Hank's own innate loneliness and his incapacity to make the kind of friendships that could alleviate it. This loneliness and incapacity were fed by other problems—his childhood, his marriage—but they had an existence apart. They were basic components of Hank's personality, and they help account for a great deal in his life, including his music and his ultimate self-destruction.

For Hank Williams, idol of millions, to be desperately lonely is poignantly ironic, but it is not surprising. Loneliness of larger-than-life public heroes is a fact of our age. "You might describe it as a feeling of 'alone in a crowd,' " says a psychiatrist. "Marilyn Monroe suffered from the same thing. She was everyone's dream girl, but inside herself she was a tortured, frustrated individual. She didn't know who she was. All she knew was what the public pictured her as, a great sex idol, and she knew she wasn't that."

The gap between the public's view of Hank and his own view may not have been so great as with Marilyn Monroe, but it was the same sort of gap. It was brought on by his chronic loneliness and insecurity, which left him unable to take satisfaction from his great success and from the acclaim it brought him. Hank needed something more than success and acclaim. He never articulated what the something more was; he wasn't sure himself. But he articulated the desire for it, through set after set of song lyrics.

Thus the bitter paradox of Hank's life: the very insecurity and depth of feeling that nurtured his creative genius also drove him to self-ruin. Just as he could not live with or without his wife Audrey, neither could he live with or without the inner conflict that gave voice to his own genius. It made him, and then it destroyed him.

Success, Hank found, did not allay the loneliness that gnawed at his insides. Nor did money. It was no help to be rich, except that you could buy a few more baubles and a lot more booze to try to get your mind off your problems. Audrey couldn't, or wouldn't, understand this. Hank's success and money did solve her problems; they gave her the status and recognition she craved. But they failed to make a happy man out of Hank.

All the pressures on Hank Williams combined to make him an alcoholic. He suffered from chronic, recurring depression, and the only relief he could think of was the bottle. He sought no psychiatric help, nor did he give Alcoholics Anonymous a try. Apparently he never even considered either.

Joining A.A. would have meant admitting he had a serious drinking problem, and Hank was not willing to do that. He always acted as though getting drunk was a little indiscretion that should be overlooked because it wouldn't happen again. Inside, he must have known better. Outside, he gave no indication that he did. He was sheepish, contrite, ready to plead for sympathy but not ready to face the fact that he was destroying himself.

As for seeing a psychiatrist, his limited view of the world did not include an understanding of what "head doctors" do. One thing a head doctor might have told him is that one cannot understand drinking as a problem until he first understands it as a solution. In many cases, compulsive drinking represents a compromise between suicide on the one hand and severe psychiatric disorder on the other; that is, a means of survival, however unsuccessful in the long run, between literal death and living death. As grim as that sounds, it makes some sense as a solution. "Halitosis," in the words of one problem drinker, "is better than no breath at all."

Hank was seldom a mean drunk. He was sloppy and animal-like, toward the end disgustingly so, but he was not belligerent. However, he often was reckless or playful. One time he shot up his room at Nashville's Hermitage Hotel, pumping bullets into the walls and ceiling. Another time, holed up on a bender in the old Tulane Hotel, he accidentally set fire to his bed; his hair was singed, but he was not injured, and he got off with a fifteen-dollar fine.

These stories and others are still told around Nashville. According to one tale, policemen answering a complaint on the top floor of the Tulane once found Hank and a lady wrestler chasing each other, nude, up and down the hallway. That story may well be apocryphal, but no caper was beyond Hank when he was loaded.

Sometimes his playfulness could get downright dangerous. One night, after playing a show at a military installation, the Drifting Cowboys were lying on bunks in the barracks provided for their overnight stay. Hank, who had been out on a gun-collecting mission, had obtained a .357 Magnum pistol. "All of a sudden," says Jerry Rivers, "there was a loud explosion and the sound of a bullet winging down the row of bunks, taking chinks out of the iron bedsteads as it went."

Hank, well in his cups, had quietly taken out his gun. While examining it, he had idly pulled the trigger and fired a bullet past his ear. The Drifting Cowboys recovered quickly enough to grab the gun and hide it before the military police arrived. "What shot?" asked Rivers innocently. "I was asleep." The MPs went elsewhere to hunt, and the boys put Hank to bed—without his gun.

For the Drifting Cowboys, life with Hank, which for months had been both profitable and fun, became a trial. They seldom knew until the last minute whether he would show up drunk—or show up at all—for their dates. Promoters got edgy about booking him. Money wasn't a problem immediately: the band members were on salary, to ensure their being available to work when Hank needed them. But it was bound to become a problem when Hank started not showing up for some dates and not getting booked for others.

For a long time, Hank did not let drinking interfere with his Grand Ole Opry obligations. Whatever he did during the week, he managed to be sober enough to make his regular appearances on the Opry. What suffered were his out-of-town tours. Jim Denny, in charge of the Opry's artist service bureau, which handled its stars' traveling engagements, began including a combination detective-nursemaid as standard equipment on the Drifting Cowboys' trips. The man's job: to keep Hank Williams sober enough to fulfill his, and the Opry's, obligations.

The Denny system had at least one notable success, in Las Vegas. Hank and the band were booked as part of a country music package show playing the big Vegas hotels, and when the time came to leave Nashville, Hank was in no shape to go. Denny called Rivers and Don Helms and told them, "Hank's over at the Tulane, stoned. He was supposed to fly to Vegas, but he missed the flight. You've got to take him in the car now."

Rivers and Helms bundled Hank into the band limousine, after frisking him for hidden bottles. "He looked like any old derelict you'd see on skid row," recalls Rivers sadly. "He would've drunk anything. In fact, Don thinks he tried to drink some anti-freeze on that trip.

"The trip was a constant fight to keep Hank from drinking. We'd avoid stopping at filling stations that had beer signs out front. And when we had to stop at a place like that, we'd get out before Hank and tell the station attendant. 'This man is not to have anything.' One time we caught him trying to bribe the colored boy who was wiping off our windshield. He had some money out, and he was asking the boy, 'You got anything to drink here?' "

There was only one real squabble on the way out to

Las Vegas, Rivers recalls. "Hank got really upset with this no-drink policy, and he said, 'This is my car, and I'll say what goes.' Don was in the co-pilot seat, and he handled it. 'You're not in any condition to talk about anything,' he told Hank. 'We're goin' strictly by Denny's instructions, and that's that.' " That was that, too. Hank arrived in Las Vegas mean as a snake but stone sober.

A burly detective, hired by Denny, was there to take over the watch. He shook hands with Hank and told him, "We're gonna be the best of buddies. But if I see you take a drink of anything, I'm gonna knock you flat on the ground." This straightforward approach worked perfectly until the band's last night in Vegas. After the final show, Hank sneaked out and got gloriously drunk. (The show promoters may have felt like joining him, for although Hank was sober for every appearance, the show was not paying off. "Not many of the free-spending tourists were coming to see us," says Rivers. "The crowds were mostly farmers, cowhands, and hotel employees. They'd buy one ninety-cent Coke, watch the show, and leave.")

Hank made two tours of Canada. The first, in the fall of 1949, was highly successful. The second, a year or two later, was a near disaster. The difference was drinking. Hank wasn't on the sauce the first time around, but he definitely was the second. Nashville promoter Oscar Davis remembers a stop, on that second tour, in Peterborough, Ontario:

"Hank got stinking drunk in his hotel room, and he sent word to me that he wasn't going to appear that night. We threw him under a cold shower, and he was still drunk. I didn't want to give all that money back, though, so we persuaded him to go on. To get on stage you had to go up a little flight of steps. Well, Hank stumbled on the steps, crawled up to the mike and began singing. He repeated the lines to the song a dozen times. Finally, he fell down [reinjuring his back], and we had to drag him off stage.

"The crowd was furious. They really wanted to get to

him. We called the Mounties, and they escorted us all out of town." To this day, says a Nashville executive, "Certain areas in Canada won't book a country music show because of the way Hank broke commitments on that tour."

All this might have been bearable had there been some humor in it. But Hank was no lovable drunk. If he sometimes joked after sobering up, it was only to spare his friends embarrassment. While the boozing itself was in progress, he was dull, humorless, and utterly purposeful.

"When Hank was sobering up," says Sammy Pruett, "all he had to do was smell the stuff and he'd be gone again. I remember one time Minnie Pearl put me on a plane with him in Arizona, to bring him back to Nashville to dry out. He thought I was taking him to Florida for a little vacation. I had a half pint with me, and that got him to Nashville. Then I bought another half pint, and that was enough to get him into the hospital."

Hank usually recovered from one drunken night in time to perform the next night, but a trip to Texas and Arkansas was a glaring exception. The first date was in Dallas, and Hank flew ahead in Henry Cannon's plane. The rest of the band drove over from Nashville. When they arrived at the venerable Hotel Adolphus, Hank was not registered. As show time neared, he still had not showed up. Then Jerry Rivers spotted a tall, thin man wearing dark glasses and a white cowboy hat getting into an elevator. "Hey, isn't that Hank Williams?" Rivers asked a bellhop. "Oh, no, sir," said the bellhop. "That's Mr. Herman P. Willis, in Room 504."

Herman P. Willis was their joking name for a dummy who never does anything right, so they hurried up to 504 and, sure enough, found Hank. He was half loaded and would have been perfectly content to let the charade continue right through show time. His accomplice in that little escapade may well have been a Dallas night club manager named Jack Ruby. Hank had gotten chummy with Ruby, and the band had played a few times at his club, the Silver Spur. "Ruby was a good

old boy," recalls Don Helms. "He was a good man to
work for." When Helms next saw Ruby, a dozen years
later, he was shooting Lee Harvey Oswald on national
television.

Hank was all right in Dallas and then in Waco, but
when they headed for Greenville he got roaring drunk.
The boys put in a rush call to Hank Snow, the Nova
Scotia balladeer who had just gotten established on the
Opry. Snow flew in and did the Greenville date in
Williams' place, singing his own songs with the Drifting
Cowboys backing him up. Williams was suffering from
a monstrous hangover, and trying to convert it into
another all-out drunk, so Snow stayed with the band
into Little Rock. Williams, in no shape to perform, was
put aboard a plane and shipped back to Nashville to
dry out still another time.

16

By the end of 1951, only two and one-half years after
he had come to Nashville, Hank Williams was in deep
trouble. His marriage was foundering. His career, which
had developed with record speed, was awash in whisky.
Promoters, victimized too often by Hank's intemper-
ance, were balking at giving him any more dates. Nashville people, while sympathetic, were not anxious to risk
their own reputations by committing themselves to help
him.

Besides, Hank was giving no indication that he
wanted help. Proud and distant, he kept his private
troubles private, rebuffing offers of advice and assistance. In a sense he was reaping the harvest of loneliness he had sowed. He had never let anyone get really

close to him, and now that he desperately needed help, no one felt close enough to step in and give it to him, like it or not. Jim Denny and Fred Rose, both very influential in shaping his career, were too wrapped up in the business side of it—and probably too much older as well—to be of much help.

The Roses seem to have been unaware of Hank's real needs and problems. Even today, Wesley Rose plays down Hank's terrible drinking problem. He attributes it to "sugar in the blood producing a craving for liquor," and he concludes simply, without trying to probe for the causes, "Hank had to drink."

The Drifting Cowboys may have been in a better position than anyone to help their leader. Yet they appeared unable to do more than fret about the situation and hope it would clear up. Their inaction is understandable, even if it was shortsighted. They were all country boys with little education or exposure to the world. They were no older or more experienced than Hank. Not drinkers themselves, they had no idea how to deal with someone who was. Most important, they were the Indians and Hank was the chief. As Jerry Rivers puts it: "He held the reins. We were just employees."

"Reasoning with Hank was out of the question when he was drunk," says Don Helms. "And when he was sober he wouldn't discuss the situation. He wasn't huffy about it, just evasive. He was ashamed at his own behavior."

"When we did get him to talk about it," says Rivers, "he'd agree with us for a while, then he'd stop talking about it and turn the conversation to something else. In the end, he'd usually get panicky and have to have something more to drink." The Drifting Cowboys' complaints and ideas, advanced in the most tentative manner, fell on deaf ears. Bob McNett once approached Hank in just such a manner and got just such a response: "For quite a while Hank looked straight ahead, saying nothing. Then he said, 'Leave me alone, I don't want to talk about it.'"

The boys talked a lot about the drinking problem among themselves. They had to: it was affecting their nervous systems and their careers. But beyond an occasional attempt to talk about it with Hank, they simply rode the tide, protecting him when he was drunk, hauling him to hospitals to dry out. They all considered quitting the band many times, Rivers says, but none of them ever did. Loyalty was part of the reason; reluctance to give up what was still a damned good country music job was another part.

They did, however, begin doing an increasing amount of work for a young singer name Ray Price. With Hank canceling out of dates, they had time for other work. Price, who has gone on to become one of Nashville's biggest stars, was a sort of protégé of Hank, and when he needed a band to back him up he naturally turned to the Drifting Cowboys.

Inevitably, not only promoters but the press began to get on Hank. With the exception of Montgomery columnist Allen Rankin, he had never been close to reporters. In fact, he could not have been very receptive to them; the only serious stories of length about Hank were written after he died; apparently no one could get through to him during his lifetime. His own laconic style, part shyness and part distrust, was undoubtedly a factor in his distant press relations. Ray Jenkins, now editor of the Alabama *Journal,* remembers trying to interview Hank when the Hadacol Caravan played Columbus, Georgia. "I couldn't figure out if he was drunk or what," says Jenkins, "but he didn't say much, and I couldn't make sense out of what he did say. I didn't even write a story about him."

Although the average entertainment editor covers up for visiting stars who show their warts, Hank's transgressions were so blatant they had to draw some fire. One of the most notable broadsides was delivered by Edith Lindeman, a staffer for the Richmond (Virginia) *Times-Dispatch,* the morning after Hank bombed out at the local auditorium. Her story of January 30, 1952, is more than caustic criticism; it is also a dispassionate account of one dreadful night among many in Hank Williams' fall from grace.

Sitting through the early portions of the program, wrote Miss Lindeman, "The audience was polite, but they were waiting for Hank Williams. After about a half hour, [Ray] Price announced that Hank 'had a serious operation on his spine nine weeks ago but he made this engagement, so here he is.' To a burst of applause, Hank came in. His spine most certainly was not holding him erect. He sang, 'Cold, Cold Heart,' but did not get some of the words in the right places. Then he sang 'Lonesome Blues,' with a good deal of off-key yodeling.

"Several couples got up and left the auditorium. Then Hank sang 'I Hear that Lonesome Whistle Blow,' and some more people got up. Hank walked off and intermission was called. It lasted twenty-five minutes, during which time between fifty and seventy-five people went to the box office to get their money back. . . .

"After the intermission, Ray Price and his boys came back. They sang and played and ad libbed and whipped up extra numbers. Half the audience applauded their stalwart efforts to keep the show going. The other half yelled for Hank to come back.

"Presently Price was called off stage. When he came back, he said, 'The situation seems a lot improved,' and introduced Hank to the crowd again. This time his spine seemed to feel better. The audience greeted him with laughs and a few boos, to which he answered, 'I wish I was in as good shape as you are.' Then he looked around and said, 'Hank Williams is a lot of things but he ain't a liar. If they's a doctor in the house, I'll show him I've been in the hospital for eight weeks and this is my first show since then. And if you ain't nice to me, I'll turn around and walk right off.'

"Price, who deserved some special place in hillbilly heaven after his stint last night, jumped in and said, 'We all love you, Hank, don't we, folks?' And the audience applauded and laughed.

"Then Hank sang 'Move It On Over,' and it sounded

pretty good—almost as good as one of his records after it has been played a few hundred times. He also introduced the instrumentalists all over again, and sang 'I Can't Help It.'

"As a finish he sang, 'Cold, Cold Heart' once more, remembering all the words. Then he walked out, and got in his big yellow automobile with a chauffeur to drive him home."

The show was booked for the Richmond auditorium again the following night, and the place was packed in anticipation of another boozy performance by the great Hank Williams. Hank, however, was relatively sober. And he turned Miss Lindeman's onslaught to his own advantage by announcing at the outset, "I want to dedicate my first number to a gracious lady writer"— and then singing "Mind Your Own Business."

The Richmond trip was one of the tours for which Jim Denny provided a special escort to try to keep Hank sober. The escort in this case was Charlie Sanders, a veteran backstage employee at the Grand Ole Opry. "Denny told me, 'I can't get nobody else to watch out for Hank. Will you do it?' I said okay, for Denny's sake, not for Hank's. The idea was to get him to all these auditoriums and get him there sober."

Sanders adapted a policy of parceling out booze to his ward, just enough to keep him content, not enough to make him drunk for his show dates. "He was pretty drunk when he left Nashville, and he told me, 'I can't go without some more whisky.' So I went out to get him a pint." When Sanders returned to the car, Hank was sitting there with a paper sack in his lap and a look of studied innocence on his face.

"I went out to the fruit store," said Hank.

"Let's see what kind of fruit you got," said Sanders. He opened the bag and found two bottles, one of gin, one of wine. Sanders took them both back to the store.

That one pint was all Hank got from Nashville to Richmond. It was more than enough, on top of his already full load, to keep him well oiled. At an overnight stop, Sanders recalls, he took away Hank's matches and cigarettes before putting him to bed, a sensible precaution in light of his penchant for falling asleep while smoking. Next morning, however, there was a burned place on Hank's sheet and mattress. Hank had awakened in the middle of the night, bummed a cigarette and match, and proceeded to fall asleep smoking. Hank shrugged off the incident, told Sanders to find out how much the damage was, and paid for it.

That day, on the way into Richmond, Hank developed a furious, hangover thirst. He spotted an old well near a farmhouse and got Sanders to stop there. A man standing at the house eyed the group suspiciously until Sanders volunteered, "This here's Hank Williams."

The man brightened and said, "I listen to him all the time on the radio. I'd be honored to give him a drink." Hank normally would have caught the word "drink" like a radar catches blips, but this time regular thirst got the best of him. He gulped down almost half a bucket of water without stopping.

"Hank," said Sanders jokingly, "what was that water worth to you?"

"How much money you got in your pocket?" Hank replied.

Sanders fished out a five-dollar bill, and Hank said to the man who owned the well, "Friend, is five dollars enough for this bucket of water?" The man protested: "You don't owe me one thing in the world. I'm honored to do it."

Hank waved his hand impatiently. "Give the man the money," he told Sanders, and slouched back to the car. Sanders pushed the bill into the man's hand, and they drove off.

Sanders swears Hank was sober when he delivered him to the Richmond auditorium that evening. "But when I walked into the dressing room later, he was drunk. Some of his buddies had started givin' him drinks. I said to him, 'What's the score? I done sweated out eighteen hours gettin' you sober, and you got drunk again in ten minutes.' And he said, 'I needed a drink bad.' "

On stage, Sanders recalls, Hank was every bit as bad as Edith Lindeman said he was. "When he finally went off, he could hardly find the opening in the curtain. We bundled him into a car and carried him around to a drive-in and put some coffee and a sandwich in him. There was another show that night, and he was goin' to be ready for it.

"When we headed back to the auditorium, I got the driver to put me and Hank out ten or twelve blocks away. It was about ten above zero, and he was still in his stage clothes, with no coat or nothin'. But we were gonna sober up, I'll tell you. He complained, but when he said how cold he was I just walked him faster. When we got back, he was as sober as anybody in the world, and the second show went fine."

Sanders shepherded Hank back to the hotel, and when he left him he said, "I'll see you at one tomorrow afternoon. If you're gonna drink, let it be over by then." When Sanders arrived at the appointed hour next day, he found Hank in predictably bad shape. "He had a fifth cut down pretty good, and he had several bottles of beer with part gone out of each bottle. We called the doctor, and when he showed up we got him to give Hank a hypo. I remember telling the doctor, 'He's got to work tonight, so make sure that hypo wears off by then.'" It did wear off, and Hank performed to the satisfaction of everyone, including Miss Lindeman.

Cedric Rainwater, the Drifting Cowboys' bass player, was so embarrassed by Hank's on-stage display that first night in Richmond that he promptly went back to Nashville. "We found a note in his hotel room," says Jerry Rivers, "saying he had to fly home because his little boy was sick. We didn't know the real reason till Don saw Ced when we got back and asked him how his little boy was. 'Huh?' Ced said. 'He's all right I guess.' Then he did a double take and said, 'Oh! Yeah. . . . Why, the pore little feller done had a risin' riz up in his ear.'"

Reflecting on the Richmond trip not long ago, Charlie Sanders delivered this simple epitaph for Hank: "He was no deadbeat at all. He wasn't tryin' to beat anybody. The only one he ever beat was hisself."

Certainly he seldom tried to beat his audience. In a sense he cheated them, by getting too drunk to perform properly, but that was the act of a compulsive drinker, not a calculating cheater. Hank treated his audiences with whatever measure of respect his state of insobriety would allow. There was nothing mysterious about that. Like any great entertainer, he loved his audiences. They nourished him; in fact, in his declining months they kept him going; without them, and without the music he loved to bring to them, his life would have ended even more prematurely than it did.

The audiences, for their part, were remarkably tolerant of Hank. He was their favorite, drunk or sober, as he has remained their favorite, dead or alive. Some people, as in Richmond, walked out when he stumbled on stage or jumbled the lyrics of songs he knew by heart. Most people laughed at him good-naturedly and waited patiently while he pulled himself sufficiently together to get through the show. A few people were moved to tears, struck by the pitiful condition of a man who seemed to have so much: so much talent, so much success, so much to live for and enjoy.

Hillous Butrum recalls a show at the Dallas Sportatorium when Hank arrived four and one-half hours late. It had taken that long to get him sober enough to appear. "It was 12:30 A.M.," says Butrum, "and nobody had left the place. Hank walked on stage with a grin and said, 'Mornin' friends, nice to see y'all.' They gave him a terrific cheer. One of the big names in country music, I think it was Hank Snow, was standing next to me, and he just shook his head, saying, 'I don't understand it.' "

"Hank got some heckling on stage," says Don Helms, "but he was no more temperamental about it than any other star would be. Once in a while if a heckler kept on him, he'd put him down good. The clincher usually would be gesturing in the guy's direction and saying, 'Would some of you friends get a shovel and try to cover that up?' " Hank also had a put down for the occasional heckler who needled him about singing "Lovesick Blues" so often. "So far I've made twenty-four thousand dollars outta this here song," he'd say. "You tell me what song you've made twenty-four thousand dollars out of, and I'll stop singing it."

There were times when Hank's love for the audience turned to anger and when the audience's good-natured laughter at him turned to derision. On one occasion, he fell off the stage, staggered back up, and shouted over the mocking laughter of the audience: "Don't give me any of that crap. I'm gonna finish this song." And there were times when he didn't even realize the mockery in the laughter, when he mistook it for real enthusiasm. At such times he was likely to grin broadly and say, "Y'all liked that song, did yuh? All right, I'll sing y'all another one." The other one was as bad as the first, but he went ahead with it anyway.

This sort of aggressive egotism now surfaced more frequently, always induced by alcohol. One time, in New Orleans, Billy Walker was scheduled to appear just before Hank, who was to close the show. Hank was drunk, and when the time came for Walker to go on, Hank said to him, "You been on yet, son?" "No," replied Walker. "Well, you're too late," mumbled Hank. "I'm goin' on." And he did. Walker did get to perform —after Hank had finished and most of the audience had left.

Another time, reportedly in Las Vegas, Hank ran across a jukebox that did not offer any of his songs or records. He went to a jukebox distributing house, bought the best machine in the place, stocked it entirely with Hank Williams numbers, and had it delivered to the offending night spot. "Throw that other machine out," he told the owner. "This one's got records worth playing."

So it went from tour to tour, from town to town; a good, sober show here, a drunk, terrible show there. Local promoters booked Hank with trepidation, if at all.

The Drifting Cowboys talked and worried, but they went along with him. Clearly, Hank was headed downhill, and a crash was inevitable. Yet no one took strong action to prevent it. Some who might have felt powerless to do so. Others didn't realize the lateness of the hour.

Back in Nashville, Hank's troubles were increasing at home and at work. His marriage to Audrey, already shaky, was strained unbearably by his ever-increasing drinking sprees. His affiliation with the Grand Ole Opry was strained also; when he failed to appear or appeared drunk on a show date somewhere, the waves of indignation were felt all the way back to the Opry.

"Sure, the other artists on the show would be there, but Hank was the big draw," says Irving Waugh, now president of WSM. "When he didn't show up the people wanted their money back. You can't let that happen many times and still maintain decent relations with the public and the promoters. If the guy is ill, you've got a legitimate excuse, and maybe you can send a substitute. But if he doesn't show, you're in real trouble."

Hank also was missing some of his radio shows on WSM. Usually he called in to say he was sick and couldn't make it. When he came to the studio in noticeably bad shape, he would grin weakly and say, "Well, them bones done riz again."

Early in January 1952, Audrey left Hank and filed for separate maintenance. Her action caused only a slight stir in Nashville's country music circles. One story is that Audrey made her final decision to leave after Hank fired at her four times when he burst into the house following a New Year's Eve party. Perhaps that is what happened, but nothing so dramatic was necessary. The marriage had run its course.

Audrey later changed her suit from separate maintenance to outright divorce. At the divorce proceeding, she secured an injunction tying up more than 133,000 dollars in real and personal property owned by Hank. And she estimated her husband's 1951 income at more than 90,000 dollars—a long way from the quarter-million he was earning a year or so earlier but still the basis for a fat settlement.

Hank, stunned and deeply hurt, did not contest the suit. He was in no shape to do so successfully. Audrey's allegations of "cruel and inhuman treatment" were all too true, and the counterclaims he might have made, however valid, would have been pale by comparison.

On May 29, Audrey was granted a divorce in Nashville chancery court. Under the decree, she received a healthy chunk of Hank's property and earnings, past and future. She also received custody of three-year-old Randall, with the provision that Hank could have the boy during the summer, beginning in 1953, and could visit him a reasonable number of times during the rest of the year.

Details of the settlement gave Audrey: the family home on Franklin Road, which she valued at $55,000 minus a $13,599 mortgaged indebtedness; a Cadillac with outstanding notes amounting to $706; $1,000 in cash; $4,000 to pay the fees of her attorneys; one-half of all royalties due Hank from Acuff-Rose and M-G-M Records at the time her divorce action was filed and one-half of all royalties forthcoming in the future.

The last-named provision was to make Audrey Williams a wealthy woman, for the royalties on Hank's published songs and records mounted steadily in the years following his death, reaching a combined total of 220,000 dollars for the year 1966. Audrey could not have anticipated they would climb as high as they did, but she was shrewd enough to know that her financial security lay with her husband's future royalties rather than with his current assets. Meanwhile, she was taking no chances: a provision of the decree stated that, should royalties fail to net Audrey at least 10,000 dollars a year, the difference would be made up to her from other sources.

Audrey herself had to give up something, but not much. She relinquished her interest in the farm in Franklin and in Hank and Audrey's Corral, the Western-style clothing store in Nashville. She also agreed to support and educate young Randall except for the periods he spent in his father's custody.

The divorce shattered Hank. It removed one of the few props he had left—his home and children. It did not remove his love for Audrey, as well it might have; he remained passionately, helplessly in love with her till the end of his life. But now he went spinning off on longer sprees, missing more show dates than ever, even dates at the Opry itself. The pills and non-addictive drugs he had been taking for his back pains became—like alcohol—a regular part of his diet.

Well before the divorce was granted, Hank had moved out of the house on Franklin Road, paying Audrey a modest amount monthly for separate maintenance. He moved into a two-story house on Natchez Trace in Nashville, living in the downstairs part and renting the upstairs to young singer Ray Price. Hank had met Price several months before, had taken an instant liking to him, and had made him a sort of protégé. He booked Price on many of his tour shows, which was a good break for a young entertainer, and on one occasion, in Norfolk, Virginia, Price filled in for Hank when he was too drunk to perform. Hank got Price his first spot on the Opry, insisting Price be signed on even though he hadn't had a hit song.

"We got pretty close," says Price, who has gone on to become one of country music's premier performers. "Hank was a lonely person, and when he wanted to talk to somebody he'd call all over the country trying to find me. I think he drank because he wanted people to pay attention to him. He wanted people to show him they loved him, and this was his way of testing them."

Price says Hank moved to Natchez Trace with the idea of straightening himself out and trying to patch things up with Audrey. "He was doing real fine when he thought she wasn't actually going to divorce him. Our deal worked okay. I did most of the housework and sort of took care of him. But when the divorce came it got real bad."

Price accompanied Hank to the lawyer's office to sign the divorce papers. When the lawyer said he didn't have to give Audrey half of his future royalties, Hank said crisply, "I want to." His idea, says Price, was to "show her he loved her and wanted her to come back."

There was little chance of Audrey's coming back, and Hank soon realized it. He sank into fits of deep depression, punctuated by long sessions with the bottle and occasional lively times with girls. "He wasn't too bad before the divorce," says Price, a little too generously, "but after it he went off the deep end. Don Helms and I wound up taking him to a sanitarium up in Madison. Then his mother sent a niece from Montgomery, and she took him back to Alabama for a while. When he came back, he started raising cane again."

Hank's visits to sanitariums became almost routine. Sometimes he had to be carried in, struggling, and kept at the institution forcefully. Other times he seemed resigned to a drying-out period, and he joked with the friends who took him and the nurses who cared for him while he was there. Either way, his recovery was often complicated by his ingenious knack for getting more booze. He would bribe an orderly to produce a bottle of something—he hardly cared what kind or what size —and he'd get himself as loaded as possible before he was discovered.

His trips in and out of sanitariums and his visibly deteriorating physical condition gave rise to considerable gossip that he was not going to live much longer. One story had Hank willing his body to a medical school for use in research. Another one, widely circulated among artists and fans alike, was that Hank suffered from a mysterious ailment that was slowly turning him to stone. Many people doubtless were surprised, and perhaps a little disappointed, when he died of almost ordinary diseases.

Price says he never saw Hank take any drugs. "His trouble was the bottle, and the fact that he wouldn't eat when he drank. If we could start him eating, we could get him straightened out pretty good. But he had no interest in food. If he ate and the food came flying back up, he'd take another drink right away. Naw, he wasn't a public drunk. He'd do all his drinking right in a room. The problem was to get him out once he got started."

Drunk or sober, Hank was getting to be an unpleasant companion, and Price made up his mind to leave the house on Natchez Trace. "I called the boy who was running his Western store and got him to come to the house, so he could verify that I wasn't taking anything of Hank's when I packed up. While I was packing, Hank came in and asked me where I was going.

" 'I just can't take it any more,' I told him.

" 'Don't leave me,' he said, 'I'm gonna be all right.'

"I got to," said Price, and he did.

About that time, Hank played a show date in El Paso. It was a package show, with Ernest Tubb the other featured entertainer. Minnie Pearl arrived to play the El Paso date and found Hank in bad shape. "They had a male nurse with him," recalls Pearl, "and they were trying to get him to finish the tour. We played the first show that evening, and he sang a couple of songs. They were pretty bad, but the audience didn't care. They'd take it from him, where they wouldn't from the rest of us.

"Hank was drunk and had no business being on stage. But the promoters had to make him try to work, they had so much money riding on him. So after the first show we drove him around to see if we could sober him up. He kept trying to get us to stop and get him a drink. Finally he said, 'Let's sing.' 'Okay,' we said, 'what?' We'd have done anything to keep pleasin' him and keep him occupied.

"He wanted to sing that great old hymn of his, 'I Saw the Light.' So we started singing it. All of a sudden Hank stopped, and he cried out, 'That's the trouble. It's all dark. There ain't no light!' "

17

On the morning of August 11, country music executive Harry Stone walked behind the WSM studio. "A Cadillac was parked there, with a hillbilly at the wheel," recalls Stone. "And there in the back seat lay Hank Williams. He was the most pitiful-looking thing I'd ever seen."

Hank looked up at Stone and said, "Mr. Harry, they just fired me."

"The hell you say," replied Stone. "What for?"

"For drinkin'."

"What're you gonna do now?" asked Stone.

"I'm goin' back to Shreveport," said Hank.

Three years and several hundred thousand dollars after he hit the Grand Ole Opry, Hank Williams was fired from it. A sensation at twenty-five, a washout at twenty-eight. Actually, it is a minor miracle that he lasted as long at the Opry as he did. Opry officials in those days started trembling at the mere mention of alcohol, and Hank's recurring bouts with it left them faint with fear about propriety, the Opry image, and so on. They had tolerated his escapades in the hinterlands, even though these escapades reflected poorly on Mother Opry herself. But when Hank brought his drinking problem right into Ryman Auditorium, something had to be done.

Hank came close to being fired a number of times, only the strong pleas of Jim Denny and a couple of other supporters saved him. National Life, the Opry's sponsor, was becoming extremely nervous about having an out and out drunk as one of the show's star performers. The powers were reluctant to act while Hank was making his regular Opry appearances. But then, says Irving Waugh, "It got to a point where he'd disappear for weeks at a time. Nobody would know where he was."

There is a difference of opinion over precisely which affront caused the Opry finally to fire Hank. One story is that he missed a Friday night WSM show he was told he had to make. Another is that it was his showing up drunk one time too many for a Saturday night Opry appearance. Ray Price says it was his failing to show at all for an Opry-sponsored date in Reading, Pennsylvania.

In any event, the decision was made by a group that included the top executives at WSM, the Opry, and National Life: Jim Denny; Jack Dewitt, president of WSM; Irving Waugh, then head of the station's advertising department; Jack Stapp, then program manager, and George Reynolds, the station's chief engineer. Two other influential men also were consulted: Fred Rose and Edwin Craig, president of National Life.

The actual firing was left to Jack Stapp, who is now one of Nashville's most successful music publishers. Stapp summoned Hank into his office at WSM, motioned for him to sit on a big, green leather couch ("all the guys sat there") placed along one of the black, decorator-done walls. A speaker on one wall was putting forth the station's current program. Stapp told Hank straight off that he was being suspended from both WSM and the Opry. Hank took the news well, Stapp says, and did not make a fuss.

Later that day, Don Helms drove up to Hank's house to return some hunting gear Hank had left in his car. Hank came out and told Helms simply, "I'll be gone for a while. I'll be seein' you boys around." He said he'd been fired and was going to Shreveport. Then he grinned and added one of his favorite expressions: "Don't worry about anything—nothin's gonna be all right anyhow."

Next day the Nashville newspapers ran a small,

crisply worded item that said Hank Williams had been released by WSM "for failing to appear on scheduled radio programs and missing personal appearance performances."

A few days later, Hank was on his way back to Shreveport, deeply troubled and in danger of a complete breakdown. His wife and family were gone, his career tarnished, his body sick and addicted to alcohol. The decision to send him back to Shreveport was apparently made by his two chief advisers, Fred Rose and Jim Denny. It was a logical move, the country music equivalent of sending a slumping or sore-armed baseball star to the minors to rehabilitate him.

Wesley Rose, indulging his taste for euphemism, says Hank's departure was "not really a firing but a leave of absence. It was better for Hank to be out of Nashville, off the merry-go-round for a while. I think he was glad to leave at that particular time." Perhaps, but the testimony of others indicated Hank acquiesced only reluctantly in the decision to ship him away.

Rose insists that WSM and the Opry were willing, indeed planning, to take Hank back if he straightened out in Shreveport. Again, there is conflicting testimony. Harry Stone says bluntly, "They wouldn't have given him a job back for anything in the world." The important thing is that Hank himself believed he could make a comeback. Whether he had been told so or not, he was convinced to the end that he could and would get back on the Opry.

Shreveport's Louisiana Hayride took Hank again for the simple reason that, drinking or no drinking, he was still a big draw. "Sure it was a risk," says Frank Page of station KWKH, "but we thought the risk was worth it. There are a lot of 'risky' artists in this business, and we've taken quite a few under the conditions that we took Hank. Some work out, some don't. Anyway, the people loved Hank partly *because* of his problems."

They also loved him because of his awesome, irrepressible talent, which kept shining through all the whisky and heartache that seemed ready to drown it.

As much as he might stagger around on stage, Hank remained a thoroughly professional recording artist. He never showed up drunk for a recording session, and the quality of his records held at a consistently high level.

Indeed, judging from Hank's recordings and the success they were enjoying, he was doing as well as ever. Throughout troubled 1952, his records sold at the usual brisk pace, and several of them reached the charts. If anything, he became a bigger hit as a recording artist: when he died in January 1953, he had two of the top three and three of the top ten singles in *Billboard's* country and Western listings—"Jambalaya," "I'll Never Get Out of This World Alive," and "Settin' the Woods on Fire," in that order.

Whether Hank had a premonition of death when he wrote "I'll Never Get Out of This World Alive" is hard to say, but it is not unreasonable to think he did. That same year he told a Nashville *Tennessean* reporter who came to interview him, "I'll never live long enough for you to write about me." The song, however, is not a morbid piece but a bit of down and out country humor.

In addition, Hank's songwriting genius did not diminish. Some of the best songs were written after the break with Audrey, that is, during the most doleful, drunken months of his life. Naturally, some of them were based on his then-current relationship with Audrey, just as some had been based on that relationship when the two of them were together.

"He couldn't sleep at night anyway," a close friend has said, "so he'd sit up writing songs. It was like he had a feeling that something terrible would happen to him if he didn't stay there and get them finished. Then, early in the morning, he'd call me or Don Helms or Webb Pierce, either because he wanted someone to listen to his songs or because, now that he was finished, he wanted someone to drink with. He never drank while he was writing, because he couldn't write while he was drinking."

Hank was a success all over again in Shreveport. The

audiences loved him, even though he continued his habits of appearing under the influence for some shows and completely skipping others. "I had to apologize for him a lot to our audiences," says Frank Page. "I'd say, 'Hank is sick tonight and can't make it.' I never said he was drunk, though sometimes it was evident that's what he was."

The high times on tour continued, too. Page recalls one Hayride trip to Brownwood, Texas, when "we fought him all the way on the bus, trying to keep liquor away from him. Somehow he got a couple of pints, and he was hard to hold up by the time he hit the stage. You know, he couldn't sing at all when he was drunk. Some people can, but he'd flat out all over the place."

When he reached Shreveport, it was evident that Hank wasn't carrying the torch for Audrey to an extreme point. A girl was at his side. Her name was Billie Jean Jones Eshlimar, and she was to play a major role in the final months of Hank's life.

Billie Jean, nineteen years old, was a native of the Shreveport area, the daughter of a Bossier City police officer. Slender but full-blown, she had a pretty, rather sensuous face, and a glorious mass of dark red hair. In the memorable words of a Nashville music executive, she was "so pretty you couldn't look at her."

Billie Jean had quit high school in her senior year to marry a handsome young airman named Harrison Eshlimar. The marriage didn't work out, and they separated. By the summer of 1952, Billie Jean was keeping company with country artist Faron Young, who was then moving up from the Louisiana Hayride to the Grand Ole Opry. She met Hank backstage at Ryman Auditorium the night Young was making his first Opry appearance.

"I was nineteen and had never been out of Shreveport before," says Billie Jean. "Hank came up to me and said, "If you ain't married, Ol' Hank's gonna marry you. You're about the purtiest thing I ever saw.' "

Later, Young and Billie Jean double dated with Hank and a Nashville girl, and soon after that Hank was giving Billie Jean the rush—telephoning her in Shreveport, taking her out when she came to Nashville. Conveniently for Hank, Young broke up with Billie Jean about this time, although he says the breakup had nothing to do with the attention Hank was paying her.

When Hank left Nashville in September, in a chauffeur-driven limousine, Billie Jean was with him. She recalls that they went by way of Montgomery and stopped at his mother's boardinghouse. Hank took Billie Jean in to see a woman who occupied one of the rooms —a little something, she realized, he had stashed away for trips to Montgomery. She also realized that Hank was trying to tell the woman that Billie Jean was his wife-to-be and that she (the woman) was finished. "They got into a fight," Billie Jean recalls, "a real fight, with fists and everything. He finally threw her out."

Understandably upset, Billie Jean got the chauffeur to drive her to the bus station, where she caught a Greyhound for Shreveport. "A few weeks later, Hank called. I wouldn't have been surprised to have never seen him again. But he said, 'Honey, I'm comin' down. We're gonna get married.' "

Hank arrived in Shreveport with two Cadillacs, loaded to the roof, followed by a couple of small trailers. He and Billie Jean decided to get married in mid-October, as soon as her divorce from Eshlimar became final. Billie Jean recalls vividly Hank's first meeting with her family:

"We drove up to my parents' house in Hank's Cadillac. I said, 'Momma, this is Hank Williams.' She scowled at him and said, 'Shoot, you ain't no Hank Williams.' He didn't look like it, all right. He had on the baseball hat and jeans he usually wore when he traveled in the car. But he ran over to Momma and pulled off his hat and showed her—'I really *am* Ol' Hank.' And he started singing 'Lovesick Blues' to prove it to her!"

Billie Jean had been a telephone operator, and when they got to Shreveport she became one again. She was wild about Hank, even on the job: "I used to run out on the street with my headset on to meet him." Hank wanted to start touring right away, and Billie Jean said she'd go with him before they were married—if he hired her brother as lead guitarist and took the brother's wife along as chaperone. That worked well until one day she came back to the hotel room and found Hank on his knees, looking under the bed.

"God damn, baby," he said cheerfully, "I was just lookin' for my shoes."

"Hank," said Billie Jean, "you got your shoes on." She looked under the bed and found two cases of beer. She promptly opened every can and poured the contents into the sink.

Later, however, Billie Jean let Hank have beer, which he had come to love. She had a two-can limit for him. "If he got more, I'd force milk and two raw eggs down him, then I'd call my brothers to pack him off to the hospital. He'd go up the elevator singing, 'Good-by, Joe, me gotta go, me oh my oh. . . .' "

When drying out in confinement, Hank maintained his passion for comic books. "I brought him every weird, crazy funny book on the stands," says Billie Jean, "hundreds of them. He called them 'goof books,' and he never read anything else, not even a newspaper."

Billie Jean says she never put up with the type of drunken foolishness in which Hank had indulged in Nashville. "I told him, 'You either walk as a man as my husband, or you don't walk at all.' He treated me like a lady, too. Unlike Audrey, I wanted no part of show business. I didn't want a maid or high-falutin' dresses. I just wanted him."

Although she is now a shrewd woman with an eye for a dollar, Billie Jean insists that when she married Hank it was for love, not for money. "He needed me, too," she says. "He needed somebody who'd be kind to him without wanting anything from him. I was his last hope in humans." Hank's big problem, she is convinced, was "too many leeches around him. Everybody wanted his money."

The wedding was one of the memorable productions of American show business. It was a two-stage affair, the first stage conducted in runaway fashion before a justice of the peace in the middle of the night, the second conducted at the New Orleans Municipal Auditorium before several thousand paying "guests," who were treated to matinee and evening performances.

The auditorium wedding was well planned, of course, but the J.P. ceremony was decided on rather hurriedly. Hank had gotten word that Audrey was highly displeased by his proposed marriage to Billie Jean, so he decided to get it done swiftly and quietly, before things got fouled up. After a Hayride show at the Shreveport auditorium, a couple of nights before the New Orleans spectacular was scheduled to come off, he and Billie Jean drove to the nearby town of Minden, woke up a J.P., and got him to marry them.

Also along on that midnight ride was Paul Howard, a country musician and songwriter who was a sort of adviser to Hank in Shreveport. "On the way back from the J.P.'s," recalls Howard, "we ran out of gas—way out in the bow-jacks, the real country. Hank got the biggest bang out of standing out on the highway, in his gaudy show uniform and big hat, flagging down traffic. Finally a soldier picked us up and took us in for gas."

Billie Jean remembers the man who picked them up: "Hank wanted the guy to go home with us. Paul said, 'Hell no, Hank, not on your wedding night.' They argued about it for a couple of hours, and I finally got rid of the guy. Then Hank sat in my rouge, which had spilled in the car, and he walked into the restaurant for breakfast with red all over the seat of his white show uniform."

The New Orleans wedding was as lavish and well planned as the Minden ceremony was seedy and spontaneous. It was handled for Hank by promoter Oscar Davis, in concert with a New Orleans entrepreneur. "I knew I could promote some goods for him," says Davis. "He didn't have any money, and he needed some stuff to start the marriage with, especially furniture." New

Orleans was chosen because it was a large city near Shreveport and because "Jambalaya" already had made Hank popular there.

Davis solicited various New Orleans stores and came up with a collection of goodies: champagne, flowers, a wardrobe for Billie Jean, the usual assortment of wedding gifts. He lined up the municipal auditorium for a 3 P.M. "rehearsal" and a 7 P.M. "wedding." "All the folks want to see me get married," Hank explained to the press, "and all of 'em can't get in at one time." Tickets were priced from 75 cents to $1.50. No mention was made of the fact that the two were already married, and both shows were sellouts.

A group of country music artists performed at each show, but the top Nashville stars and executives, including Jim Denny and Fred and Wesley Rose, were pointedly absent. "To us, it was no place to get married," says Wesley Rose. "My father felt he'd be part of a carnival if he went." Also absent was Audrey Williams, whom Hank had had the brass to invite; "there's nothing I wouldn't do to spite her," he told friends.

So Billie Jean, stunning in her wedding gown, and Hank, bleary-eyed in a dark fringed stage uniform, stood before the Reverend L. R. Shelton, pastor of the Algiers, Louisiana, First Baptist Church. At three and again at seven, they exchanged vows, kissed, and swept majestically out of the hall, to the sighs, tears, and cheers of the faithful.

According to Billie Jean, the newlyweds were supposed to depart immediately for a honeymoon in Cuba —but Hank had too much champagne at the reception and passed out in his hotel room. That left Billie Jean to face the press alone, and she says she responded to that challenge by appearing, in wide-eyed innocence, in a translucent negligee and no shoes. Hank, she announced, was "resting."

The New Orleans spectacular was the high point of the brief marriage. Hank, according to Billie Jean, was ill to the point of needing regular nursing-type attention. Still, they had some good times. A number of the good times were generated by Hank's unceasing generosity. Even now, when his net worth had been sliced in half and his earning power was greatly reduced, he displayed the same old desire to please other people, loved ones and strangers alike.

Billie·Jean recalls that, on trips to see her grandparents, who lived on welfare, Hank would present them with huge quantities of groceries. "He did that with everybody poor who gave him a sob story. I think he gave everybody down here a gun. He gave away uniforms too. 'You like this one?' he'd say to somebody. 'Here, take it.' " Hank lavished gifts on Billie Jean herself, but she says she refused them: "I wouldn't even let him buy me a ring for the wedding. He wanted to buy me a hen's egg, but we used my sister-in-law's ring instead."

During his Shreveport stay, Hank virtually lost contact with most of his Nashville friends and business associates. The Drifting Cowboys, who had long since ceased relying on Hank for steady work, were backing up Ray Price on show dates. Hank occasionally would engage them for a specific date, but generally he relied on musicians around the Hayride.

Other people who saw a good deal of Hank during that period disagree. They say he was worn out and obviously sick, still very much on the bottle, probably very much on pills. He was suffering from hepatitis and from a heart condition. As he was getting set to start one tour, through southern Louisiana, he spread his hands across his chest and complained to a fellow entertainer: "My chest is ready to bust. I can hardly breathe." He shrugged off a suggestion that he cancel the tour and see a doctor.

Oscar Davis, who promoted show dates for Hank during the Shreveport interlude, says flatly, "Hank was gone. His health was declining, and he couldn't straighten out. When he sang 'Lovesick Blues,' which he still used to close his shows, it took the guts right out of him." What about drinking? "He'd beg for whisky like a baby begs for milk, and he'd think up a million ways to get it. I'd let him go all night. But the next morning I'd go up to his room about ten-thirty, and I wouldn't let him out of my sight till show time.

"He didn't care how he lived at that point. He still loved his ex-wife, and he loved the boy too, but he couldn't cut out the drugs and the booze. I'd tell him, 'You ought to think of the boy,' and he'd cry and ask for another drink."

Davis' comments on the money Hank received in those last months are stark evidence of how far down he'd come: "His top had been about fifteen hundred dollars a day in his prime, but now, in towns around Louisiana, we just got whatever we could. No local promoter would handle him. It was too risky. We'd have to buy the radio time, hire the auditorium, do it all—and then take our chances." Even at that, it was a good risk. Hank Williams was still a powerful name, and there were lots of people willing to pay just to see if the rumors about his downfall were true.

On the southern Louisiana tour he made despite shortness of breath, Hank ran into trouble with one of his audiences. He got a pint of whisky from a local disk jockey, got sick, and, at the show, stubbornly refused to sing "Lovesick Blues" despite repeated calls for it from the audience. Angry fans mobbed his car after the performance and rocked it until police arrived. The next town on the itinerary, Jennings, sent word that if Hank couldn't arrive sober he'd better not arrive at all.

Back in Shreveport, after the tour, Hank told the Hayride manager he wanted to take a vacation. The manager readily agreed, advising him to take two or three weeks off. Hank went back to Montgomery, ostensibly to rest, but he wound up playing show dates and coming back to Shreveport in no better shape than when he'd left.

Somehow that fall, Hank came under the influence of a quack doctor whose drugs were to have an uncertain but hardly beneficial effect on the singer's health. The man's name was Horace R. "Toby" Marshall. He was a convicted forger who practiced medicine under phony doctors' degrees. A reformed alcoholic, he specialized in treatment of other alcoholics, although he had not gone beyond high school and knew virtually nothing about medicine.

Toby Marshall was a classic charlatan and, when caught at the game shortly after Hank died, a candid one as well. He told an Oklahoma legislative committee investigating narcotics abuse that he bought his medical "degree" from a magazine sales crew in an Oklahoma City filling station: "I paid thirty-five dollars for it. The magazine salesman had a machine that ground out diplomas and degrees while the customer waited."

Marshall made himself sound like a selfless servant of the ill and depressed. "A drunk, as anyone knows, is disagreeable to live with," he wrote for his personnel file when admitted to San Quentin to serve an armed robbery term. "Most wives won't do it. And few relatives will. I made myself available to families who needed me, and often spent twenty-four to thirty-six hours at a time giving the alcoholic the attention his family wouldn't. I'd sit hours. I'd be there when he woke, and I'd talk with him. I'd show him he was wanted.

"That's how I worked with Hank Williams. He drank without reserve. . . ."

Unfortunately for Hank, that is not the only way Marshall worked with him. Marshall gave him drugs as well as attention, prescribing them by means of a simple but effective ruse: he would telephone a doctor's office and get the doctor's registry number by posing as a pharmacy clerk; then he would call a pharmacy and place his order for drugs, using the number to make the order legitimate. By this method, Marshall managed to get Hank all the "bennies" (amphetamines) and Seconal he wanted. He also managed to get him chloral hydrate, a sedative.

Marshall first met Hank in Oklahoma City, where, he later said, he was called in to minister to Hank's drunkenness. He succeeded to the point where Hank was able to stagger onto the stage. Minnie Pearl, who was working that show, doesn't recall Marshall's presence, but she does recall Hank's pitiful attempt to perform:

"When Hank was ready to walk on stage, he turned to me with that little-boy look, and I said, 'Hank, you oughtn't go out there and try to work.' He said, 'Don't worry about ol' Hank, it's gonna be all right.' He stood out there, swaying, trying to sing but not being able to. He'd forget the words so often he could hardly get through a song. His voice was like the cry of a child or a wounded animal."

That was the start of Hank's relationship with Toby Marshall, and it lasted until the week he died. When the two traveled together, as they often did that fall, Hank paid Marshall a fee of three hundred dollars a week. Marshall also received unspecified sums for telephone "consultations" and for keeping Hank supplied with drug prescriptions. The last prescription, apparently, was one written in December for twenty-four grains of chloral hydrate. Hank had it filled, and then refilled, at a drugstore in Montgomery.

After Hank's death, Marshall had the gall to present Billie Jean Williams with a bill for $736.39, for medical services rendered her late husband. The bill was never paid, and some two months later Marshall was put in jail in Oklahoma.

At the Oklahoma legislative hearing that resulted in revocation of Marshall's parole, Billie Jean testified that she believed prescriptions provided by Marshall contributed to Hank's death. Marshall, she said, followed Hank everywhere "with a little black bag. Every time my husband went to fill a singing date and got away from me, that guy with the bag would meet him and administer to him. I destroyed all the drugs he brought home. One time when he was in Oklahoma City . . . he made three thousand dollars and returned home with five hundred. He said he spent some money for expenses and other money for treatment."

At the same hearing, Marshall's parole officer produced a letter written by Marshall about Hank a week after the latter's death. The letter claimed Hank might have committed suicide—to escape "parasites" and "fair-weather friends." Far-fetched, perhaps, but other sections of the letter showed medical quack Marshall to have had a surprisingly clear understanding of his patient's basic personality problems.

After telling a self-laudatory story of long vigils over Hank during drunken periods and of strong efforts to prevent him from sinking to ever-lower depths, Marshall wrote: "Although he [Hank] had a multiplicity of emotional problems, basically he was a very lonely person, and couldn't stand being alone. . . . This, in spite of the fact that he had a host of fair-weather friends, most of whom were parasites who fawned on him, played up to him, kept him supplied with liquor and women, and usually wound up getting to him for a chunk. . . .

"I can't overlook the fact that . . . he had been on a rapid decline. Most of his bookings were of the honky-tonk beer joint variety that he simply hated. If he came to this conclusion [suicide] . . . he still had enough prestige left as a star to make a first-class production out of it . . . whereas, six months from now, unless he pulled himself back up into some high-class bookings, he might have been playing for nickels and dimes on skid row."

There are conflicting stories about Hank's state of health in the late fall of 1952. Some people say he was a physical wreck, unable to control even such basic body functions as urination. Others say his health seemed to be improving, that his bony frame had some meat on it, that he seemed more relaxed and more confident of the future than he'd been in a long time.

Ray Price recalls seeing Hank at the "Big D Jamboree," shortly before Christmas. A "Dr." Marshall was with him, says Price, but except for having "his head skinned up a little," Hank was in pretty good shape. He worked the Jamboree and performed reasonably well. "His spirits were high one day, down the next. He told me, 'I'm comin' back to Nashville to go to work.' "

Returning to Nashville and the big time was very much on Hank's mind as the year drew to a close. Perhaps he never would have made it, but he was certainly trying. He was making an effort, however halting, to pull himself together. The best evidence of this comes from people who saw him on his trip home over the Christmas holiday.

"At the Jamboree," says Price, "Hank was feeling lonesome, and he said to my mother and me, 'Say, I might just come over and spend Christmas Day with you.' 'Well, c'mon,' we said. But he went back to Alabama instead."

In his last remaining Cadillac, a blue convertible, Hank and Billie Jean arrived in Georgiana a couple of days before Christmas. They did not head for Lon Williams' house but for Taft and Erlene Skippers'. Taft was Hank's cousin and boyhood friend, and he and Erlene lived in a small house east of town. A plain-spoken but genial man, Skipper had worked hard to build up two nice little businesses, raising pure-bred hogs and running a small general store.

The Skippers gave their guests the best bedroom in the house, and on the following day, Hank, Billie Jean, Taft Skipper, and another cousin drove up to Montgomery to see the annual Blue-Gray football game. On Sunday morning they all went to the East Chapman Baptist Church. Hank was no churchgoer, but with memories of his childhood and church with Mama flooding back to him, he joined in the singing and praying with apparent pleasure.

After services, a group of neighbors came over to hear Hank sing. They had asked him to play in church, but he had told them no, he couldn't sing that kind of music in church. "He played 'Kaw-liga' and 'Jambalaya,' " recalls Skipper, "plus a new one I'd never heard. Something about logging trains. It was a purty tune." He strummed and sang right in the Skippers' little store, and customers as well as "guests" got in on the free concert.

The Skippers were quite taken by Billie Jean. "Some people at church," says Taft with a shy smile, "said she was the purtiest girl they ever saw." Erlene remembers that she was quiet and polite and that after the meal was over, "she got right up and cleaned off the table."

To the Skippers, Hank and Billie Jean seemed to be a happy couple. "He told me he loved Billie," Taft says, "and that she was a nice girl too. He said I should remember that, regardless of what anybody might tell me about her marrying him for money or fame. Anyway, it seemed like Hank was pretty near broke. He had a four-thousand-dollar certified check in his pocket, from a radio station in Shreveport, and he said that was the only money he had in Alabama that Audrey didn't have tied up.

"He said he was gonna settle down and try to lead a decent life and that him and Billie had plans to rebuild his life. The way they talked at supper that night, I believe they'd-a done it."

On Christmas Day, Hank drove the twenty-five-odd miles to his father's house in McWilliams. Lon had gone to Selma to spend the day with friends, for his son had not bothered to let him know he was coming. That was the way father and son treated each other when Hank was grown; each made occasional forays into the other's territory, and if they didn't make connections it didn't much matter. Lon's chief memories of Hank's trips to McWilliams involve drying out from an overdose of booze. "If he took a notion to get drunk," says Lon, "he'd sometimes lay up at my place, and I'd take care of him." Lon's home in those days was a small white frame bungalow only a short distance from his present house and an even shorter distance from the run-down old building where Hank attended a couple of early school grades.

With Lon gone for the day, Hank and Billie Jean went on to Lon's sister's house, in nearby Pine Apple, and had Christmas dinner with her. Lon recalls, with evident satisfaction, that Hank left Christmas presents for him with the sister.

Mrs. Edna Curry Lamkin, a neighbor and old boyhood friend, remembers seeing Hank that day. "He looked marvelous," she wrote the Montgomery *Advertiser* after his death. "He was feeling good too. . . . [but] I believe Hank had a premonition that time was 'running out' on him, and that, unconsciously, he had come to tell us all good-by." Another premonition attributed to Hank; more were still to come.

Hank and Billie Jean drove to Montgomery, where they spent a few quiet days. They stayed, as Hank always did, at Lilly's boardinghouse, and if Hank and his Mama got into one of their battles, there is no record of it. One of the purposes of the stay was to get Lilly better acquainted with Billie Jean. Lilly's heart still was with Audrey, who in her mind would always be Hank's wife, but she made a reasonably smooth accommodation to the change. (Lilly by that time was remarried, to a man named W. W. Stone. It was her third or fourth marriage, and her last.)

Hank performed at least once during that final stay in Montgomery, at a private holiday party given by the American Federation of Musicians local on Sunday, December 28. Although few of the AFM members were practitioners of country music, they gave Hank a warm reception. "We listened attentively, as if attending a concert by Benny Goodman or hearing the cultivated voice of some operatic star," Tom Hewlett, president of the local, later wrote. "We forgot our talent, technical skill, and musical training; we truly enjoyed every note of song. . . . his magnetic personality—plain and honest as it was—will be a lasting memory to all who were present. His was a God-given talent projecting through him into his music and lyrics."

Hank was restless in Montgomery, and with good reason. He had landed a show date for New Year's night, in Canton, Ohio. It was to be his first date out of the South since his release from the Opry and retreat from Nashville. If he got through it, sober and singing like the old Hank, it would be a big step toward reestablishing the career he had thrown away.

That week at Lilly's house, Hank telephoned Don Helms in Nashville. Could the Drifting Cowboys work the Canton date with him? he asked Helms. They could drive up in Hank's old limousine, and he would fly up from Montgomery to meet them. Helms thought for a moment. The band already was committed to work with Ray Price on New Year's night, at a concert in Cleveland. But Price wouldn't mind sparing a Drifting Cowboy or two. How about Helms himself? His wailing steel guitar had been the band's characteristic sound during the good years. Hank readily agreed, so the evening was set: Price to continue his rapid rise up the country music ladder with a date in Cleveland; Hank Williams, in many ways his mentor, to try to get another foothold on the same ladder with a date in Canton; and the old reliable Drifting Cowboys to back them both on stage.

On December 30, the day before he was to leave for Canton, Hank spent a bad evening. According to Billie Jean, he was up off and on during the night. "Hank," she said, "what the devil is the matter with you?"

"Billie, I think I see God comin' down the road."

"Oh, Hank, don't say that," she said, tears welling in her eyes.

December 31 dawned with snow on the ground and more falling. Flying was out of the question, so Hank quickly made plans to go by car. He had been using drivers, rather than driving himself, at various times during the past few months; he'd paid men large sums to drive him from Nashville or Shreveport to Montgomery, while he rested or tried to sleep off a drunk in the back seat. This time he engaged an eighteen-year-old Montgomeryite named Charles Carr, an off-duty taxi driver.

"When Hank was ready to leave," recalls Billie Jean, "he came in and sat down on the edge of the bed. He just looked at me, not saying a word. 'What're you lookin' at, Hank?' I asked him. 'I just wanted to look at you one more time,' he said. I stood in front of the mirror, my back to him, and he came over and kissed me on the cheek. Then he said good-by and left."

Several years later, says Billie Jean, her third husband, country singer Johnny Horton, kissed her on precisely the same spot on the cheek before he left on a similar trip. He was killed in a traffic accident on that trip.

While Hank headed north in the back seat of his Cadillac, young Charles Carr at the wheel, Ray Price was catching one of the few available flights from Nashville to Cleveland, and Don Helms was starting out for Canton in Hank's limousine. With Helms were the Nashville promoter of the Canton show and the other members of the pickup band. Jerry Rivers and the rest of the Drifting Cowboys headed for Cleveland in Price's car. By the time the Rivers group reached Louisville, they turned their car around and began the long trip back to Nashville. Price would just have to pick up a band in Cleveland or make it on his own.

Meanwhile, Hank, Price, and Don Helms kept pushing ahead for their Ohio destinations. Hank, lounging in the back seat of the Cadillac, had a bottle of whisky, and some chloral hydrate from Toby Marshall's last prescription, to sustain him on the long, lonely drive.

18

That New Year's Eve, Hank's sister Irene and her husband were attending a party near their home in Virginia. Shortly after midnight, she vividly recalls, she clutched her throat and cried out, "Hank has just died!"

Irene, a long-time devotee of ESP and other mystic arts, urgently told her husband she had to go home

immediately, pack a suitcase, and get ready to go after
Hank. Her husband put her off for a while but finally
took her home around 2 A.M. There she packed a bag
and waited. She "knew" she would be notified by the
highway patrol.

A few hours later, says Irene, a highway patrolman
knocked on the door and told her to telephone a certain relative. She did, asking the relative straight off,
"Where did Hank die, and where is my mother?"

"How did you know he was dead?" asked the astonished relative.

"I knew it last night when he died," replied Irene impatiently. "Now, where is his body, and where's my
mother?"

The news came scarcely less dramatically to the
people assembled that evening at Canton's Memorial
Auditorium. Almost none of them had gotten word by
the time they arrived for the show. Neither had Don
Helms and the other musicians who had driven up from
Nashville to work with Hank. They had pulled into
Canton, dead tired, early that morning and had slept at
their hotel until it was time to eat and go to the auditorium. There, in the dressing room, the Nashville
promoter said to them, "I don't guess you've heard the
bad news." Receiving nothing but blank stares, he
blurted out, "Hank passed away." Says Helms, "We
were simply astounded."

At show time, Cliff Rodgers, a local disk jockey who
was to act as master of ceremonies came on stage and
announced that Hank Williams had died. There were
cries of disbelief and anguish from the audience. Hank,
said Rodgers, would have wanted the show to go on,
so it would. But first, there would be a small tribute.
The whole cast for that night's show, standing behind
closed curtains, then played and sang "I Saw the Light."
Most members of the audience rose to their feet and
sang along, many of them in tear-chocked voices. After
that, the regular show proceeded, with the big acts—
Hawkshaw Hawkins, Homer and Jethro, June Webb—
performing in an unusually subdued manner. The Nash-

ville band that had come to back up Hank played some of the songs he would have sung.

"A lot of people actually shed tears," Helms recalls. "Hundreds of them, I'd say, all through the show. I played an instrumental on 'Cold, Cold Heart,' and I barely got through it. I was pretty shook up."

Back in Nashville, Fred and Wesley Rose were shook up too, all the more so because they had been convinced Hank was making a solid recovery and soon would be back in the big time. The Roses went to a small gathering of old friends on New Year's Eve, where they drank a toast to a successful comeback for Hank. Soon after midnight, they went home to bed.

"At 3 or 4 A.M.," says Wesley Rose, "I got a phone call from my father. 'Let me know when you're awake,' he told me, so I walked around a little and came back to the phone. 'Sit down,' my father said, 'or this might knock you down. . . . Hank Williams died tonight. . . . Now don't fall all to pieces."

Over the next few days, the story of Hank's death emerged. His Cadillac, with young Charles Carr driving, had picked its way through the snow and sleet toward Canton. A tedious trip under the best of conditions, it became grueling and grim in the storm. Hank slept off and on, taking occasional nips of whisky and perhaps some chloral hydrate to keep himself comfortably relaxed. In Tennessee he stopped to see a physician, who apparently gave him an injection. The reason for this medication has never been determined, but the most plausible theory is that his back was bothering him.

In any case, Hank was dead several hours after that stop. The end came silently and in an ironically anticlimactic fashion. Near Rutledge, Tennessee, about an hour out of Knoxville, a state trooper pulled the Cadillac over for speeding. The trooper gave Carr a ticket, and, in the process, couldn't help noticing the tall, slender figure stretched across the back seat.

"That guy looks dead," he said. Carr replied that the man, whom he didn't bother identifying as Hank Williams, had taken a sedative and was sleeping. Satisfied with that explanation, the trooper collected a twenty-five-dollar fine and let the Cadillac drive away without a further check. Hank gave no sign that he was awake, nor indeed alive, throughout the episode. This is not surprising, since the combination of alcohol and barbiturates or amphetamines makes a powerful sedative.

As Carr drove on, across the western tip of Virginia and into West Virginia, he worried increasingly about the inert body on the seat behind him. Should he wake Hank up, just to see that everything was all right? Or should he stick to his driving and not risk getting bawled out? For a surprisingly long time, some five hours after the encounter with the Tennessee state trooper, Carr stuck to his driving. Finally, at Oak Hill, West Virginia, a town of about 3,500, he decided he had to take a look. He pulled the car into a Pure Oil Station, reached back to touch Hank's hand, and found it cold. Then he tried to awaken Hank and couldn't.

Carr drove quickly to the Oak Hill hospital, where Hank was pronounced dead on arrival. He had died, without a sound and quite alone, after barely making it into the year 1953.

After an autopsy, Fayette County officials announced that death had been caused by heart failure. There was no evidence of foul play, they said. There was alcohol in the bloodstream; how much was not specified. No mention was made of evidence of drugs in the system, but the doctor may not have been looking for it.

Interestingly, the autopsy report indicates that Hank's body overall was in fairly good condition, better than one might expect of a problem drinker. There were, however, signs of alcoholism leading to serious physical disorders. His liver contained fatty deposits, a major step on the road to the hard drinker's dreaded disease, cirrhosis. His lungs showed evidence of edema, or accumulation of excessive fluids. The lining of parts of his digestive system was inflamed and shredded, an indication of prolonged ingestion of a damaging substance such as alcohol.

Although the doctor who performed the autopsy did not specifically say so, a fresh appraisal of the report suggests that Hank died of alcoholic cardiomyopathy, that is, of heart disease directly traceable to excessive drinking. Medical researchers have discovered comparatively recently that prolonged ingestion of alcohol can lead to the presence of small foreign bodies within the cells of the heart and to irregularities in the heartbeat. When this condition has reached a certain stage, the heart will stop functioning, even though the person may be relatively free of alcohol at that time.

That is apparently what killed Hank: failure of the heart muscle associated with the fatty metamorphosis of the liver, with both related to his unchecked consumption of alcohol.

Among those who really knew Hank and his situation, there were two basic reactions to Hank's death: one of genuine shock, the other of feigned shock. Those genuinely shocked believed, as did Wesley Rose, that Hank was on the road to recovering both his health and his career. The others believed, as did Harry Stone, that Hank was beyond hope of recovery and that death or serious illness was only a matter of time. As Jerry Rivers has said:

". . . to me and the other Drifting Cowboys, the news was shocking, but not unbelievable. The past months had been nothing but a series of surprises and disappointments for us, and this came almost inevitably as the closing chapter."

Among country music people in general, there were the usual public lamentations that are uttered when one of the fraternity dies. Everyone who could make himself heard said something about Hank's genius and the awful tragedy of his premature death. M-G-M Records' Frank Walker, who had in fact been fairly close to Hank, showed a bit of originality when he dashed off a highly sentimental letter addressed to "Mr. Hank

Williams, c/o Songwriter's Paradise." Dated January 1, the day Hank died, the letter read in part:

> . . . an hour or so ago I received a phone call from Nashville. It was a rather sad call too, Hank, for it told me that you had died early this morning. I don't know much about the circumstances and it really doesn't matter, does it? What does matter though is that the World is ever so much better for the fact that you have lived with us, even for such a short time. . . .
>
> Remember the time the newspaperman asked you how you wrote a song? I'll never forget your answer—"I just sit down for a few minutes, do a little thinking about things, and God writes them for me." You were so right, Hank, and do you know I think HE wanted to have you just a bit closer to him, Nashville's pretty far away, so HE just sent word this morning Hank that HE wanted you with HIM. You're going to be kept busy too. There's lots of work to be done way up there for we aren't improving too much here on earth. You'll be writing for the greatest singers too, the Angels, they're so wonderful—I know they'll want you to join them. . . . I guess that's all I have to write about on this New Year's Day, Hank. Thanks so much for being with us, and until I see you again,
>
> HAPPY NEW YEAR, HANK,
Your Pal
Frank

Actually, Walker had been writing Hank a sort of open letter every year since he had signed Hank to an M-G-M contract. This final letter seemed so appropriate, and so well suited to the effort to push Hank's record sales higher than ever, that M-G-M ran it in full on the back of the Hank Williams memorial album, which was issued soon after the singer's death.

By far the most significant and impressive reaction to

Hank's death came from the public at large. Newspapers and radio stations, especially in the South but in other regions too, began to get a flood of tributes to Hank. Some were gushing in their praise, others were awkwardly shy; but almost without exception they were spontaneous and heartfelt. Special requests also came in large numbers: requests for more pictures of Hank to be printed in the paper; for extra copies of the editions carrying stories of his death; for memorial programs, featuring song after Hank Williams song, to be presented on the radio.

All across the country, sales of Hank's records increased at a tremendous rate. Not just his current hits, such as "I'll Never Get Out of This World Alive," but everything he had recorded was suddenly in great demand. *Billboard* reported record dealers sending rush orders to M-G-M Records; a dealer in Durham, North Carolina, said everybody was asking for Williams records—and many customers wanted two copies of each one.

A month later, the demand for Hank's records remained so great that one of M-G-M's plants was devoting itself exclusively to pressing them, and the company was announcing that its next package of new releases would be cut from twelve to six records to try to catch up on Hank. In Troy, New York, a radio station used Hank's disks to help put over a local March of Dimes drive; anyone sending a contribution would get a picture of Hank, and the first hundred sending twenty-five dollars or more would receive a special white-label copy of "Kaw-liga" and "Your Cheatin' Heart." The station's first mail after the offer was announced included five hundred March of Dimes contributions.

The demand persisted. For close to six months, reported *Billboard*, Hank's records were "the most sought-after waxings in the country music field." Although Hank did not live a day of it, 1953 became the best year his music had ever had. He won, posthumously, a number of country music awards. Among them was a

Downbeat poll naming him the most popular country and Western performer of all time.

"According to experts in the field of hillbilly music," said one writer, Hank "would have earned half a million dollars in 1953—that is, if he had been around to cash in on the publicity attending his death."

The Montgomery newspapers received a staggering number of tributes and requests. There were letters from every state in the nation, requests for pictures and extra papers from states from Florida to Idaho. A letter from Willard, Missouri, said: "We were greatly grieved. . . . He never wrote a song that did not touch the heart with its simple message of longing and love." Another letter said, "He was loved greatly by all St. Louis." A fan from Milwaukee wrote:

". . . we felt he was a friend of ours; someone we had known for a long time. Hank seemed to put his own feelings and emotions into each song he sang. . . . it would seem at times he was telling us a story about himself." The Milwaukee letter concluded: "Above all, I cannot tell you how much we would appreciate a true-life picture of Hank."

In its first edition after Hank's death, the Montgomery *Advertiser* devoted the entire front page to news of the event and reactions to it. More copies of that issue were sold than of any in the newspaper's history. Ten days later, the *Advertiser* gave Hank another full page. Most of this one was devoted to reminiscences of south Alabamians who had known the man during the years he spent playing the dance halls. Many of the reminiscences were unabashed in their adulation of him as a person and as a performer, and all of them were bursting with pride over the fact that he was a local boy.

Jeanette Davis, of Pepperell, wrote: "This letter is to tell you how much I love Hank and his music. Hank was not for any certain time, but for all time and all people. . . . No one will ever take Hank's place in the hearts of millions of people, as well as my own. . . . I sincerely hope this little bit of information on Hank will tell you what a wonderful guy 'My' Hank and 'Our' Hank was and always will be."

Said Bonnie Green, of Montgomery: "He came, it seemed, from nowhere, to melt millions of 'Cold, Cold Hearts,' and I was no exception."

The page contained a number of maudlin expressions as well. A Montgomery man who claimed to have talked to Hank shortly before he died wrote, "I hope to meet him hereafter and know him . . . for my best friend has gone. I am carrying a picture clipped from the paper to remember him by." And Mrs. Lillian Swindall of Montgomery, who said her two daughters had sung on Hank's old radio show, expressed the hope that "we can all sing together by and by."

Carolyn Lewis, of Ramer, outstripped them all by saying, "I only wish he could have outlived me."

Inevitably, there were a couple of primitive poetic tributes, which the *Advertiser,* with more space than taste, ran at full length. One spelled out Hank's name in daisy-plucking style: "W—is for the will to be a success/I—is for the beautiful island in the sky where he may rest," and so on. The other rambled through six verses linking God and Hank in divine purpose. One verse ran:

"I know he will be singing in the angels' band,
Waiting to greet us and shake our hand.
I picture him now there with God above,
Singing softly a song of heavenly love.
We miss him so much now that he is gone,
But the Master has called him, God upon the
    throne.
Yes, we will always love and remember Hank."

Carolyn Quartararo, who had met Hank backstage at a New Orleans show, provided a country version of Shakespeare's "noblest Roman of them all." Wrote Miss Quartararo: "I cried my heart out to think we lost the best hillbilly we've ever known. . . . nobody could ever take his place, no matter how hard they try."

Common to all the letters and telegrams and phone calls triggered by Hank's death was this feeling of irreplaceable loss. Each said, in its own way, that there would never be another Hank Williams. But the outpouring that followed his death was tame compared with that which accompanied his funeral.

The funeral was held Sunday, January 4 in Montgomery. It was one of the most spectacular the South has ever seen, perhaps second only to the awesome turnout for the martyred Dr. Martin Luther King, Jr., in Atlanta in 1968. And it is regarded in Montgomery as the greatest emotional plunge that city has taken since the inauguration of Jefferson Davis as president of the Confederacy.

People converged on Montgomery from all over the South, and in some cases from beyond. Everybody who was anybody in country music, and not irrevocably committed elsewhere, was present. A Nashville florist drove a two-ton truck full of flower arrangements to the ceremony. The designs were so large that only ten of them could be placed in the truck. Jerry Rivers, driving in from Nashville with a group of musicians, got snarled in a traffic jam before he even reached the city. When he got to Lilly's boardinghouse, where the body reposed, "there was such a crowd we could hardly get near the place. Two of the active pallbearers got stuck in traffic, so I was enlisted as a temporary pallbearer to help get the casket to the auditorium."

It was a bright, crisp winter day, and a single, twisted tree stood leafless in the small front yard of the boardinghouse. The shutterless, weather-beaten structure, a homemade "Room and Board" sign tacked on its front, projected a stoic simplicity. As the mourners stood with heads bared, the pallbearers carried the silver casket down the worn steps and placed it in the hearse for the short ride to the municipal auditorium.

The crowd had begun forming in front of the auditorium at 9 A.M., and when the funeral cortege arrived, four hours later, its number had swelled to nearly twenty-five thousand. Some people had lunches or thermoses of hot coffee. Many women carried babies in their arms. At 1 P.M. the casket was placed at the foot of the auditorium stage, and fifteen minutes later the top was raised. It revealed a somber, composed-looking Hank, laid out in a suit designed by Audrey and tailored by Nudie, the country and Western specialist.

Not everyone thought Hank looked beautiful in his coffin. "Hank did not look like himself at all in death," wrote a woman who'd lived in Lilly's boardinghouse. "For one thing, his beautiful smile is missing."

Only 2,750 people were able to get into the auditorium, but after they had viewed the remains, some of the thousands waiting outside were allowed to file by the casket. It was a notably heterogeneous group, just as the admirers of his songs and singing had been. It was proof, wrote Eddie Jones, who covered the funeral for the Nashville *Banner,* that "the followers of Hank Williams knew no class barriers:

"A silver-templed executive clad in a conservative blue suit was closely followed by a weeping young woman in a brilliant satin jacket.

"There were old women with shawls and young men in leather jackets, men in the uniform of the armed forces and men in the traditional Western garb of hillbilly performers."

(Not only did the Montgomery and Nashville newspapers cover the funeral in force, two Montgomery radio stations broadcast the proceedings—the first time that had been done in the city. "Public pressure demanded it," explained an executive of one of the stations.)

The casket was surrounded by large and elaborate floral pieces, one in the shape of one of Hank's old guitars, another designed as the cover of a Bible. Across the front of the Bible piece were the first few notes of "I Saw the Light." During the course of the procession and the service that followed, four women fainted. A fifth fell at the foot of the casket and had to be carried from the auditorium in hysterics. Weeping women were everywhere, and there were many moist-eyed men in the crowd too.

At 2:30 P.M., when it became obvious that nowhere near the entire line would be able to pass before the casket, the auditorium doors were closed and the funeral service was started. Backstage, Little Jimmy Dickens, who had often worked with Hank, wept openly. On stage, other Nashville stars sang their tributes. Ernest Tubb led off with "Beyond the Sunset." Then Roy Acuff, in his unmistakable country tenor, sang Hank's finest hymn, "I Saw the Light"; he was joined on the choruses by Red Foley, Carl Smith, Webb Pierce, and several other artists. They sang the hymn, not mournfully, but in the spirited fashion that Hank intended it be sung.

Foley, his voice almost breaking under the emotional strain, sang "Peace in the Valley," an old country standard. Foley himself was in tears by the time he finished the song. The eulogy was delivered by the Reverend Henry L. Lyon, pastor of Montgomery's Highland Avenue Baptist Church. "I can't preach Hank's funeral," Dr. Lyon told the crowd. "He preached it himself in song. He had a message written in the language of all the people. His life was a real personification of what can happen in this country to one little insignificant speck of humanity."

Touching on the man's success, Dr. Lyon said: "I'll tell you the secret of Hank Williams' greatness. It was a message of the heart. . . . they listened everywhere."

When the service ended, thousands of people dashed for their cars, hoping to get to the cemetery in time to see the burial. The result was another huge traffic jam, and the long procession passed slowly through streets lined on both sides with onlookers. Several thousand massed at the grave site (many had been there since before the service started), with the front ranks pressing so near the coffin they were in danger of falling into the hole that had been dug for it. The graveside ceremony was mercifully brief, and the minister concluded it by presenting a rosebud to each surviving member of the family.

Behind all the pageantry and emotion at the funeral, a number of intra-family skirmishes were being fought. In a way, they presaged the more intense struggles between family members that are still being waged today. The first skirmishes occurred at Oak Hill, West Virginia, the day after Hank died.

In Montgomery, most of the fussing took place in Lilly's boardinghouse, where Hank was lying in state and while the final steps before the services were being taken. One of the principals rushed into the room where the body lay, crying, "If I kiss him, he'll come back to life!" She was restrained by several bystanders.

Billie Jean Jones Williams, the widow of record, cheerfully admits she wore slacks to view the body, treating all protests with disdain. Her mother and brother came to the funeral too, and the whole family, she says, stayed in one room, "with me on the floor. We couldn't afford a lot of rooms at the hotel." She went back to Shreveport, she says, in a Greyhound bus, on a ticket paid for by her father.

Hank's sister Irene recalls one struggle between the Shreveport group and the surviving Williamses: "Billie Jean told somebody she didn't like the outfit Hank was to be buried in. I said, 'Billie, if you don't like it, go out with me to the store and we'll find something else.' She said, 'No, your mother's running this show.' I said, 'Billie, this is no show, this is my brother's funeral.' " True, but it was also destined to be a show, not only for Billie Jean but for thousands of fans who would have felt let down had Hank gone out any other way.

According to one neutral observer, the funeral infighting wasn't that unseemly. "With the wife, ex-wife, sister, and mother there, you had a real uncomfortable situation," he says, "and it was handled about as well as it could have been, considering you were burying an idol." At the funeral service itself, he says, Irene was delegated to be a symbolic peacemaker, taking "a wife on each arm."

A spectacular funeral had to be matched by a spectacular monument. Hank was assured one of the most impressive monuments possible when Montgomery's Willie Gayle stepped to the forefront. Gayle is now a highly successful purveyor of sales techniques ("Keep America Strong Through Professional Selling" is his motto), but at the time of Hank's death he was a designer with the Henley memorial company. Audrey and Lilly, Gayle says, did not know exactly what they wanted for Hank's memorial. They knew it had to be grand, however, and money was no object.

Thinking big comes naturally to Willie Gayle, and he managed to fend off all sorts of competition. "Every large monument company in North America and Canada flew in here to try and make the sale," he says. "People from the Columbia school of design and all over. We were just eatin' 'em up like ice cream." Gayle drew the contract-winning design on the back of a menu in Montgomery's old Pickwick Café; "They closed the place up but we stayed there till three in the morning, while the waiters kept bringing coffee." The price of the job was "a good five figures," with the money provided by Hank's estate.

Gayle's monument is a slender slab of Vermont granite standing on a two-step pedestal. Across the top of the slab are the opening notes of "I Saw the Light." On the front are a small bronze plaque of Hank playing the guitar and, etched into the stone, rays of heavenly sunshine coming through a cloud. On the back is a poem entitled "Thank You, Darling." It reads in part:

> Thank you for all the love you gave me
> There could be one no stronger
> Thank you for the many beautiful songs
> They will live long and longer . . .
> There are no words in the dictionary
> That can express my love for you
> Someday beyond the blue
> Audrey Williams

The poem, indeed the whole monument, indicated that not only was Audrey asserting her right to Hank's money, she was asserting her right to his memory as well. No matter that she had divorced him less than a year before. No matter that he had remarried. The second wife was to be frozen out of the picture. Audrey was to be remembered, forever more, as Hank's loving wife.

At the base of the monument was a marble cowboy hat, which Willie Gayle had had made in Tate, Georgia, as an exact replica of Hank's own hat. Spread across the base, etched into the stone, are front pages of the sheet music for some of Hank's biggest hits: "Kaw-liga," "Hey, Good Lookin'," "Jambalaya," and so forth. Flanking the monument are various shrubs and flowers plus two simple white urns with the initials "HW" inscribed on them.

Gaudy as the monument sounds, it is actually fairly tasteful, considering the jumble of elements it contains. At least it is of modest proportions and does not stand out from everything else in that part of the cemetery. It is in a lovely spot, and a visitor lucky enough to be there alone can hear the birds chirping and the wind rustling the flowers and shrubs around the grave.

19

One way to judge the impact of a man's life is by the tributes he receives after his death. By this measure, Hank Williams had a heavy impact. The letters, the public praise, the funeral all are evidence of the man's stature with the public and with the country music industry. In Hank's case, however, the impact went far beyond that. It went into memorial celebrations and musical tributes and re-released recordings that continued for years after his death and, in some instances, continue even today.

While one cannot attach commercial meaning to the letters and what not that followed hard on his death, one can hardly help but attach that meaning to most of what has followed since then. A tremendously salable commodity when alive, he was even more salable after he died. The sudden nature and mysterious circumstances of his death contributed to the salability; so did his youth and his short but meteoric career.

In this way, Hank was another James Dean, the "rebel without a cause" who flamed out at a similarly early age, leaving a cult of devout worshippers. Hank had an appeal so broad that he made Dean and many other popular culture heroes look as though they were appealing to a special interest group. Hank's popularity, it became more and more evident, was rooted in no one age group or income level or social class. It transcended them all, as easily as Hank had transcended the artificial boundaries separating popular from country music.

Perhaps the first spin-offs from his death that smacked of commercialism were the "tribute records," songs written and recorded by country artists to mourn a great one's passing. There were fifteen or more such tributes to Hank, and almost every Nashville record company put out at least one of them. No other country music artist, probably no musical performer of any kind, has ever had such a flock of songs written about him.

The tribute records tumbled onto the market, one after another, within a couple of weeks after Hank's death. Capitol put out one numbered 2397 and another numbered 2401, while King did even better, issuing only one other record between the tributes offered by Jack Cardwell (number 1172) and Hawkshaw Hawkins (1174). That in itself is a good indication of the prime motivation behind the records: to make money. It was not the sole motivation, however, and it would be unjustly cynical to imply that it was. Included among the writers and artists who produced the tribute records were a few fairly close friends of Hank plus a number of men who genuinely respected him, as a talent and as a man.

Among the latter, the respecters, was Jack Cardwell, the heavy-set, genial man who played in a country band around Mobile, disk-jockeyed for a local radio station, and wrote songs in his spare time. Cardwell had met Hank in Mobile a couple of times during his spell at the shipyard, and he followed Hank's subsequent career with great interest and admiration. As soon as a new Williams song came out, he had his band playing it. Cardwell had signed a recording contract with King Records in December of 1952. On New Year's morning, he arrived at his radio station about 2 A.M., pulled out the records he wanted to play on his show and glanced at the news ticker.

"It hit me right between the eyes," Cardwell recalls, " 'Cowboy singer Hank Williams dies.' " He tore the story off the machine and went straight home, ignoring his disk jockey show. His wife was in tears, having heard the news on the radio. Cardwell turned the dial to WCKY, Cincinnati, and heard disk jockey Nelson King intone, "It's true, he's dead. Hank Williams is dead." Cardwell stood dumbfounded for a few minutes, then flopped on his bed and, with only the brief news story to guide him, began writing "The Death of Hank Williams."

"What I ended up with actually was a dirge," says Cardwell, "only eight bars of melody repeated over and over." By any standard, including Cardwell's, it was not great music, but it was from the heart and, more important, it was swiftly done. That afternoon, he got a band together, recorded the song at a local studio and shipped it off to King Records. King had four Cardwell sides ready for release on January 8, so they simply knocked off one of them—a romantic ballad called "My Love for You Would Fill Ten Pots"—and substituted "The Death of Hank Williams." A couple of days later it was on its way to disk jockeys across the country.

Cardwell, of course, played the record on his own show. "The reaction was unbelievable," he says. "We were bombarded with calls. Some people screamed and cussed and said, 'Don't never play that horrible thing no more.' The others begged us to 'Please play it one more time.' It was about a fifty-fifty split." Cardwell says he got a call from Hank's mother threatening to sue him, but he put her off with the suggestion that she contact King's attorneys in Nashville. Within about a month, he says, his "tribute" had reached number two on the charts: "The only thing that kept it from the top was one of the master's own songs."

Sales of "The Death of Hank Williams," according to Cardwell, exceeded 107,000, with over 40,000 being sold in one four-day period. Several of the other tribute records did quite well too, although none of them was paid much heed by the industry in Nashville. Among the others were a second "The Death of Hank Williams" and a "The Life of Hank Williams"; "Hank, It Will Never Be the Same Without You," by Ernest Tubb; "Hank Williams Meets Jimmie Rodgers" and "There's a New Star in Hillbilly Heaven," both by Virginia Rounders; and "The Last Letter," by Jimmy Swan. Swan has gone on to greater glories: he ran as an arch-segregationist candidate for governor of Mississippi in 1967.

Lilly Stone may have been averse to having anyone else make money from her son's death, but she was not averse to doing so herself. The dirt had hardly settled in the grave before Lilly had engaged a Montgomery photographer to put together a booklet on Hank for her. The photographer in turn engaged a writer, and the two of them turned out *Our Hank Williams*. It was a mawkish, skin-deep series of reminiscences, and, under Lilly's direction, it conveniently omitted the unpleasant aspects of Hank's life: his drinking problem;

his hell-raising antics; his use of pills; his divorce from Audrey and marriage to Billie Jean. Lilly attributed his problems and premature death not to deep emotional stresses, but to his back injury and "the obsession to capture for himself and the world all the thousands of words and melodies that flew through his mind." Hank was so popular that even such a piece of nonsense as that enjoyed reasonably good sales.

Back in Shreveport, Billie Jean was in a bad spot. Hank's estate was tied up in litigation, and she was practically broke: "I was nineteen and had no collateral. Who was going to lend me money?" Paul Howard, who had been their friend in Shreveport, offered her this advice:

"Billie, I don't know if you can sing, but if you can, you can clean up. I can book you as Mrs. Hank Williams." Billie Jean was skeptical but Howard assured her, "You must go out there looking sad and tell 'em, 'How d'ya do, ladies and gentlemen, I'm Mrs. Hank Williams. . . . I sure wish Hank could be here tonight.' You'll have 'em crying all over the place."

So Billie Jean limbered up her voice, which wasn't bad, memorized a few of Hank's songs and hit the road. Howard served as her manager, getting fifty per cent of the take after expenses had been skimmed off the top. "We packed 'em in, all right," recalls Billie Jean with relish. "Even the nigger houses. I hung 'em off every rafter. There were people falling out on the floor and fainting." The only problem was keeping her suitably sorrowful in front of audiences. A naturally ebullient sort, she tended to come on stage with a cherry greeting for the fans. They didn't seem to notice, however, and the show rolled profitably along.

Not surprisingly, Audrey Williams came up with the same idea. Audrey had been a singer of sorts, and she too hit the road to capitalize on the Hank Williams name. There was enough demand to support both acts, but Audrey decided to do away with the competition. As part of a financial settlement with Billie Jean, Audrey got her to drop the use of the name Mrs. Hank

Williams. "Even though she was never legally married to Hank," says Audrey, "this was just a simple and easy way to make sure there would be no problems."

Audrey proceeded to make plans for taking up musically where Hank had left off. She told Montgomery reporters she was planning on starting a "Drifting Cowgirls" band. She had already organized a band of girls, she said, and was now going to change the name "in memory of Hank." More interestingly, Audrey also told the reporters that she and Hank were to remarry sometime in February. "There could never be another love like Hank Williams and myself," she said. (Billie Jean denied the remarriage story and charged that Audrey had attempted to persuade Hank to remarry her "the day of our wedding.")

All this was lighthearted banter compared to the intense struggles for Hank's assets that were soon to begin. The struggle pitted, at first, Lilly, Irene, and Audrey against Billie Jean, and later, Irene against Audrey. Later still, Billie Jean jousted with M-G-M, and a child fathered by Hank illegitimately became a contender for a hunk of the money. Only Lon remained aloof from the legal wrangling. He probably had no tenable claim on the money anyway, but his silence amid so much unseemly bickering gave him a new measure of dignity.

Hank's estate was surprisingly small. An assessment in Montgomery placed the total value at only $13,329.25. There was $4,394 in cash, $4,000 of which was in the cashier's check Hank had shown Taft Skipper several days before he died. The remainder, some $8,900, was comprised of miscellaneous personal items and mementos, including numerous Nudie-tailored suits, five cowboy hats, nine pairs of hand-tooled boots, several pistols, and a saddle. This assortment was gathered together by his mother and displayed in glass cabinets in "Hank's old room" at the Montgomery boardinghouse.

The estate was small for two reasons: Hank was not earning much when he died, and his savings had pretty well disappeared; Audrey, in addition to getting half of everything he made, had been given the single most valuable piece of property, the home in Nashville, as part of their divorce settlement.

Yet the cash value of the estate by no means indicated its true worth, for it also contained the rights to Hank's record and publishing royalties. As all parties with a claim on Hank were soon to discover, these royalties became much more valuable as the years passed and the Hank Williams legend flourished. They came to mean tens of thousands of dollars a year.

The involvement of three states—Alabama, Tennessee, and Louisiana—complicated the legal proceedings. So did the involvement of four women—Lilly, Irene, Audrey, and Billie Jean. Normally, Lilly, as the mother of a married man who had died intestate, would have had little control over the legal outcome. But Audrey had been properly divorced from Hank, and there now became a question of whether Billie Jean had been properly married to him.

Lilly asserted that Billie Jean had married Hank before her divorce from Harrison Eshlimar had become final. Billie Jean hotly denied the assertion and countered, "I can't see what business Mrs. Stone has in the estate at all." She added: "I don't want to fight over Hank's estate. He wouldn't have wanted it that way. If it were left up to me and Audrey, we could work this thing out on friendly terms."

Dubious as that contention was, there was no chance of proving it, for Lilly was not about to get out of the contest. She figured rightly that if neither Audrey nor Billie Jean was married to Hank when he died, that left her in command. Hence she filed a petition seeking to be named administratrix of the estate.

Lilly's case got a decided boost on January 15, when a Shreveport judge ruled that Billie Jean had married Hank ten days before her divorce from Eshlimar was final. Billie Jean claimed her lawyer had told her, at the time she married Hank, that she *was* legally divorced and that she had proceeded on that assurance. Her new lawyer carried that a step further, claiming that Billie Jean's understanding made the marriage valid under Louisiana law, because she had married Hank "in good faith." Whether this also made the marriage valid in Alabama and Tennessee was another question.

So much smoke arose during the hassle over the legality of the marriage that Lilly and her attorneys were left in some doubt on the point. For that reason, apparently, they decided to make an out-of-court settlement with Billie Jean, to buy her off, in effect, rather than face a chancery court fight. Their first offer was a few thousand dollars. They raised that to ten thousand dollars, then to fifteen thousand dollars. Billie Jean, says a friend, was tempted to take each offer, but she held off. As the ante went up, in five-thousand-dollar increments, she became more tempted yet.

Billie Jean finally settled for thirty thousand tax-paid dollars and went to Nashville to sign the agreement. She surrendered all claims on the estate and all rights to use Hank's name in commercial ventures. That same year, 1953, the estate made some 73,000 dollars in royalties. Half of that, minus taxes, was almost as much as Billie Jean received for her entire final settlement. But, had she gambled on a court fight, would she have won—or lost everything?

Lilly was named administratrix of the estate. When she died, in February 1955, Irene was appointed to the post. Irene managed the estate with a firm hand, fending off periodic attempts by Audrey to have things run more to her liking. Irene's tenure came to a surprising end in 1969, when she was convicted of possession of illegal drugs by a federal district court in Texas. She is now serving a seven-year term in the federal prison at Alderson, West Virginia. Montgomery attorney Robert B. Stewart is currently serving as administrator.

Billie Jean, for her part, has little regard for either of the other two women—but particularly little for Audrey. A country girl at first, Billie Jean has become a shrewd, sophisticated woman, and her feeling of live and let live

toward Audrey at times gives way to a feeling of pure
and undisguised dislike.

The legal wrangling represents much more than mere
personal animosity, however. A great deal of money is
at stake, for Hank's estate has prospered beyond anyone's dreams. In the twenty years from 1953 through
the end of 1972, the estate has received royalties from
Acuff-Rose and M-G-M totaling about $2.7 million
dollars, or an average of almost 135,000 dollars a year;
under the terms of her divorce from Hank, Audrey has
received an equal amount, meaning that Hank's songs
have generated well over $5 million in royalties since
his death. Acuff-Rose has provided almost two-thirds
of the total pot.

The figures bear out magnificently the statement
made by Fred Rose at the time of Hank's death: "We're
going to treat his songs just as if his death never occurred." Acuff-Rose and M-G-M have combined to do
just that. Shortly after the funeral, Rose assembled the
Drifting Cowboys in his recording studio and bade them
provide the backup instrumentation for a number of
Hank's unreleased vocal recordings. These were rushed
onto the market, where they were snapped up.

That was only the beginning. M-G-M has issued numerous Hank Williams albums since his death, bringing
to about forty the total number of Williams albums
on the M-G-M label. Almost thirty of these are still in
print.

Hank Williams, Jr. has become big box office. A
tall, blond young man with a pleasant if rather vapid
face, Hank, Jr. has achieved star status partly because
of his name, and the similarity of his voice to his
father's, and partly because of his own ability. The
general opinion around Nashville seems to be that he
might have carved out a musical career anyway but that
being Hank Williams, Jr. helped a hell of a lot.

The old Drifting Cowboys reorganized in the late
1960s. The band, with most of the original Nashville
personnel, worked about a hundred show dates in 1968,

seventy-five per cent of them with Hank, Jr. In Little Rock, their opening week, they drew the biggest auditorium crowd since Hank himself had played there some seventeen years before. M-G-M issued, in the spring of 1969, a Drifting Cowboy album entitled "We Remember Hank Williams" (what else?). Jerry Rivers still plays on Hank Jr.'s dates. The other Drifting Cowboys are scattered through the country music business.

M-G-M already has issued 29 albums of Hank, Jr.— many of them featuring his father's songs. Hank, Jr. is now demanding and getting three thousand five-hundred dollars a shot for personal appearances. He is worth the price, because he is proving to be a great drawing card: in Greensboro, North Carolina, in December of 1968, a promoter booking Hank, Jr., the Drifting Cowboys, and three or four other acts grossed forty-one thousand dollars for a one-night stand—more than ten times what he paid to hire the talent; thirty-three thousand of it was in advance sales. A year later, Hank, Jr. pulled in a huge gross at Cobo Hall in Detroit. The son has done at least one thing the daddy didn't: he has starred in a movie, a country music production called *A Time to Sing*. Hank, Jr. may never be an actor, but the movie has done a lot for his career nonetheless.

Various other interests have turned a dollar on Hank's name and talent. A mail-order company called Currier/Nast Enterprises purchased the rights to some of Hank's less promoted albums from M-G-M and, in 1971, began merchandising them in an aggressive national campaign. Currier/Nast used such predictable media as *True* magazine but also advertised repeatedly on television in New York City—one of the last major holdouts against the advance of country music. By the first of 1973, the promotion was still going strong, having sold—according to Currier/Nast—"many thousands" of "deluxe 4-record Hank Williams Memorial Albums" at the low-low price of $12.95.

Meanwhile, Audrey Williams has been managing a few enterprises almost unrelated to Hank, Sr. Foremost among them are Ly-Rann Music, a music publishing house, and Bonanza Productions, Inc., a record company; both are located on Nashville's Record Row. When ill health forced her to curtail her activities a couple of years ago, she sold both companies to Acuff-Rose. Audrey has proved herself a tough business woman, and chances are she would have made out well even without the hundreds of thousands of dollars she has received from Hank's estate.

Hank's money has cost Audrey one thing: the admiration of some of her country music brethren. Among Hank's old friends, one does not often hear a good word about Audrey. She is criticized (always privately, for she is a woman of consequence) for capitalizing on Hank's name after casting him aside through divorce.

Whatever one thinks of Audrey, she cannot be blamed for the tortured, tragic life her husband led. Plagued by inner conflicts and weaknesses, Hank brought about his own destruction.

Since Hank's death, there has been an almost constant legal battle over his estate and related matters. Most of it involves who gets how much of what. This is natural enough, people being what they are, but it has been accompanied by too many unctuous declarations of devotion to the man alone, rather than to his money as well.

Most of the litigation has been conducted in the Montgomery County courtroom of Judge Richard Emmet, a genial young fellow who happens to be a Hank Williams fan. The issues that have come before the court include the following:

1. The guardianship of Hank, Jr. It was awarded in Alabama to his grandmother, Lilly Stone, and to Irene when Lilly died. Later, a second guardianship was set up in Tennessee, with Audrey Williams as the guardian, to handle the income generated by the young man. That turned out to be some 400,000 dollars over a three-year period, and when Audrey subsequently failed to give a satisfactory accounting of her guardian expenditures when it was due, Hank, Jr. waived legal

claims against her; she later gave the accounting required by the court.

(Hank, Jr. reached his majority in 1967, and before long he had broken publicly with his mother on business and professional matters. He now conducts his own affairs, with great success. Hank, Jr. can afford to be independent-minded: aside from his show business career, he is his father's sole legal heir, and when the estate is terminated, that half of the royalty income will go to him.)

2. The renewal of publishing rights to Hank's songs. Irene, acting for the estate, sold the renewal rights to Acuff-Rose for a bonus of twenty-five thousand dollars and the payment of royalties in accordance with the prevailing contract. Audrey and Hank, Jr., in a suit four years later, contended that the deal was made too soon—sixteen years before it was necessary to renew—and that the rights were worth much more; a New York publisher, Audrey claimed, had valued the songs at a half million dollars. Each side produced expert witnesses, including Mitch Miller, Frank Loesser, and other names from the world of popular music. The judge ruled that the renewal fee was sufficiently high in view of the fact that the new contract was likely to produce two million dollars in royalties.

3. The ownership of various properties once belonging to Hank. Audrey asked the U.S. district court in Montgomery to order Irene and her Montgomery attorney to turn over "certain items of personal property, records of business transactions, monies, and assets." The suit was dismissed on the ground that broader matters concerning the estate and guardianship were pending in state court.

4. The inheritance status of a child Hank was alleged to have fathered illegitimately. Attorneys representing the child never actually brought a claim against the estate, because Alabama law, like that of most states, provides that an illegitimate child cannot inherit from its father and because the child's adopted parents did not want the whole thing brought into the open. The

issue is not dead, however. Legislation has been proposed that would permit paternal inheritance in copyright situations, and the child may someday be back to claim a slice of the pie.

While most of the circumstances surrounding the birth remain a mystery, a few fascinating bits have come to light. The child, a girl, was born a couple of months after Hank's death. The mother was a brunette in her late twenties, whom Hank apparently had met in Tennessee. Lilly Stone virtually acknowledged her son's paternity by caring for the woman before the birth and for the child afterward, until the local welfare agency found an adopted home. However, the entire matter remained a family secret until it came out in a court hearing in 1967.

It was inevitable that a movie about Hank's life, at least a simplified version of it, would be made. When Hank was riding high in Nashville, there was talk that he himself would play the title role. He in effect squashed that prospect by failing to grab his chance to play a sheriff in *Small Town Girl* and by becoming too risky and controversial a performer. After his death, M-G-M purchased the rights to do what amounted to the authorized film version, but the film itself was not done until 1964. A low-budget enterprise called *Your Cheatin' Heart,* it turned—and continues to turn—a healthy profit.

Originally, the project was in the hands of Hollywood producer Joe Pasternak. Pasternak had a couple of scripts prepared before he abandoned the whole idea. "Somehow," he says, "I could never find a suitable person to play Hank's part." M-G-M thereupon dropped the idea in the lap of another producer, Sam Katzman.

Katzman started from scratch, and his big hangup, like Pasternak's, was finding somebody to play Hank. "We looked at a half dozen possibilities," Katzman recalls, "including Jimmy Stewart and even Burt Lancaster. Then we looked at George Hamilton. I had him read the part, and that was it. He was Hank Williams to me." He wasn't to anyone who'd known Hank, but he was admittedly a better choice than Lancaster—or Sammy Davis, Jr.—would have been. Susan Oliver, a capable if uninspiring actress, was chosen to play Audrey and Arthur O'Connell to play Fred Rose. In a bit of fabrication that was to typify the whole movie, a fictional character named Shorty, a sort of composite of Hank's musician buddies, was invented, and Red Buttons was retained for the part. Under the agreement by which M-G-M secured the rights, Audrey Williams became in effect an adviser for the film project.

Your Cheatin' Heart was frankly a cornball moneymaker, with short shrift given both accuracy and artistry. Katzman readily acknowledges this. "We didn't go for any art in it. We had to exaggerate a lot of spots and make a lot of points that didn't really exist, just to get a story out of it."

Even making these allowances, the movie was guilty of one major and several minor distortions. The minor distortions included: having Tee-tot, the old black guitar player, die in young Hank's arms, a scene so improbable it boggles the imagination; omitting the Toby Marshall interlude and Hank's use of drugs in general; intimating that Hank was on the wagon when he departed on his last trip and that his craving on the trip was for "a bottle of soda," not whisky.

The major distortion involved Audrey. The movie completely omitted her divorce from Hank and his subsequent marriage to Billie Jean. Instead, it blithely pictured her as sticking with him to the end, right down to a closing scene of Audrey, together with the children, fighting back the tears in the Canton theater on New Year's night. "Yes, we left out parts," says Katzman. "Like the second marriage. We didn't want to get involved with the second wife."

In the fall of 1968, four years after the film appeared, Billie Jean decided to get involved with M-G-M. She filed suit in federal court, for a total of 2.2 million dollars, against M-G-M and two broadcasting companies that showed *Your Cheatin' Heart* on television.

She charged that although the movie was advertised as "the real life story of Hank Williams," it deliberately misrepresented her marital status with Hank. This, she said, cast "shame" on her and resulted in her being "held out to the public as being guilty of lewd, improper, and unchaste conduct."

A federal district court in Atlanta found Billie Jean to be the legal widow but found no malice intended by the movie and therefore disallowed her claim for damages. A second suit was dismissed on pleadings.

Curiously, Audrey permitted herself to be portrayed in the film as an ambitious, almost grasping woman, not a very nice person compared to Hank, who was shown as a down-to-earth country boy deeply troubled by success and all its demands. She apparently overlooked that characterization in favor of the one that portrayed her as the pillar of strength and soul of reason behind an erratic, phlegmatic husband.

Your Cheatin' Heart premiered at Montgomery's Paramount Theater, complete with a two-hour stage show that featured Tex Ritter, Johnny Cash, and Roy Acuff. Governor George C. Wallace, who had proclaimed "Hank Williams Week," was also on hand. The *Advertiser* reviewer, awed by a few scenes of drunkenness, proclaimed that "The realism of the story was almost harsh in its honesty. . . ." but another *Advertiser* writer commented: "How well the film depicts Hank's troubles and dazzling successes, his marital tangles and long battle with the bottle, remains to be seen."

Despite its distortions, the movie was good entertainment, with Hamilton doing a passable job as Hank and Hank, Jr. singing some of his father's greatest songs. (*Time* called it a movie "better heard than seen.") Audiences loved it, particularly in the South, where it has made the rounds a half-dozen times and, like a small-time *Gone with the Wind,* shows no signs of expiring. In fact, says M-G-M, *Your Cheatin' Heart* is the most successful country film ever made; it has grossed almost ten million dollars, on an initial investment of 1.2 million.

Acuff-Rose had little to do with the movie, largely because Wesley Rose judged the emphasis on Hank's drinking to be in bad taste. "Mr. Rose struck me as a man in love with legends," observes a man closely connected with *Your Cheatin' Heart,* "and he didn't want anything to tarnish that of his father or of Hank."

But Acuff-Rose has its own piece of the action in what has become the Hank Williams legend. Not only does the company hold the rights to the songs already published, and seemingly imperishable, it holds the rights to more than one hundred lyrics and fragments of lyrics that have never been published. The value of this material is incalculable, and all the contending parties would dearly love to lay hands on it. There has, in fact, been a legal struggle in this area, with Audrey trying to establish her right to share in future proceeds.

The unpublished material grew to such proportions because of Hank's habit of scribbling verses at random and then either sticking them in some little nook or turning them over to Fred Rose. They are the property of Acuff-Rose because of Hank's exclusive songwriting contract with the company. Hank used to keep many of these lyrics in a shoe box, according to Wesley Rose. "Some are four lines, some a full song, some just a title," says Rose. "I can't say what they're worth. It depends how good each song is and how we treat it. If it isn't a good song, we wouldn't even want to put it out. Anyway, ten publishers would earn ten different amounts with the same song."

Rose admits frankly he has been in no hurry to publish the leftover material because the songs already published have been doing so well. "We've made a super-human effort to build Hank up since his death, and his earnings have been probably ten times what he got in his lifetime. When you have a great artist, you want to keep everything you do in the right light, because you don't want the bubble to break." For sixteen years after Hank's death, Rose saw "no reason at all to reach back into those lyrics. We were going to wait till people said, 'Those songs [Hank's old songs] are overexposed. We want something new.' "

In 1969, that time arrived. That year, Acuff-Rose commissioned Hank Williams, Jr. (who, unlike his father, can read and write music), to turn a number of the leftover fragments into songs. M-G-M released an album of the first batch—"Songs My Father Left Me"; one of the numbers in the album, "Cajun Baby," became a hit single. Acuff-Rose has turned additional lyric fragments over to Hank, Jr. and presumably all of them will become full-fledged songs—in due time, of course.

The enduring interest in Hank and his music virtually assure the financial success of such ventures, for M-G-M as well as for Acuff-Rose. As Eli Waldron wrote, with only slight exaggeration, in the *Reporter,* if those two firms "could somehow contrive to get Williams' dirty laundry to spin at 45 rpm, they'd make a fortune on that too. Williams had ten million fans in this country and another five million abroad. They literally, quite literally, worshipped him."

20

Estimates of fifteen million Hank Williams fans are by no means inflated. A few other country music artists— Jimmie Rodgers, Roy Acuff—have had as many. The remarkable thing about Hank's fans is their unending devotion to the man and his music and their efforts in keeping the legend alive. Their ranks have been swelled by millions of other people too young to recall Hank's life and times but captivated by his music nonetheless.

Who are the fans? People from every section of the

country—indeed, of the world—from every walk of life, of every musical taste. Because Hank's songs spanned the country and pop fields, his enthusiasts span them too. He is even considered, along with a select few other country artists, acceptable to most folk music fans. When guitar pickers gather, one will inevitably say, "Let's do this old Hank Williams song. . . ." (The song will not be a commercial hit like "Your Cheatin' Heart" but a hymn or one of the less-celebrated ballads of unrequited love.)

The whole process, legend and money-making and durability of music, has been greatly aided by what Roy Acuff calls Hank's "very timely death." Like James Dean, Hank died at a most propitious time: in Hank's case, after he had rocketed to the top of his field, then fallen and was striving to regain the heights again. It is no surprise that this story, involved as it was with love and alcohol and loneliness, has touched the hearts of millions. Coupled with the man's songs, it will last as long as country music itself.

The efforts, both commercial and non-commercial, to perpetuate Hank have been so successful that large numbers of people think he is still alive. The Grand Ole Opry, Jerry Rivers notes, still gets requests from Japan (where Hank has always been popular) to "Send Mr. Hank Williams to sing for us."

One of the reasons for this apparently endless appeal is the ever-widening circle of artists who record Hank's songs. They range from country to pop to folk to soul and even jazz, and they include various sub-species within those categories. "Your Cheatin' Heart," for example, has been recorded by such diverse types as Ray Anthony, Ramsey Lewis, Frankie Avalon, Roberta Sherwood, Fats Domino, Ray Charles, Les Paul and Mary Ford, and the Pete King Chorale, not to mention a dozen or two country artists—some seventy-five artists in all. A song getting this kind of recording action finds its way onto a lot of turntables that would not touch a pure country number.

M-G-M itself has catered to this broad market. Its

catalogue includes a version of Hank Williams' songs for just about everybody. For the real devotee, there is album after album of Hank and the Drifting Cowboys —the genuine, original stuff; for followers of Hank and Audrey and all that, an album called "Mr. and Mrs. Hank Williams," featuring their duets; for those partial to a smoother sound, a couple of albums offering the songs done sweetly with strings; for fans of Hank, Jr. albums with his voice superimposed on that of his father, in one of those "recording miracles" we are blessed with these days; and for everybody, the usual run of "Unforgettable" and "Immortal" albums, plus one that capitalizes on what M-G-M seems to regard as Hank's third Coming—"The Legend Lives Anew." If the company had the Beatles or the Boston Pops under contract, there would surely be Williams albums by them too.

The slicked-up, fully orchestrated reissues of Hank's music have not found universal approval. Using strings, horns, and vocal groups as backing for country singers is a matter of controversy within the trade these days. "We can only have praise for the few remaining A&R men who have resisted the modern approach and continue to record their artists with simple backing," wrote Everett Corbin, editor of Nashville's *Music City News,* a few years ago. Corbin lamented that country music will continue to be modernized "unless there are enough country music fans left to rally to its cause."

The modernized treatment of Hank Williams is largely the work of Jim Vienneau, an M-G-M Records executive who is also the nephew of the late Frank Walker. Vienneau, according to some observers, has "revitalized" Williams' music. According to others, he has defiled it. "Perhaps the worst thing ever to happen to country music is the recording of the late Hank Williams with strings," wrote an English enthusiast, John Atkins, in a letter to *Music City News.* "Hank was one of the most gifted and talented men ever to grace this earth. . . . His music will live on forever in its ORIGINAL FORM, and anything short of this can only serve to tarnish his memory."

Adding strings to Hank's singing, said Atkins indignantly, "is about as reasonable as someone painting a mustache on the *Mona Lisa* to bring it up to date. Hank Williams' recordings, too, are a work of art, and they need no alteration or addition. Never again will there be a singer and composer as great as Hank Williams, and he will live on forever as the greatest country singer of all time, and not as someone who merely fronted an orchestra as M-G-M would have some people believe."

M-G-M, Acuff-Rose, and others with a commercial interest in the Hank Williams legend do not fret over such criticism. It helps keep the legend alive. It also proves what they have long believed: that the markets for Hank's music are many and varied. One man's "mustache on the *Mona Lisa*" is another man's favorite album. You take your choice, and you pay your money.

Successful as the efforts at "revitalizing" the music have been, the simple versions of Hank's songs remain the most popular. At times the popularity has been awesome. In the late 1950s, in many areas, Hank's records were outselling those of the phenomenon of the day, Elvis Presley. Radio stations from Georgia to Texas were reporting Hank still leading the pack in requests from listeners.

Former members of the Drifting Cowboys, most of whom are still working musicians, are besieged with requests to play Hank's songs or to reminisce about the old days almost everywhere they go. "You can tell the M.C.'s on your shows not to introduce you as 'one of the original Drifting Cowboys' or some such, but they still do it," says Don Helms. "And when the show is over, people come crowding backstage looking for you. They don't ask for the stars on the show either. They just ask everybody, 'Where's that boy that used to work with Hank Williams?' "

Bob McNett, who now runs a country music park in

Pennsylvania, says the enduring interest in Hank is "a little fantastic. I get phone calls, letters, people trying to find his original recordings." And, adds Hillous Butrum, one must be careful about the kind of reminiscences he provides: "If you got up and said Hank was no good, there'd be plenty of people ready to knock you in the head."

Jerry Rivers receives requests for information on Hank, his songs, the band, and so forth, from all over the world. Although a few inevitably involve money-making schemes, the great majority are earnest attempts simply to dig out this fact or confirm that bit of gossip. The detailed knowledge of many of the correspondents is surprising. A young Berliner named Hans-Peter Rehfeldt wrote Rivers a series of questions on the precise order and composition of various Drifting Cowboys recording sessions. Hank "made the finest records I have heard in my life," wrote Rehfeldt, "and it fills my heart with joy to listen to them. One day I will come to Nashville and visit his grave; may it be the last thing I do in this world."

Such fervent personal promises are not unusual among country music fans, who take their favorite artists very seriously indeed. In Hank's case, they are positively common. All sorts of people, foreigners as well as Americans, still observe little rituals and memorial ceremonies to demonstrate their devotion to the man. Charles Steiner, of Basel, Switzerland, presumably is still commemorating Hank's death in the same way he did several years ago—by listening to his entire collection of Hank Williams records each New Year's Day. It takes four hours to get through them all, but Steiner finds it so satisfying that he has been repeating the process each September 17 as well, to celebrate Hank's birthday.

On the other side of the world, in New Zealand, Hank has a fervent fan in Garth Gibson, who edits *Country & Western Spolight,* in Otago, South Island. In a profile of Hank eleven years after his death, Gibson wrote: "I am quite sure that, with the exception of

Jimmie Rodgers, no other country singer alive or in death will reach the prominence that Hank Williams did in a few short years. Nor will any other country artist make such a great contribution to the library of country music. . . . Hank Williams left us a priceless heritage of the best country music which ever has, or ever will be, recorded. Yes, Hank may be dead, but his music will never die."

Another foreign-born fan, Eva Weissmann, an Austrian who now lives in Chicago, has been president of the Hank and Audrey Williams International Fan Club for the past fifteen years—"the ONLY OFFICIAL fan club," Miss Weissman declares. Founded by a Jacksonville, Texas, woman in 1948, the club at one time had three thousand members; that was when public interest in Hank soared right after his death. Membership has dwindled, but Eva Weissmann keeps the faith. Audrey Williams sends her pictures and what not for the club's informal archives and invites her to the house on Franklin Road when she comes to Nashville. Miss Weismann got hooked on Hank shortly after she arrived in this country, and before she knew a word of English: "I liked the voice that went with his songs."

Miss Weissmann confesses to a decade-old dream about Hank "which sometimes still haunts me today." In the dream, she was standing by Hank's grave with Audrey and the family, when "a familiar voice began singing—'Mansion on the Hill.' I turned to see who it was and there stood Hank. I said to him, isn't that your grave? And he said—'Yes, but I forgot to sing my song,' and slowly walked away, still singing."

Among country music fans, there is a sharp difference of approach: those interested in the whole artist versus those interested only in his music. Miss Weissmann stands firmly with the latter group. "I never go beyond [into] personal problems of any star and I won't knock any person for what they are. I liked Hank, his music and his voice and that's all that mattered to me. What he did with his personal life was his business. If he wouldn't have been the way he was—would we have these songs of his today?"

In the country music business, says one long-time Nashville publisher, "Nobody has ever had so many artists try to imitate him as Hank did." Also, nobody has had so few do it successfully. Yet the Williams influence has been pervasive. It has touched numerous songwriters and such contemporary singers as Ray Price and Roger Miller. Outside of country music, where he was the first country writer-performer to make a lasting impression, his influence reaches all the way to Bob Dylan, one of the major figures on the folk and protest scenes of the 1960s. As the New York *Times'* Robert Shelton noted, in his 1967 review of the Dylan album "John Wesley Harding":

"His voice has that warm and buoyant quality associated with the best of Nashville recording. . . . behind nearly all of Dylan's albums, there is a discernible 'ghost singer,' whose recent influences seems to be infusing the singer with inspiration. Those have included Woody Guthrie, Buddy Holly, Ray Charles, and Chuck Berry. On 'John Wesley Harding,' the ghost singer is Hank Williams, 'the hillbilly Shakespeare,' who called himself Luke the Drifter and who sang of mockingbirds and sorrow."

Not long after Hank's death, a thousand-dollar music scholarship in his name was established at the University of Alabama. The first thousand was given by American Folk Publications. A writer in the Alabama *Journal* was moved to suggest, only partly in jest, that a recipient of the scholarship:

"Shouldn't know one note from another;

"Should have a voice like the whine of an electric saw going through pine timber;

"Should be a lank, gaunt, unschooled, mixed up, and sorrowful country boy;

"Should sing only what he feels, not what he is supposed to feel;

"Should be a 'natural' and, in his field, a genius."

For a while in Montgomery, civic boosters—and real

fans too—worked hard to keep the legend alive. In September of 1954, to honor Hank's birthday, the Alcazar Temple of the Shrine sponsored a two-day memorial celebration. Sixty thousand people packed the sidewalks to watch the opening parade, which included among the marchers three governors, Alabama governor-elect Jim Folsom, Alabama senator Lister Hill, and more than fifty country artists. Ten thousand people came to the first show, at which everyone paid to get in and no one was paid to perform. The money, of course, went to Shrine charities, but the local businessmen got in their plugs too. "You are invited to read your souvenir program carefully," read the program forward, "so you may know the business firms of Montgomery who have made this book possible." Willie Gayle's marble monument was dramatically unveiled to the singing of "I Saw the Light," then placed at the graveside in a solemn ceremony. Another memorial celebration, on a slightly smaller scale, was held three years later.

Nowadays Montgomery residents usually take visitors to see two historic sites: the spot at the top of the capitol steps where Jefferson Davis took the oath as president of the Confederacy; and Hank Williams' grave in Oakwood Cemetery Annex. The grave is about the only memorial to Hank remaining. Lilly's old boardinghouses have given way to new buildings. The Empire Theater, where Hank sang his "WPA Blues," is still operating, but it takes no special cognizance of that occasion. The civic boosters now let Hank's anniversaries go by without fanfare, perhaps because business is good anyway; they have not even put up markers directing people to Oakwood Cemetery Annex.

Yet the people come, many thousands of them every year. They ask directions at gas stations and cafés, and they drive slowly up the red dirt road leading into the cemetery. Often they have to hunt up the cemetery caretaker, a black named Willie Embry, to locate the grave site, because again there are no signs and because the grave, monument and all, is almost indistinguishable from its neighbors until one is standing in front of it.

The grave has been the target of various forms of vandalism over the years, with people stealing the small urns or digging up plants or chipping souvenir pieces from the monument as if it were Plymouth Rock. In December of 1969, after a long spell without incident, the urns and the marble cowboy hat were stolen. They were recovered, undamaged, the following day.

Nonetheless, Hank's grave remains the best-kept in the annex. The Montgomery attorney who represents his estate replaces the stolen material and tips caretaker Embry to make sure the plot is always neat. Audrey regularly sends fresh flowers, which are placed in a yellow pot with a card reading. "From Audrey and the children." On warm weekends, the dirt road often is lined with cars, the grave surrounded by visitors. "There's been some drop off," says Willie Embry with a chuckle. "You can nearly count the cars that come now."

Not long ago, a young gravedigger stopped his work nearby to point out for a visitor some of the details of Hank's grave. "I know a lot of boys around here who carried him home when he was drunk," he said. Then he shook his head and added, "Hank Williams ain't never gonna die in Montgomery."

Nor in Nashville. Hank's old house on Franklin Road, greatly embellished by Audrey, is a tourist attraction in its own right. Describing a bus tour of Nashville, Larry L. King wrote in *Harper's* in 1968, "Our longest pause was at the home of Audrey Williams, widow of the legendary Hank. 'That 1952 Cadillac in the driveway is the one Hank Williams died in,' our guide said, prompting the greatest camera action since Iwo Jima." Other attractions at the house include the "Hank Williams museum" inside and the "$40,000 cabana decorated in true Hawaiian style" in the rear.

The czars of Nashville's music industry have not seen fit to make shrines out of the hotels Hank got drunk in and the sanitariums he dried out in, but that would hardly be in keeping with the image the industry tries to project. They have chosen instead to memorialize him through the Country Music Hall of Fame and Museum, an historical-promotional enterprise housed in a tastefully modernistic structure on Record Row. The Hall of Fame, which features color pictures and recordings and artifacts of some sixty artists, has attracted almost one million paying visitors, plus innumerable non-paying school children, since it opened in April, 1967. The visitors are almost reverent as they make their way through the treasures. Souvenir snitching is unheard of, as Dorothy Gable, the attendant, explained a few years back:

"When we put Gentleman Jim Reeves' clothes on a manikin and placed it right in the open, we were told, 'People will cut the fringe off his jacket, you watch.' Well, it hasn't happened. If this were a rhythm and blues or rock and roll place, maybe it would. But the people who came in here are devoted to these artists. Why I believe if our visitors saw somebody taking something, they'd knock him down."

Only a few of Hank's possessions are in the museum. (The rest of them are either in the possession of Hank, Jr. or in storage in Montgomery.) There is a guitar to be inspected plus a handful of pictures and a book of his songs with Japanese lyrics. Most visitors, however, prefer to stand silently in front of his plaque or his picture in the "Artists' Gallery." "The first remark you usually hear is, 'Isn't it a shame he died so young?'" said Dorothy Gable. "Once in a while you hear, 'Isn't it a shame the way he died?' but then the same person adds, 'But he must have had a reason.'"

In 1961, the Country Music Association made the first selections for its Hall of Fame. Three men were chosen out of the thousands of performers, writers, and executives who have molded American country music. One was Jimmie Rodgers, "the Singing Brakeman." The other two were the integral parts of Hank Williams' success: Hank himself and Fred Rose.

Hank's Hall of Fame plaque reads: "Hank Williams

will live on in the memories of millions of Americans. The simple, beautiful melodies and straightforward, plaintive stories in his lyrics of life as he knew it will never die. His songs appealed not only to the country music field, but brought him great acclaim in the 'pop' music world as well."

So the legend lives—in records and royalties, in simple, stirring memorials as well as in hokey, tasteless ones. It shows no sign of dying; sustained by commercial interests and by a legion of fans, old and new, it may live forever. Yet the life remains more intriguing than the legend, as any great life must. To the average fan, it is a dimly perceived blend of color and chaos, joy and anguish, with an awesome, mysterious end. The fan doesn't know why Hank burned himself out at twenty-nine, but he knows it was a terrible waste. And he knows, as the people who visit the Hall of Fame know, that Hank "must have had a reason."

Afterword

"A couple of years after Hank died, we thought the 'legend,' too, was pretty much dead," says Jerry Rivers of the Drifting Cowboys. "Were we ever wrong. It looks now as if there's no end in sight."

Rivers is, if anything, understating the situation. Interest in Hank Williams, in the man and the music and the legend, stands at an all-time high. It is far greater than when *Sing a Sad Song* was written, twelve years ago; and as Rivers says, there's no end in sight. A sort of Hank Williams industry has developed, with headquarters in Nashville and operations of varying size scattered around North America. While "Hank Williams, Inc.," does not rival the Elvis Presley industry, either in size or in the amount of space devoted by fan magazines and tabloid weeklies, it encompasses an impressive array of commercial and artistic activity.

In early 1980, the following spinoffs, ripoffs, and signs of undying interest were evident:

• Not one, but two, on-stage imitators: American Jim Owen and Canadian "Sneezy" Waters. Owen and Waters are country musicians in their own right, but they are reaching wider audiences with Williams imitations than they could hope to reach otherwise. The flat-out imitation is not new to American entertainment. In recent years, it has been used by actors ranging from the talented Hal Holbrook (as Mark Twain) to low-grade copycats of Presley. To my knowledge, however, it has never before been brought to bear in sustained fashion on a country music figure. It constitutes the sincerest form of flattery, show-biz style.

Owen, a Nashville singer/songwriter, presents a show composed essentially of Williams songs done in the Williams manner. Waters, on the other hand, puts on a dramatic musical based on the fateful trip to Canton, Ohio. Both are moderately successful from an artistic standpoint and, thus far, highly successful at the box office. To anyone who saw the original in action, neither Owen nor Waters seems much better than a fuzzy reproduction. But for those who know Hank only through recordings, certainly the heavy majority of today's audiences, each man does a creditable job of evoking the Williams voice and personality. Says Bob Pinson of the Country Music Foundation, speaking of Owen: "When the lighting is just right, kind of shadowy across his face, he can look a lot like Hank."

• A two-hour television special on Williams's life. Filmed in Nashville with such stars as Johnny Cash, Waylon Jennings, and Kris Kristofferson, the show seemed likely, at this writing, to gain a spot on one of the networks. Knowledgeable observers say this film, a musical in biographical form, is far more faithful to the Williams story than was MGM's *Your Cheatin' Heart,* which omitted the divorce and remarriage as well as the drug problem.

• Continued life for *Your Cheatin' Heart* itself. Among country music movies, it is one of the top money earners of all time; given its low budget (a mere $1.2 million), it may well have yielded a higher return on investment than any other country film. MGM's Hollywood office reports that *Your Cheatin' Heart,* while no longer circulating in commercial theaters in this country, is "probably still playing" abroad. And it is doing nicely in the United States as a special rental property. Films, Inc., circulates eleven retail prints— "a fairly standard number for us"—in 35 mm to customers ranging from colleges to social clubs. (For those interested in renting *Your Cheatin' Heart,* Films, Inc., has offices in New York City, Los Angeles, Atlanta, and Wilmette, Illinois.)

• Persistent rumors of another Hollywood film about Hank's life, as well as a second book already published about him, a third in progress, and a fourth —a memoir by his sister, Irene—in the talking stage.

• A new career for the Drifting Cowboys. Almost two decades after their leader's death, the boys in the band are a popular act without him—yet unquestionably because of him. They have cut three albums of the old songs, including one with Jim Owen. Fully reorganized three years ago, the band has been playing a sizable and increasing number of show dates: 100 in 1979, 100 to 125 projected for 1980. The dates are spread across the United States and Western Europe; this year's European tour includes concerts in Germany, Norway, England, and Scotland.

Lead guitarist Bob McNett, steel guitarist Don Helms, bassist Hillous Butrum, and fiddler Rivers—the group that backed Hank during most of his two years at the top—form the nucleus of today's Cowboys. (Another bass and drums have been added for a fuller sound.) The "boys" look like the middle-aged men they've become—Rivers has put on weight, Helms wears glasses —but they play the music the way it ought to be played. All but McNett still live and work in Nashville; Helms and Rivers hold regular jobs at Buddy Lee Attractions, a talent agency that books the Cowboys' dates.

And would ol' Hank be amazed at some of the dates. In March of this year, the Cowboys played the Smithsonian Institution, as part of the institution's country music series. In July, they'll appear with the New Orleans Pops Symphony—at the New Orleans Municipal Auditorium, site of Hank's two gaudy second-marriage ceremonies. Rivers reports that the Smithsonian concert was sold out a year in advance. "It's a funny thing," he says. "The more sophisticated the audience, the better they seem able to interpret and appreciate our music. Our best audiences should be rednecks. But a lot of them are too busy whoopin' and makin' noise to hear us. When it gets down to really enjoying the music, people like the crowd at the Smithsonian stand out. So do a lot of those British audiences. Lord, you should have heard 'em in Ireland and Scotland last year. They're worse'n here about Hank. They just idol-worship the man."

• A seemingly undiminished public acclaim and curiosity. A couple of straws in the wind: Records kept by librarians at the Country Music Hall of Fame show more inquiries about Hank Williams than about any other star, past or present; and "in 1977," according to author Jay Caress, "a national organization of CB truck drivers voted 'Your Cheatin' Heart' as their favorite record of all time."

A few light years from the world of CB, in a church on Manhattan's East Side, I recently heard Hank invoked by singer Don McLean. Not by name; that wasn't necessary. McLean, who was giving a benefit concert, simply started singing "Lovesick Blues," and the audience, 90 percent of it under thirty, burst into spontaneous applause. ("Lovesick Blues" remains a Williams anachronism. The song still bears his stamp as indelibly as if he wrote it himself, and almost everybody in the church that night probably thinks he did.)

The legend grows in other ways, too. Towns and cities that figured prominently in Hank's career have recently seen fit to honor him. Nashville now has a small Hank Williams museum. Audrey Williams's secretary organized it, with a dedication by Hank, Jr. The main display contains an assortment of Hank's stage costumes and boots plus one of his guitars and some of Audrey's show paraphernalia. Another room houses an authentic bit of morbid Americana—the Cadillac in which he died. Photos are for sale, and a projector screens two of the very few Williams film clips: a segment from the Kate Smith TV program and some silent footage taken backstage at Ryman Auditorium. (The Smith segment, closely guarded by the few who possessed copies of it in the 1960s, is now widely available.)

In Butler County, Alabama, where Hank lived until his early teens, local entrepreneurs have been staging an annual "Hank Williams Memorial Festival." To their credit, they have kept the show low-key and oriented toward hometown talent, with a couple of Nashville figures imported as headliners. Since the number of would-be Williamses is limited, even in Butler County, the acts often wander away from the master's material; last year, one young man did a Presley routine. The outdoor setting, near Mt. Olive, is pleasantly informal, and the crowds are good-sized; seven thousand or more attended in 1979. Taft Skipper, Hank's cousin, plays a major role in putting on the festival.

Montgomery still has no big Hank Williams memorials, living or inanimate. That's probably just as well, considering what some people tried to erect there several years ago: an eighty-foot-high monument in the shape of a cowboy boot. As it is, the elaborate grave in Oakwood Cemetery Annex remains the city's lone shrine to Hank. Since Audrey died, in 1975, the grave has not been so well tended. But now it contains her coffin as well as his, nestled together beneath Willie Gayle's elaborate marble stonework.

It would be nice to be able to report how many millions of Williams recordings (albums and singles) have been sold since those first Sterling sides were cut. A decade ago, MGM Records wouldn't divulge sales information. MGM has since been sold to Polydor Records; Polydor is willing to provide figures, but those available for total sales are so low and obviously incomplete as to be meaningless. Polydor currently lists six Williams albums in its active catalogue. All are on the MGM label, and the latest two are repackagings of material issued earlier. "For a guy who passed away almost thirty years ago," says Polydor's Herb Cohen, "Hank does very well."

The songwriting royalty picture has changed considerably. Hank, Jr., collects the lion's share: 100 percent of foreign royalties and 50 percent of domestic. The

other 50 percent belongs to Hank's second wife, Billie
Jean, who has established herself as his legal widow;
that is, it belongs to Billie Jean and to the Hill and
Range music-publishing company, which bought her
rights once she had secured them in court and which
now pays her a stipulated percentage of the song royalties. (A how-the-world-turns note: A friend of mine
from college days, now a Manhattan attorney, has handled Hill and Range's end of the tangled litigation.
"From the standpoint of the personalities, the weird
happenings, and the legal issues raised," he says, "it's
the most interesting case I've ever worked on.")

Success for Billie Jean and Hill and Range has come
at the expense of Acuff-Rose publishers. While this has
meant a substantial loss of income for Acuff-Rose, the
firm obviously still makes lots of money on Hank Williams. Says Bud Brown of Acuff-Rose, "He earns more
than any living writer we have, and we've got some
pretty big ones. The sales of Hank's songs increase almost every year. Foreign sales have been coming up
pretty strong—to about 30 percent of the total."

What of Hank's uncompleted songs, which several
years ago seemed to promise another bonanza for
Acuff-Rose? Hank, Jr., has finished them as planned,
adding music and making slight changes in the original
lyrics. About ten "new" Williams songs have resulted.
They bear such titles as "Cajun Baby," "Your Turn to
Cry," and "I Just Didn't Have the Heart to Say Goodbye."

As for Hank, Jr., he is now a mature man who has
survived some of the pitfalls that trapped his father
as well as one his father never faced: a disfiguring and
nearly fatal accident, followed by a long series of sur-
gical operations. Hank, Jr., has left Nashville to live
in slower-paced Cullman, Alabama. He remains a mid-
dling-big name in contemporary country music and living evidence that a son can escape—if only painfully—
the legacy of a famous and tragic father.

ROGER M. WILLIAMS

New York City
April, 1980

Discography

This discography represents a complete listing of Sterling and MGM commercial (nonpromotional) record releases in the United States of non-overdubbed Hank Williams recordings. Interspersed with the Sterling/ MGM material are transcribed programs for the Le-Blanc Corporation and for the March of Dimes, some of which (in the case of the LeBlanc Corporation) were made available to MGM for commercial release several years after Williams's death, and a partial listing of Armed Forces Radio Service 16″ transcription discs containing Grand Ole Opry appearances by Williams. Not included are outside manufacturers' packages made available through leasing arrangements with Polydor/ MGM, or foreign releases of any type.

The discographical format employed here is self-explanatory; however, it should be noted that the composer credits are based only on the data found on the initial record release. No attempt has been made to expand upon these disc credits. "No CC" merely means no composer credit is given on the first Williams record release of the song in question.

Much credit is due Jerry Rivers (whose fine fiddlin' is evident on most of Hank Williams's prime-time recordings) for his 1967 Hank Williams discography, which first appeared in his own *Hank Williams: From Life to Legend,* published by Heather Enterprises, and which has subsequently been reproduced in several other publications. Jerry's discography has been an invaluable resource for this compilation. Polydor's archivist, Dick Campbell, and his staff generously provided several hundred pages of recording data. Ex-Polydor executives Ed Outwater and Jim Vienneau also contributed to the project. Dean May extracted important data from the Acuff-Rose files that was unavailable elsewhere. Thanks to fellow collectors Nick Benedetto, Bill MacEwen, and Ronnie Pugh for their tremendous help, too.

Additional acknowledgments will be made in a more comprehensive Williams discography to be published by the Country Music Foundation Press. Many musicians have contributed session personnel data that will be used therein. This expanded discography will also include matrix data, more A.F.R.S. Grand Ole Opry data, and spoken word recordings, as well as many photographs of Williams, some of which have never been published. Anyone interested should write to me at the address below. All inquirers will be notified when the new discography is available.

BOB PINSON

Country Music Foundation
4 Music Square East
Nashville,Tenn. 37203

Session Recordings

STERLING RECORDS

TITLE & COMPOSER CREDIT	78 RPM	45 RPM	33 1/3 RPM
Castle Recording Co. WSM Studio D Nashville, Tenn. December 11, 1946			
Calling You (Hank Williams)	*Ster.* 201, MGM 11628	*MGM* K11628, X4110 (EP) in set X243, X1648 (EP)	*MGM* E243 (10"), E3331, 3-E2, SE4576
Never Again (Will I Knock on Your Door) (Hank Williams)	*Ster.* 201, MGM 10352	*MGM* K10352, X1639 (EP)	*MGM* E3733, 3-E4, SE4576; *Metro* M602, MS602
Wealth Won't Save Your Soul (Hank Williams)	*Ster.* 204, MGM 30455 in album 107	*MGM* K30455 in boxed set K107, X1102 (EP), X4110 (EP) in set X243, X1648 (EP)	*MGM* E107 (10"), E243 (10"), E3331, SE4576
When God Comes and Gathers His Jewels (Hank Williams)	*Ster.* 204, MGM 11628	*MGM* K11628, X4111 (EP) in set X243, X1649 (EP)	*MGM* E243 (10"), E3331, 3-E2, SE4576

NOTES: Acuff-Rose Publications acquired release rights to all Sterling sides in May, 1948. MGM Records acquired the rights from Acuff-Rose in July, 1948. Artist credits on *Sterling* issues for these four sides are given as *Hank Williams and the Country Boys.* MGM labels credit the sides to *Hank Williams with His Drifting Cowboys.* The recording sequence for these four sides has not been established.

The MGM stereo LP release, SE4576, exists in both unaltered and overdubbed form. The unaltered version bears additional master numbers in the wax near the label as follows: XSBV 131682-3A//XSBV 131683-3A. Otherwise, both products look identical.

Castle Recording Co.
WSM Studio D
Nashville, Tenn.
February 13, 1947

MGM RECORDS

TITLE & COMPOSER CREDIT	78 RPM	45 RPM	33 1/3 RPM
I Don't Care (If Tomorrow Never Comes) (Williams)	*Ster.* 208, *MGM* 10226	*MGM* K10226, X1637 (EP)	*MGM* E3733, SE4576; *Metro* M602, MS602
My Love For You (Has Turned to Hate) (Williams)	*Ster.* 208, *MGM* 11533	*MGM* K11533, X1637 (EP)	*MGM* E3733, 3-E4, SE4576
Honky Tonkin' (Williams)	*Ster.* 210		
Pan American (Williams)	*Ster.* 210, *MGM* 10226	*MGM* K10226, X1076 (EP), X1554 (EP)	*MGM* E3605, E3928, E4576, SE4576 (both original and revised releases); *Metro* M572, MS572, M602, MS602

NOTE: The band's name is now listed as *Drifting Cowboys* on all issues. The recording sequence for these four sides has not been established.

Castle Recording Co.
Nashville, Tenn.
April 21, 1947

Move It On Over (Hank Williams)	*MGM* 10033	*MGM* K10033, X1076 (EP), X1636 (EP)	*MGM* E3272, 3-E2, E3923, SE3923, E4040, E4211, SE4211, 2E-12, 2SE-12, E4267-4, E4300, SE4300, SE4576, SE4651, SE4680, SE4690, SE4755-2, 2-SES-4865, M3F-4954
I Saw the Light (Hank Williams)	*MGM* 10271, 30454 in album 107	*MGM* K30454 in boxed set K107, X1101 (EP), X4110 (EP) in set X243, X1648 (EP)	*MGM* E107 (10"), E243 (10"), E3331, 3-E2, E4109
(Last Night) I Heard You Crying in Your Sleep (Hank Williams)	*MGM* 10033	*MGM* K10033, X1492 (EP)	*MGM* E3560, E3924, E4267-4, SE4576
Six More Miles (to the Graveyard) (Hank Williams)	*MGM* 10271, 30454 in album 107	*MGM* K30454 in boxed set K107, X1101 (EP), X1493 (EP)	*MGM* E107 (10"), E3560, E3924, E4254, SE4254

NOTE: The cuts of "Move It On Over" on SE4576 (revised issue) and SE4690 are unaltered in terms of overdubbing, but *are* altered to the extent that the electric guitar break between verses three and four has been removed.

265

Castle Recording Co.
Nashville, Tenn.
August 4, 1947

Fly Trouble (Wilds – Biggs – Rose)	*MGM* 10073	*MGM* K10073, X1076 (EP), X1555 (EP)	*MGM* E3605, 3-E4, E3928, E4300, SE4300
Honky Tonk Blues	Unissued		
I'm Satisfied with You (Rose)	*MGM* 11768	*MGM* K11768, X1555 (EP)	*MGM* E3605, E3928
On the Banks of the Old Ponchartrain (Williams – Vincent)	*MGM* 10073	*MGM* K10073, X1638 (EP)	*MGM* E3733, E4140, SE4140, SE4576

Castle Studios
Tulane Hotel
Nashville, Tenn.
November 6, 1947

Rootie Tootie (Rose)	*MGM* 10124	*MGM* K10124, X1319 (EP)	*MGM* E3412, 3-E4, E4140, E4267-4
I Can't Get You Off of My Mind (Williams)	*MGM* 10328	*MGM* K10328, X1637 (EP)	*MGM* 3-E4, E3733
I'm a Long Gone Daddy (Williams)	*MGM* 10212, 30638 in album 168	*MGM* K10212, K30638 in boxed set K168, X4042 (EP) in set X168, X1217 (EP)	*MGM* E168 (10"), E3330, 3-E4, E3926, E4140, E4267-4

Honky Tonkin' (Williams)	*MGM* 10171	*MGM* K10171, X4108 (EP) in set X242, X1318 (EP)	*MGM* E242 (10"), E3412, 3-E2, E3918, E4168, E4267-4, SE4576, SE4651, SE4755-2, M3F-4954

NOTE: "Honky Tonkin'" appears only on revised versions of SE4576. On the original mono and stereo versions of this album, an overdubbed recording of "Honky Tonk Blues" is mistakenly used, despite label and sleeve credits to "Honky Tonkin'."

Castle Studios
Tulane Hotel
Nashville, Tenn.
November 7, 1947

My Sweet Love Ain't Around (Williams)	*MGM* 10124, 30638 in album 168	*MGM* K10124, K30638 in boxed set K168, X4041 (EP) in set X168, X1216 (EP)	*MGM* E168 (10"), E3330, E3926, E4040, E4267-4
The Blues Come Around (Williams)	*MGM* 10212, 30637 in album 168	*MGM* K10212, K30637 in boxed set K168, X4042 (EP) in set X168, X1217 (EP)	*MGM* E168 (10"), E3330, 3-E4, E3926, E3999, E4109, E4140, E4267-4
Mansion on the Hill (Rose – Williams)	*MGM* 10328, 30455 in album 107	*MGM* K10328, K30455 in boxed set K107, X1101 (EP), X1492 (EP)	*MGM* E107 (10"), 3-E2, E3560, E3924, E4040, E4227, SE4227, E4267-4, SE4680, MBC39, MG-2-5401

I'll Be a Bachelor 'til I Die (Williams)	MGM 10171	MGM K10171, X1638 (EP)	MGM 3-E4, E3733, E4040; *Metro* M509, MS509

NOTE: On E4109 the last verse, chorus, and repeat chorus of "The Blues Come Around" are omitted.

Herzog Studios
Cincinnati, Ohio
December 22, 1948

Lost on the River (Williams)	*MGM* 10434	*MGM* K10434	*MGM* 3-E4, E3955; *Metro* M547, MS547
There'll Be No Teardrops Tonight (Williams)	*MGM* 10461	*MGM* K10461, X1082 (EP), X1650 (EP)	*MGM* E3219, 3-E2, E3918, E3925, E4211, SE4211, 2E-12, 2SE-12, E4267-4
I Heard My Mother Praying for Me (A. Williams)	*MGM* 10813	*MGM* K10813	
Lovesick Blues (No CC)	*MGM* 10352, 30636 in album 168	*MGM* K10352, K30636 in boxed set K168, X4042 (EP) in set X168, X1217 (EP), KGC107, K13305	*MGM* E168 (10"), E3330, 3-E2, E3825, E3926, E4109, SE4651, M3F-4954; *Metro* M530, MS530

NOTE: "Lost on the River" and "I Heard My Mother Praying for Me" are duets by Hank and Audrey Williams. Artist credits are to *Hank and Audrey*.

Castle Studios
Tulane Hotel
Nashville, Tenn.
7:30 P.M.–10:30 P.M.
March 1, 1949

Dear Brother (Williams)	MGM 10434	MGM K10434, X4110 (EP) in set X243, X1648 (EP)	MGM E243 (10"), E3331, 3-E4, E3955; Metro M547, MS547
Jesus Remembered Me (H. Williams)	MGM 10813	MGM K10813, X4111 (EP) in set X243, X1649 (EP)	MGM E243 (10"), E3331, M3G-4991; Metro M547, MS547
Lost Highway (Payne)	MGM 10506, 30453 in album 107	MGM K10506, K30453 in boxed set K107, X1102 (EP), X1491 (EP)	MGM E107 (10"), E3560, 3-E4, E3924, E4140, E4227, SE4227, E4254, SE4254, E42674, MG-2-5401
May You Never Be Alone (Williams)	MGM 10609	MGM K10609, X1491 (EP)	MGM E3560, 3-E4, E3924, E4140, E4227, SE4227, E4267-4, SE4651, SE4755-2, M3F-4954; Metro M602, MS602

NOTE: "Dear Brother" and "Jesus Remembered Me" are duets by Hank and Audrey Williams. Artist credits are to *Hank and Audrey*.

269

Castle Studios
Tulane Hotel
Nashville, Tenn.
11 P.M. – 2 A.M.
March 1 and 2, 1949

Honky Tonk Blues	Unissued		
Mind Your Own Business (Williams)	*MGM* 10461	*MGM* K10461, X1082 (EP), X1319 (EP)	*MGM* E3412, 3-E2, E4140, E4227, SE4227, E4267-4, E4300, SE4300, SE4755-2
You're Gonna Change (or I'm Gonna Leave) (Williams)	*MGM* 10506	*MGM* K10506, X1082 (EP), X1650 (EP)	*MGM* E3219, 3-E2, E3925, E4140, SE4140, E4267-4, MG-2-5401
My Son Calls Another Man Daddy	Unissued		

NOTE: "Mind Your Own Business" on SE4755-2 has been electronically re-channeled to simulate stereo. However, the recording is free from any overdubbing of additional instrumentation.

Castle Studios
Tulane Hotel
Nashville, Tenn.
7:30 P.M.–9 P.M. (approx.)
March 20, 1949

Wedding Bells
(Claude Boone)

MGM 10401, 30456 in album 107

MGM K10401, K30456 in boxed set K107, X1101 (EP), X1491 (EP)

MGM E107 (10"), 3-E2, E3560, E3924, SE4755-2; *Metro* M509, MS509

I've Just Told Mama Goodbye
(Sweet – Kinsey)

MGM 10401, 30453 in album 107

MGM K10401, K30453 in boxed set K107, X1102 (EP), X1493 (EP)

MGM E107 (10"), E3560, 3-E4, E3924, E4140, E4254, SE4254, E4267-4

Herzog Studios
Cincinnati, Ohio
2 P.M.–5:30 P.M.
August 30, 1949

I'm So Lonesome I Could Cry
(Williams)

MGM 10560, 30637 in album 168

MGM K10560, K30637 in boxed set K168, X4041 (EP) in set X168, X1216 (EP), KGC113

MGM E168 (10"), E3330, 3-E2, E3918, E3926, E4168, E4267-4, SE4651, SE4755-2, SE4787, 2-SES-4865, M3F-4954

A House without Love
(Williams)

MGM 10696, 30456 in album 107

MGM K10696, K30456 in boxed set K107, X1102 (EP), X1493 (EP)

MGM E107 (10"), E3560, 3-E4, E3924, E4267-4, MG-2-5401

I Just Don't Like This Kind of Livin'
(Williams)

MGM 10609 — MGM K10609, X4223 (EP) in set, X291, X1136 (EP) — MGM E3219, 3-E4, E3925, E4040, MG-2-5401

My Bucket's Got a Hole in It
(Williams)

MGM 10560 — MGM K10560, X4108 (EP) in set, X242, X1318 (EP), K12635, KGC127 — MGM E242 (10"), E3412, 3-E2, E4254, SE4254, E4267-4, SE4651, M3F-4954, M3HB-4975, MG-2-5401

NOTE: The composer credit "Williams" for "My Bucket's Got a Hole in It" refers to the late jazz pianist/composer Clarence Williams, not to Hank Williams.

TITLE & COMPOSER CREDIT	FEATURED PERFORMER	33 1/3 RPM (16" ET)	33 1/3 RPM (LP)

THE LE BLANC CORPORATION

Castle Studios
Tulane Hotel
Nashville, Tenn.
October, 1949

TITLE & COMPOSER CREDIT	FEATURED PERFORMER	33 1/3 RPM (16" ET)	33 1/3 RPM (LP)
(Show #1)			
Rovin' Cowboy (theme) (No CC)	Hank Williams	Le Blanc EO-QM-11102	MGM E3999 (side 1)
Wedding Bells (Boone)	Hank Williams	Le Blanc EO-QM-11102	MGM E3999, E4168, E4267-4

Song	Performer	Le Blanc	MGM
Lovesick Blues (Mills – Friend)	Hank Williams	*Le Blanc* EO-QM-11102	*MGM* E3999, E4168, E4267-4; *Metro* M602, MS602
Joe Clark (P.D.)	Jerry Rivers, fiddle inst.	*Le Blanc* EO-QM-11102	*MGM* E3999
Where the Soul of Man Never Dies (Raney)	H. & A. Williams, duet	*Le Blanc* EO-QM-11102	*MGM* E3999
Sally Goodin' (closing theme)	Jerry Rivers, fiddle inst.	*Le Blanc* EO-QM-11102	
(Show #2) **Happy Rovin' Cowboy** (theme) (Knowland)	Hank Williams	*Le Blanc* EO-QM-11103	*MGM* E4109 (side 1 opening & closing; side 2 closing)
You're Gonna Change (or I'm Gonna Leave) (Williams)	Hank Williams	*Le Blanc* EO-QM-11103	*MGM* E4109
There's a Bluebird on Your Windowsill (Clarke)	Audrey Williams	*Le Blanc* EO-QM-11103	*MGM* E4109
Fiddle tune (Fire on the Mountain) (P.D.)	Jerry Rivers, fiddle inst.	*Le Blanc* EO-QM-11103	*MGM* E4109
Tramp on the Street (Cole)	Hank Williams	*Le Blanc* EO-QM-11103	*MGM* E4109

273

Song	Performer	Le Blanc	MGM
Sally Goodin' (closing theme)	Jerry Rivers, fiddle inst.	*Le Blanc* EO-QM-11103	
(Show #3)			
Rovin' Cowboy (theme) (No CC)	Hank Williams	*Le Blanc* EO-QM-11104	*MGM* E3999 (side 2)
I'm a Long Gone Daddy (Williams)	Hank Williams	*Le Blanc* EO-QM-11104	*MGM* E3999
I'm Tellin' You (Hughes – Lewis)	Audrey Williams	*Le Blanc* EO-QM-11104	*MGM* E3999
Bill Cheatam (P.D.)	Jerry Rivers, fiddle inst.	*Le Blanc* EO-QM-11104	*MGM* E3999
When God Comes and Gathers His Jewels (Williams)	Hank Williams	*Le Blanc* EO-QM-11104	*MGM* E3999
Sally Goodin' (closing theme)	Jerry Rivers, fiddle inst.	*Le Blanc* EO-QM-11104	
(Show #4)			
Happy Rovin' Cowboy (theme) (Knowland)	Hank Williams	*Le Blanc* EO-QM-11105	*MGM* E4109 (side 2 opening)
Lost Highway (Payne)	Hank Williams	*Le Blanc* EO-QM-11105	*MGM* E3999
I Wanna Live and Love Always (P.D.)	H. & A. Williams, duet	*Le Blanc* EO-QM-11105	*MGM* E3999
Boil Them Cabbage Down	Jerry Rivers, fiddle inst.	*Le Blanc* EO-QM-11105	

Title	Performer	Le Blanc	MGM
I'll Have a New Body (P.D.)	Hank Williams and band	Le Blanc EO-QM-11105	*MGM* E3999
Fingers on Fire (Smith)	Bob McNett, gtr. inst.	Le Blanc EO-QM-11105	*MGM* E4109
Sally Goodin' (closing theme)	Jerry Rivers, fiddle inst.	Le Blanc EO-QM-11105	
(Show #5) **Happy Rovin' Cowboy** (theme)	Hank Williams	Le Blanc EO-QM-11106	
Mansion on the Hill	Hank Williams	Le Blanc EO-QM-11106	
There'll Be No Teardrops Tonight	Hank Williams	Le Blanc EO-QM-11106	
Wagner	Jerry Rivers, fiddle inst.	Le Blanc EO-QM-11106	
The Prodigal Son (Eudy)	Hank Williams	Le Blanc EO-QM-11106	*MGM* E3850 (titled "The Prodigal")
Sally Goodin' (closing theme)	Jerry Rivers, fiddle inst.	Le Blanc EO-QM-11106	
(Show #6) **Happy Rovin' Cowboy** (theme)	Hank Williams	Le Blanc EO-QM-11107	
Pan American	Hank Williams	Le Blanc EO-QM-11107	
Lovesick Blues	Hank Williams	Le Blanc EO-QM-11107	

Song	Performer	Label
Arkansas Traveler	Jerry Rivers, fiddle inst.	*Le Blanc* EO-QM-11107
I Saw the Light	Hank Williams, Don Helms, & Hillous Butrum	*Le Blanc* EO-QM-11107
Sally Goodin' (closing theme)	Jerry Rivers, fiddle inst.	*Le Blanc* EO-QM-11107
(Show #7) **Happy Rovin' Cowboy** (theme)	Hank Williams	*Le Blanc* EO-QM-11108
Mind Your Own Business	Hank Williams	*Le Blanc* EO-QM-11108
Wedding Bells	Hank Williams	*Le Blanc* EO-QM-11108
Cotton Eyed Joe	Jerry Rivers, fiddle inst.	*Le Blanc* EO-QM-11108
I've Just Told Mama Goodbye	Hank Williams	*Le Blanc* EO-QM-11108
Sally Goodin' (closing theme)	Jerry Rivers, fiddle inst.	*Le Blanc* EO-QM-11108
(Show #8) **Happy Rovin' Cowboy** (theme)	Hank Williams	*Le Blanc* EO-QM-11109
I Can't Get You Off of My Mind	Hank Williams	*Le Blanc* EO-QM-11109
I'm So Lonesome I Could Cry	Hank Williams	*Le Blanc* EO-QM-11109

Fisher's Hornpipe   Jerry Rivers,   *Le Blanc* EO-QM-11109
                                         fiddle inst.

Thy Burdens Are Greater than Mine   Hank Williams   *Le Blanc* EO-QM-11109

Sally Goodin' (closing theme)   Jerry Rivers,   *Le Blanc* EO-QM-11109
                                         fiddle inst.

NOTES: For the sake of completeness, all performances from each show are listed whether Hank Williams was the featured performer or not.

The *Le Blanc* 16" ET records were for radio station use only and were not sold to the general public. Title and composer credits are gleaned from the MGM LP releases where possible. Other title data are obtained aurally from the *Le Blanc* ETs since the labels carry no title or composer credits.

TITLE & COMPOSER CREDIT	33 1/3 RPM (16" ET)	33 1/3 RPM (LP)

ARMED FORCES RADIO SERVICE TRANSCRIPTIONS

Grand Ole Opry   *AFRS* END-18, Program 103
Ryman Auditorium
Nashville, Tenn.
November 12, 1949

You're Gonna Change (or I'm Gonna Leave)   *MGM* MG-1-5019
(Hank Williams)

NOTE: AFRS 16" ET records were for radio use only and were not sold to the general public. Title and composer credits are from the MGM LP release.

277

MGM RECORDS

TITLE & COMPOSER CREDIT	78 RPM	45 RPM	33 1/3 RPM
Castle Studios Nashville, Tenn. 2 P.M.–5 P.M. January 9, 1950			
Long Gone Lonesome Blues (Williams)	*MGM* 10645, 30639 in album 168	*MGM* K10645, K30639 in boxed set K168, X4042 (EP) in set X168, X1217 (EP), KGC134	*MGM* E168 (10"), E3330, 3-E2, E3926, E4140, E4254, SE4254, E4267-4, SE4651, 2-SES-4865, M3F-4954
Why Don't You Love Me (Williams)	*MGM* 10696	*MGM* K10696, X4223 (EP) in set X291, X1136 (EP), K12611, KGC108	*MGM* E3219, 3-E2, E3918, E3925, E4168, E4267-4
Why Should We Try Anymore (Williams)	*MGM* 10760	*MGM* K10760, X1491 (EP)	*MGM* E3560, 3-E4, E3924, E4267-4, MG-2-5401
My Son Calls Another Man Daddy (Williams)	*MGM* 10645	*MGM* K10645, X4222 (EP) in set X291, X1135 (EP), KGC134	*MGM* E3219, 3-E4, E3925, E4267-4, 1SE-33ST

Castle Studios
Nashville, Tenn.
2 P.M.–5 P.M.
January 10, 1950

Too Many Parties and Too Many Pals (Rose – Dixon – Henderson)	*MGM* 10718, 30758 in album 203	*MGM* K10718, K30758 in boxed set K203, X1047 (EP), X1643 (EP)	*MGM* E203 (10"), E3267, E3927, E4138; *Metro* M509, MS509
Beyond the Sunset (Brock – Rowswell)	*MGM* 10630, 30758 in album 203	*MGM* K10630, K30758 in boxed set K203, X1644 (EP)	*MGM* E203 (10"), E3267, E3927, E4138
The Funeral (No CC)	*MGM* 10630, 30757 in album 203	*MGM* K10630, K30757 in boxed set K203, X1644 (EP)	*MGM* E203 (10"), E3267, E3927, E4138
Everything's Okay (Williams)	*MGM* 10718	*MGM* K10718, X1165 (EP)	*MGM* E3267, E3927, E4138

NOTE: These four sides were recorded under Hank Williams's alias, Luke the Drifter.

279

TITLE & COMPOSER CREDIT	33 1/3 RPM (16" ET)	33 1/3 RPM (LP)
	A.F.R.S.	
Grand Ole Opry Ryman Auditorium Nashville, Tenn. February 18, 1950		
I Just Don't Like This Kind of Livin' (Hank Williams)	*AFRS* END-18, Program 116	*MGM* MG-1-5019
Lovesick Blues (I. Mills – C. Friend)	*AFRS* END-18, Program 116	*MGM* MG-1-5019
Grand Ole Opry Ryman Auditorium Nashville, Tenn. June 10, 1950		
Long Gone Lonesome Blues (Hank Williams)	*AFRS* END-18, Program 130	*MGM* MG-1-5019
Why Don't You Love Me	*AFRS* END-18, Program 130	
Talk with Minnie Pearl	*AFRS* END-18, Program 130	*MGM* MG-1-5019

TITLE & COMPOSER CREDIT	78 RPM	45 RPM	33 1/3 RPM

MGM RECORDS

Castle Studios
Nashville, Tenn.
Noon – 1:30 P.M. (approx.)
June 14, 1950

They'll Never Take Her Love from Me (Payne)	*MGM* 10760	*MGM* K10760, X1492 (EP)	*MGM* E3560, 3-E4, E3924, E4040, E4227, SE4227, MG-2-5401
Honky Tonk Blues	Unissued		

TITLE & COMPOSER CREDIT	33 1/3 RPM (16" ET)	45 RPM	33 1/3 RPM (LP)

A.F.R.S.

Grand Ole Opry
Ryman Auditorium
Nashville, Tenn.
August 12, 1950

Why Don't You Love Me (Hank Williams)		*AFRS* END-18, Program 139	*MGM* MG-1-5019
Talk with Minnie Pearl		*AFRS* END-18, Program 139	*MGM* MG-1-5019
They'll Never Take Her Love from Me (Leon Payne)		*AFRS* END-18, Program 139	*MGM* MG-1-5019

MGM RECORDS

TITLE & COMPOSER CREDIT	78 RPM	45 RPM	33 1/3 RPM
Castle Studios Nashville, Tenn. 2 P.M.–5 P.M. August 31, 1950			
Nobody's Lonesome for Me (Williams)	*MGM* 10832	*MGM* K10832, X1082 (EP), X4222 (EP) in set X291, X1135 (EP)	*MGM* E3219, 3-E2, E3925, E4040, E4267-4, E4300, SE4300
Moanin' the Blues (Williams)	*MGM* 10832, 30636 in album 168	*MGM* K10832, K30636 in boxed set K168, X4041 (EP) in set X168, X1216 (EP), KGC112	*MGM* E168 (10"), E3330, 3-E2, E3926, E4267-4
Help Me Understand (Williams)	*MGM* 10806, 30757 in album 203	*MGM* K10806, K30757 in boxed set K203, X1047 (EP), X1643 (EP)	*MGM* E203 (10"), E3267, E3927, E4109, E4138
No, No, Joe (Rose)	*MGM* 10806	*MGM* K10806	

NOTE: "Help Me Understand" and "No, No, Joe" were recorded under Hank Williams's alias, Luke the Drifter.

TITLE & COMPOSER CREDIT	33 1/3 RPM (16" ET)	33 1/3 RPM (LP)

A.F.R.S.

TITLE & COMPOSER CREDIT	33 1/3 RPM (16" ET)	33 1/3 RPM (LP)
Grand Ole Opry Ryman Auditorium Nashville, Tenn. November 11,1950		
Moanin' the Blues (Hank Williams)	*AFRS* END-18, Program 151	*MGM* MG-1-5019
Nobody's Lonesome for Me (Hank Williams)	*AFRS* END-18, Program 151	*MGM* MG-1-5019

TITLE & COMPOSER CREDIT	FEATURED PERFORMER	33 1/3 RPM (16" ET)	33 1/3 RPM (LP)

MARCH OF DIMES

TITLE & COMPOSER CREDIT	FEATURED PERFORMER	33 1/3 RPM (16" ET)
Castle Studios Nashville, Tenn. ca. early December, 1950		
Lovesick Blues (portion as theme)	Hank Williams	March of Dimes 1951
Moanin' the Blues	Hank Williams	March of Dimes 1951
There's a Bluebird on Your Windowsill	Audrey Williams	March of Dimes 1951

Help Me Understand A. Williams sings &   March of Dimes 1951
                       H. Williams recites

When God Dips His Love in My Heart Hank Williams, with   March of Dimes 1951
                                        everyone on chorus

Untitled closing theme   Don Helms, steel inst.   March of Dimes 1951

NOTES: For the sake of completeness, all performances are listed whether Hank Williams was the featured performer or not.

This 15-minute program for the March of Dimes was aired in January, 1951, to assist that organization's annual fund-raising campaign.

TITLE & COMPOSER CREDIT	78 RPM	45 RPM	33 1/3 RPM

MGM RECORDS

Castle Studios
Nashville, Tenn.
7:15 P.M. –9:50 P.M.
December 21, 1950

| **Cold, Cold Heart** (Williams) | *MGM* 10904, 30751 in album 202 | *MGM* K10904, K30751 in boxed set K202, X4103 (EP) in set X202, X1613 (EP), KGC113, K13359 | *MGM* E202 (10"), E3272, 3-E2, E3825, E3918, E3923, SE3923, E4168, E4267-4, SE4755-2, 1SE-33ST, 2-SES-4865 |

Song	Master	Releases
Dear John (Ritter – Gass)	MGM 10904	MGM K10904, X1637 (EP)	MGM 3-E4, E3733, MG-2-5401
Just Waitin' (Williams – Gazzaway)	MGM 10932	MGM K10932, X1165 (EP), K12727, KGC142	MGM E3267, 3-E4, E3927, E4138
Men with Broken Hearts (Williams)	MGM 10932, 30756 in album 203	MGM K10932, K30756 in boxed set K203, X1047 (EP), X1643 (EP)	MGM E203 (10"), E3267, E3927, E4138, M3HB-4975

NOTE: "Just Waitin'" and "Men with Broken Hearts" were recorded under Hank Williams's alias, Luke the Drifter.

Castle Studios
Nashville, Tenn.
1:30 P.M.–5 P.M.
March 16, 1951

Song	Master	Releases
I Can't Help It (If I'm Still in Love with You) (Williams)	MGM 10961	MGM K10961, X1014 (EP), K12611, KGC128, X1650 (EP)	MGM E3219, 3-E4, E3918, E3925, E4267-4, SE4680
Howlin' at the Moon (Williams)	MGM 10961	MGM K10961, X4108 (EP) in set X242, X1318 (EP)	MGM E242 (10"), E3412, 3-E2, E4040, E4227, SE4227, E4267-4, E4300, SE4300, SE4651, M3F-4954, MG-2-5401

Hey, Good Lookin' (Williams)	*MGM* 11000, 30754 in album 202	*MGM* K11000, K30754 in boxed set K202, X4102 (EP) in set X202, KGC108, X1612 (EP)	*MGM* E202 (10''), E3272, 3-E2, E3918, E3923, SE3923, E4168, E4267-4, SE4755-2, 1SE-33ST; *Metro* M602, MS602
My Heart Would Know (Williams)	*MGM* 11000	*MGM* K11000, X1014 (EP), X1636 (EP), X1650 (EP)	*MGM* E3219, E3272, 3-E2, E3923, SE3923, E3925, E4140, E4227, SE4227, E4267-4, SE4755-2

NOTE: On KGC128 (45 rpm), part of the first note of the steel guitar's introduction to "I Can't Help It" is missing.

Castle Studios
Nashville, Tenn.
9 P.M. (approx.)–10:30 P.M.
March 23, 1951

The Pale Horse and His Rider (Bailes — Staggs)	*MGM* 12394	*MGM* K12394, K13359	*MGM* E3955; *Metro* M547, MS547
A Home in Heaven (Williams)	*MGM* 12394	*MGM* K12394	*MGM* E3955; *Metro* M547, MS547

NOTE: Artist credits are to *Hank and Audrey Williams*, who perform in duet.

TITLE & COMPOSER CREDIT	33 1/3 RPM (16" ET)	33 1/3 RPM (LP)

A.F.R.S.

Grand Ole Opry
Ryman Auditorium
Nashville, Tenn.
May 5, 1951

TITLE & COMPOSER CREDIT	33 1/3 RPM (16" ET)	33 1/3 RPM (LP)
Cold, Cold Heart (Hank Williams)	*AFRS* END-18, Program 175	*MGM* MG-1-5019
Dear John (T. Ritter – A. A. Gass)	*AFRS* END-18, Program 175	*MGM* MG-1-5019

TITLE & COMPOSER CREDIT	78 RPM	45 RPM	33 1/3 RPM

MGM RECORDS

Castle Studios
Nashville, Tenn.
7 P.M. –10 P.M.
June 1, 1951

TITLE & COMPOSER CREDIT	78 RPM	45 RPM	33 1/3 RPM
Ramblin' Man (Williams)	*MGM* 11120, 11479	*MGM* K11120, K11479, X4222 (EP) in set X291, X1135 (EP), KGC111	*MGM* E3219, 3-E2, E3925, E4040, E4168, E4254, SE4254, E42674, SE4651, M3F-4954

Pictures from Life's Other Side (No CC)	*MGM* 11120, 30755 in album 203	*MGM* K11120, K30755 in boxed set K203, X1047 (EP), X1643 (EP)	*MGM* E203 (10"), E3267, 3-E4, E3927, E4138, E4254, SE4254, M3HB-4975
I've Been Down That Road Before (Williams)	*MGM* 11017	*MGM* K11017, X1165 (EP)	*MGM* E3267, 3-E4, E3927, E4138
I Dreamed about Mama Last Night (Rose)	*MGM* 11017, 30756 in album 203	*MGM* K11017, K30756 in boxed set K203, X1644 (EP)	*MGM* E203 (10"), E3267, 3-E4, E3927, E4138, M3HB-4975; *Metro* M547, MS547

NOTE: These four sides were recorded under Hank Williams's alias, Luke the Drifter.

Castle Studios
Nashville, Tenn.
7:15 P.M.–10:35 P.M.
July 25, 1951

I'd Still Want You (Williams)	*MGM* 11100	*MGM* K11100, X1639 (EP)	*MGM* 3-E4, E3733, MG-2-5401
Lonesome Whistle (Davis – Williams)	*MGM* 11054	*MGM* K11054, X4223 (EP) in set X291, X1136 (EP)	*MGM* E3219, 3-E2, E3925, E4267-4, MG-2-5401; *Metro* M509, MS509

Crazy Heart
(Rose — Murray)

MGM 11054

MGM E3272, 3-E4, E3923, SE3923, E4040

Crazy Heart
(Rose — Murray)

MGM K11054, X1636 (EP)

MGM X1014 (EP)

Baby, We're Really in Love

Unissued

NOTE: It is assumed that the slightly different version of "Crazy Heart" on MGM X1014 (EP) stems from an alternate take from this session. No relevant data could be located in the MGM files.

Castle Studios
Nashville, Tenn.
7 P.M.–10:30 P.M.
August 10, 1951

I'm Sorry for You, My Friend

Unissued

Half as Much
(C. Williams)

MGM 11202, 30754 in album 202

MGM K11202, K30754 in boxed set K202, X4103 (EP) in set K202, KGC109, X1613 (EP)

MGM E170 (10"), E202 (10"), E3272, 3-E2, E3918, E3923, SE3923, E4168, E4227, SE4227, E4267-4, SE4755-2, 1SE-33ST

I'd Still Want You

Unissued

Baby, We're Really in Love
(Williams)

	78 RPM	45 RPM	33 1/3 RPM
	MGM 11100	*MGM* K11100, X1014 (EP), X4108 (EP) in set X242, X1318 (EP)	*MGM* E242 (10"), E3412, 3-E4, E4040, E4267-4, SE4755-2

NOTE: The track of "Baby, We're Really in Love" on SE4755-2 has been re-channeled to simulate stereo. However, the recording is free from any overdubbing of additional instrumentation.

TITLE & COMPOSER CREDIT	33 1/3 RPM (16" ET)		33 1/3 RPM (LP)

A.F.R.S.

Grand Ole Opry
Ryman Auditorium
Nashville, Tenn.
September 22, 1951

	33 1/3 RPM (16" ET)		33 1/3 RPM (LP)
Hey, Good Lookin' (Hank Williams)	*AFRS* END-18, Program 197		*MGM* MG-1-5019
Cold, Cold Heart	*AFRS* END-18, Program 197		

TITLE & COMPOSER CREDIT	78 RPM	45 RPM	33 1/3 RPM

MGM RECORDS

Castle Studios
Nashville, Tenn.
10 A.M.—Noon
December 11, 1951

	78 RPM	45 RPM	33 1/3 RPM
I'm Sorry for You, My Friend (Williams)	*MGM* 11160	*MGM* K11160, X1636 (EP)	*MGM* E3272, 3-E4, E3923, SE3923, E4040, E4267-4, MG-2-5401

TITLE & COMPOSER CREDIT	33 1/3 RPM (16" ET)		33 1/3 RPM (LP)
Honky Tonk Blues (Williams)	MGM 11160, 30639 in album 168	MGM K11160, K30639 in boxed set K168, X4041 (EP) in set X168, X4109 (EP) in set X242, X1216 (EP) X1317 (EP), KGC109	MGM E168 (10"), E242 (10"), E3330, E3412, 3-E2, E3926, E4040, E4227, SE4227, E4267-4, E4300, SE4300, SE4651, SE4755-2, M3F-4954
Let's Turn Back the Years (Williams)	MGM 11202	MGM K11202, X1638 (EP)	MGM 3-E4, E3733, E4140, MG-2-5401

A.F.R.S.

Grand Ole Opry
Ryman Auditorium
Nashville, Tenn.
Apr. 5, 1952

Baby, We're Really in Love	AFRS END-18, Prog. 292, Pt. 1
The Old Country Church	AFRS END-18, Prog. 292, Pt. 1
I Can't Help It (if I'm Still in Love with You)	AFRS END-18, Prog. 292, Pt. 2

NOTE: Hank Williams acts as emcee for this show in Red Foley's absence. Hank Williams and "Little" Jimmy Dickens perform together on "The Old Country Church." Program 292, part 2, is on a separate disc from program 292, part 1.

TITLE & COMPOSER CREDIT	78 RPM	45 RPM	33 1/3 RPM
MGM RECORDS			
Castle Studios Nashville, Tenn. 10 A.M.–1 P.M. June 13, 1952			
Window Shopping (Joseph)	*MGM* 11283	*MGM* K11283, X1076 (EP)	*MGM* 3-E2, E3955, E4040, E4227, SE4227, SE4755-2
Jambalaya (on the Bayou) (Williams)	*MGM* 11283	*MGM* K11283, X4109 (EP) in set X242, X1317 (EP), KGC110	*MGM* E242 (10"), E3412, 3-E2, E3918, E4168, E4254, SE4254, E4267-4, SE4755-2, 1SE-33ST
Settin' the Woods on Fire (Nelson – Rose)	*MGM* 11318, 30752 in album 202	*MGM* K11318, K30752 in boxed set K202, X4102 (EP) in set X202, X1612 (EP)	*MGM* E202 (10"), E3272, 3-E2, E3918, E3923, SE3923, E4109, E4227, SE4227, E42674, SE4755-2
I'll Never Get Out of This World Alive (Williams – Rose)	*MGM* 11366	*MGM* K11366, X4109 (EP) in set X242, X1317 (EP), KGC110	*MGM* E242 (10"), E3412, 3-E2, E4140, E4267-4, E4300, SE4300, 2-SES-4865, MG-2-5401

NOTE: The track of "Settin' the Woods on Fire" on SE4755-2 has been re-channeled to simulate stereo. However, the recording is free from any overdubbing of additional instrumentation.

Castle Studios
Nashville, Tenn.
1:45 P.M.–3:45 P.M.
July 11, 1952

You Win Again (Williams)	*MGM* 11318, 30753 in album 202	*MGM* K11318, K30753 in boxed set K202, X4102 (EP) in set X202, KGC112, X1612 (EP)	*MGM* E202 (10"), E3272, 3-E2, E3918, E3923, SE3923, E4227, SE4227, E4267-4, SE4755-2
I Won't Be Home No More (Hank Williams)	*MGM* 11533	*MGM* K11533, X4109 (EP) in set X242, X1317 (EP)	*MGM* E242 (10"), E3412, 3-E2, E4140, E4267-4, MG-2-5401
Be Careful of Stones That You Throw (Dodd)	*MGM* 11309, 30755 in album 203	*MGM* K11309, K30755 in boxed set K203, X1644 (EP)	*MGM* E203 (10"), E3267, 3-E4, E3927, E4138, E4254, SE4254, SE4690
Why Don't You Make Up Your Mind (Williams)	*MGM* 11309	*MGM* K11309, X1165 (EP)	*MGM* E3267, 3-E4, E3927, E4138

NOTE: "Be Careful of Stones That You Throw" and "Why Don't You Make Up Your Mind" were recorded under Hank Williams's alias, Luke the Drifter. "Why Don't You Make Up Your Mind" appears as "Please Make Up Your Mind" on some later releases.

293

Castle Studios
Nashville, Tenn.
1:30 P.M. – 3:40 P.M.
September 23, 1952

I Could Never Be Ashamed of You (Williams)	*MGM* 11366, 30753 in album 202	*MGM* K11366, K30753 in boxed set K202, X4103 (EP) in set X202, X1613 (EP)	*MGM* E202 (10"), E3272, 3-E2, E3923, SE3923, E4267-4, MG-2-5401
Your Cheatin' Heart (Williams)	*MGM* 11416, 30751 in album 202	*MGM* K11416, K30751 in boxed set K202, X4102 (EP) in set X202, KGC107, X1612 (EP), K13305	*MGM* E202 (10"), E3272, 3-E2, E3825, E3918, E3923, SE3923, E4168, E4267-4, SE4755-2, 2-SES-4865
Kaw-Liga (Williams – Rose)	*MGM* 11416, 30752 in album 202	*MGM* K11416, K30752 in boxed set K202, X4103 (EP) in set X202, KGC111, X1613 (EP)	*MGM* E202 (10"), E211 (10"), E3272, 3-E2, E3918, E3923, SE3923, E4168, E4254, SE4254, E4267-4, E4300, SE4300, SE4651, SE4755-2, SE4787, 1SE-33ST, 2-SES-4865, M3F-4954
Take These Chains from My Heart (Heath – Rose)	*MGM* 11479	*MGM* K11479, X4223 (EP) in set X291, X1136 (EP)	*MGM* E3219, 3-E2, E3918, E3925, E4267-4

Nonsession Recordings

The following titles (listed alphabetically) were privately made recordings, most likely with only a rhythm guitar for accompaniment. The original recording dates are not known. Discographic data presented here are for those songs that have been released without additional overdubbing and for songs that have yet to be released in any form. For those *nonsession* recordings that have been released *only* in overdubbed form, see the "Overdubbed Nonsession Recordings" listing that follows.

TITLE & COMPOSER CREDIT	78 RPM	45 RPM	33 1/3 RPM
Alone and Forsaken (Williams)	*MGM* 12029	*MGM* K12029, X1215 (EP)	*MGM* E3330, E3926; *Metro* M509, MS509
The Battle of Armageddon (Acuff – McLeod)	*MGM* 12127	*MGM* K12127	
Blue Love (in My Heart) (Jenkins)	*MGM* 12332	*MGM* K12332, X1492 (EP), X1639 (EP)	*MGM* E3560, E3733, E3924
Faded Love and Winter Roses (Rose)	*MGM* 11928	*MGM* K11928, X1556 (EP)	*MGM* E3605, E3928
The First Fall of Snow (Rose)	*MGM* 12077	*MGM* K12077, X1556 (EP)	*MGM* E3605, E3928
I Wish I Had a Nickel (Sutton – Barnhart)	*MGM* 12244	*MGM* K12244, X1555 (EP)	*MGM* E3605, E3928
Leave Me Alone with the Blues (Pope)	*MGM* 12484	*MGM* K12484, X1639 (EP)	*MGM* E3733
Little Paper Boy	Unissued in any form.		

The Long Train	Unissued in any form.		
My Main Trial Is Yet to Come	Unissued in any form, but overdubbing was done.		
No Not Now	Unissued in any form.		
No One Will Ever Know (Rose – Foree)	*MGM* 12535	*MGM* K12535, X1556 (EP)	*MGM* E3605, E3928
Please Don't Let Me Love You (Jones)	*MGM* 11928	*MGM* K11928, X1555 (EP)	*MGM* E3605, E3928
The Prodigal Son	Unissued in any form; different from the October, 1949, recording.		
Ready to Go Home (Williams)	*MGM* 12438	*MGM* K12438	*MGM* 3-E4
Singing Waterfall (Williams)	*MGM* 12332	*MGM* K12332, X1493 (EP)	*MGM* E3560, E3924
Someday You'll Call My Name (Branch – Hill)	*MGM* 12077	*MGM* K12077, X1215 (EP)	*MGM* E3330, E3926
Thank God (Rose)	*MGM* 12127	*MGM* K12127, X1218 (EP)	*MGM* E3331, M3G-4991
There's No Room in My Heart (for the Blues) (Rose – Turner)	*MGM* 12244	*MGM* K12244, X1554 (EP)	*MGM* E3605, E3928

Thy Burdens Are Greater than Mine (Stewart – King)	*MGM* 12185		*MGM* K12185
The Tramp on the Street	Unissued in any form; different from the October, 1949, recording.		
The Waltz of the Wind (Rose)	*MGM* 12535	*MGM* K12535, X1554 (EP)	*MGM* E3605, E3928
We Planted Roses on My Darling's Grave	Unissued in any form.		
With Tears in My Eyes (Howard)	*MGM* 12484	*MGM* K12484, X1554 (EP)	*MGM* E3605, E3928
You Caused It All by Telling Lies	Unissued in any form.		

NOTES: On "Ready to Go Home," the last line of one of the choruses is also carelessly injected as an introduction to the song. The success of this is questionable because of the poor timing between the intro and the song's first verse. Omit this intro, and the recording is most likely the way Hank originally performed it.

MGM ledgers also list a song titled "Goodbye" by Hank. However, I seriously doubt this is a Hank Williams recording, since the master number tends to indicate a New York recording.

Overdubbed Nonsession Recordings

The following titles (listed alphabetically) were privately made recordings that have subsequently been overdubbed with additional instrumentation and have been released *only* in an overdubbed configuration. In some cases, titles have been released in more than one such configuration.

The Angel of Death
Are You Building a Temple in Heaven?
Are You Walkin' and Talkin' with the Lord?
California Zephyr
Cool Water
Devil's Train
Dixie Cannonball
First Year Blues
Fool about You
Going Home
A House of Gold
How Can You Refuse Him Now?
I Ain't Got Nothin' but Time
I Can't Escape from You
If You'll Be a Baby to Me
I'm Free at Last
(I'm Gonna) Sing, Sing, Sing
It Just Don't Matter Now
Jesus Died for Me (by Hank and Audrey)
Jesus Is Calling

Last Night I Dreamed of Heaven
Low Down Blues
Message to My Mother
Mother Is Gone
The Old Home
Rock My Cradle (Once Again)
Rockin' Chair Money
Roly Poly
Sundown and Sorrow
Swing Wide Your Gate of Love
A Teardrop on a Rose
Tennessee Border
Wait for the Light to Shine
Wearin' Out Your Walkin' Shoes
Weary Blues from Waitin'
We Live in Two Different Worlds
We're Getting Closer to the Grave Each Day
When the Book of Life Is Read
When You're Tired of Breaking Other Hearts
You Better Keep It on Your Mind

Long-Play Albums

The following albums are listed numerically by release number, not chronologically. For the sake of a complete LP listing of MGM/Metro *commercial* releases featuring Hank Williams, those albums that are comprised solely of overdubbed recordings are included, although they are *not* a part of the foregoing discography. These overdubbed albums are easily spotted in the column headed "Related Tracks." The stereo album SE4168, for example, stipulates "12 OD," meaning 12 overdubbed recordings. Note, however, that the 12 tracks of the mono version, E4168, are unaltered recordings. Some LPs feature a mixture of unaltered recordings and overdubs, such as SE4680, with 3 unaltered tracks and 7 overdubbed tracks.

MONO	STEREO	ALBUM TITLE	RELATED TRACKS	RELEASE DATE
		MGM		
3-E2	—	Hank Williams, Vol. 1 (3-LP boxed set)	35 + 1 OD	4/57
3-E4	—	Hank Williams, Vol. 2 (3-LP boxed set)	32 + 4 OD	9/58
2-E12	2-SE12	Great Country and Western Stars	2	4/64
—	1SE-33ST	"The Last Picture Show" (original sound track)	6 + 3 OD	12/71
—	MBC-39	Music City Classics	1	9/70
E107 (10")	—	Hank Williams Sings	8	11/9/51
E168 (10")	—	Moanin' the Blues	8	9/12/52
E170 (10")	—	Pop Parade, Vol. 2	1	8/29/52
E202 (10")	—	Memorial Album	8	3/13/53
E203 (10")	—	Hank Williams as Luke the Drifter	8	3/13/53
E211 (10")	—	Pop Parade, Vol. 3	1	7/53
—	SE240-2	24 Karat Hits/Hank Williams	24 OD	8/68
—	SE241-2	24 Karat Gold from the Country	5 OD	8/68

E242 (10")	Honky Tonkin'	—	8	9/24/54
E243 (10")	I Saw the Light	—	6 + 2 OD	2/11/55
E3219	Ramblin' Man	—	11 + 1 OD	8/55
E3267	Hank Williams as Luke the Drifter	—	12	11/18/55
E3272	Hank Williams Memorial Album	—	12	1/56
E3330	Moanin' the Blues	—	10 + 2 OD	9/56
E3331	I Saw the Light (with green cover, as on E243)	See below	7 + 5 OD	5/18/56
E3331	I Saw the Light (new cover with church photo)	See below	7 + 5 OD	'59
E3331	I Saw the Light (new cover with church photo)	SE3331	12 OD	6/68
E3412	Honky Tonkin'	—	10 + 2 OD	2/22/57
E3560	Sing Me a Blue Song	—	12	8/23/57
E3605	The Immortal Hank Williams	—	11 + 1 OD	1/24/58
E3733	The Unforgettable Hank Williams	See below	11 + 1 OD	1/59
E3733	The Unforgettable Hank Williams	SE3733	12 OD	6/68
E3803	The Lonesome Sound of Hank Williams	See below	12 OD	1/60
E3803	The Lonesome Sound of Hank Williams	SE3803	12 OD	1/69
E3825	MGM Million Sellers–Country & Western Hits	—	3	3/60
E3850	Wait For the Light to Shine	See below	1 + 11 OD	6/60
E3850	Wait For the Light to Shine	SE3850	12 OD	6/68
E3918	Hank Williams Greatest Hits	See below	14	1/61

	SE3918	Hank Williams Greatest Hits	14 OD	3/63
	See below	Hank Williams Lives Again	12	4/61
E3923	SE3923	Hank Williams Lives Again	12	1/69
	See below	Let Me Sing a Blue Song	12	4/61
E3924	SE3924	Let Me Sing a Blue Song	12 OD	10/68
	See below	Wanderin' Around	11 + 1 OD	4/61
E3925	SE3925	Wanderin' Around	12 OD	10/68
	See below	I'm Blue Inside	10 + 2 OD	4/61
E3926	SE3926	I'm Blue Inside	12 OD	10/68
E3927	—	Luke the Drifter—Hank Williams	12	4/61
	See below	First, Last and Always	11 + 1 OD	4/61
E3928	SE3928	First, Last and Always	12 OD	1/69
	See below	The Spirit of Hank Williams	5 + 7 OD	7/61
E3955	SE3955	The Spirit of Hank Williams	12 OD	1/69
	See below	On Stage! Hank Williams—Recorded Live	14	1/62
	See below	Hank Williams on Stage—Recorded Live! (new cover)	14	10/62
E3999	SE3999	Hank Williams on Stage—Recorded Live! (same new cover; black label)	14 OD	10/62
E3999	SE3999	Hank Williams on Stage—Recorded Live! (same new cover; blue and gold label)	14 new OD	2/69
	See below	14 More of Hank Williams' Greatest Hits—Vol. II	14	6/62
E4040	SE4040	14 More of Hank Williams' Greatest Hits—Vol. II	14 OD	6/62

E4109	See below	*On Stage Volume II – Hank Williams*	14	2/63
	SE4109	*On Stage Volume II – Hank Williams*	14 OD	2/63
E4138	See below	*Beyond the Sunset*	12	5/63
	SE4138	*Beyond the Sunset*	12 OD	5/63
E4140	See below	*14 More of Hank Williams' Greatest Hits – Vol. III*	14	7/63
	SE4140	*14 More of Hank Williams' Greatest Hits – Vol. III*	2 + 12 OD	7/63
E4168	See below	*The Very Best of Hank Williams*	12	9/63
	SE4168	*The Very Best of Hank Williams*	12 OD	9/63
E4211	SE4211	*Great Country Favorites*	2	3/64
E4227	SE4227	*The Very Best of Hank Williams – Volume 2*	12	6/64
E4254	SE4254	*Lost Highway and Other Folk Ballads*	10 + 2 OD	9/64
E42674	—	*The Hank Williams Story*	45 + 3 OD	10/64
E4276	SE4276	*Hank Williams, Sr. & Hank Williams, Jr., Father & Son*	12 OD	4/65
E4300	SE4300	*Hank Williams Sings "Kaw-Liga" and Other Humorous Songs*	8 + 4 OD	7/65
E4377	SE4377	*The Legend Lives Anew – Hank Williams with Strings*	12 OD	7/66
E4378	SE4378	*Hank Williams, Hank Williams, Jr. Again*	12 OD	10/66
E4380	SE4380	*Movin' On – Luke the Drifter*	12 OD	7/66
E4380	SE4380	*Luke the Drifter* (same LP; new title)	12 OD	10/68
E4429	SE4429	*More Hank Williams & Strings*	12 OD	1/67
E4481	SE4481	*I Won't Be Home No More – Hank Williams and Strings*	11 OD	7/67
E4529	SE4529	*Hank Williams and Strings – Vol. III*	11 OD	1/68

E4576	SE4576	In the Beginning	1 + 10 OD	6/68
—	SE4576	In the Beginning (revised; additional master numbers in wax XSBV ¹31682-3A/XSBV 131683-3A)	11	?
—	SE4651	The Essential Hank Williams	11	7/69
—	SE4680	Life to Legend–Hank Williams	3 + 7 OD	6/70
—	SE4690	All Star Country	2 + 1 OD	7/70
—	SE4755-2	24 of Hank Williams' Greatest Hits	18 + 6 OD	2/71
—	SE4787	All Star Country Hits	2	6/71
—	2-SES-4865	Hank Williams/Hank Williams, Jr.–The Legend of Hank Williams in Song and Story	7 + 5 OD	1/73
—	M3F-4954	Archetypes	11	4/74
—	M3HB-4975	Hank Williams/Hank Williams, Jr.–Insights into Hank Williams in Song and Story	4 + 7 OD	11/1/74
—	M3G-4991	A Home in Heaven	2 + 8 OD	4/75
—	MG-1-5019	Live at the Grand Ole Opry	13	5/76
—	MG-2-5401	24 Greatest Hits, Vol. 2	17 + 7 OD	7/77

METRO

M509	MS509	Hank Williams	5 + 5 OD	1/65
M530	MS530	Country & Western Favorites	1	5/65
M547	MS547	Mr. & Mrs. Hank Williams	6	1/66
M572	MS572	Country & Western Favorites, Volume II	1	7/66
M602	MS602	Immortal	6 + 4 OD	6/67

Index

Relationships of members of the Williams family to Hank Williams are shown in parentheses after their names.

"Abilene," 115
Abraham Baldwin Junior High School (Montgomery), 53
Acuff, Roy, 1, 63, 65, 84, 123, 127, 140, 141, 169, 225, 242, 244, 245; songs of, and HW, 33; HW inspired by, 41, 75, 131; and Fred Rose, 61; and politics, 92; and Smoky Mountain Boys and Girls, 133; and Germany, 149; and HW's funeral, 225
Acuff-Rose publishing company, 59–62, 79, 103, 121, 123–24, 236, 238–39, 243–44, 247, 260, 263
Adair, Smith, 33
"Ain't Nothin' Gonna Be All Right No How," 169
"Air Castle of the South," 79
Alabama: Drydock and Shipbuilding Co., 54; *Journal*, 184, 250; University of, 250
Alcohol, 44, 171–95; in HW's childhood, 15–18; and dance halls, 36–40; and HW's early drinking patterns, 41, 46, 48–50; and HW's unreliability, 58; and Shreveport, 70, 78–79, 198–200, 205–9; and Grand Ole Opry, 83–84, 159, 196–98; and marital problems, 191, 199, 202, 204; and songwriting, 199; and HW's death, 214, 216–18, 241

Alcoholics Anonymous, 177
"Alone and Forsaken," 295
American Federation of Musicians, 212
"The Angel of Death," 298
Anglin, Jack, 69
Anthony, Ray, 245
"Are You Building a Temple in Heaven?," 298
"Are You Walkin' and Talkin' with the Lord?," 298
"Arkansas Traveler," 276
Armed Forces Radio Service transcriptions, 261, 277, 280, 281, 283–84, 287, 290, 291
Arnold, Eddy, 82, 84, 85, 90–91, 100, 113, 169
Atkins, Chet, 111
Atkins, John, 246–47
Audiences: appeal of HW to, 74–75; and HW's drinking problem, 189–90
Automobiles, 72, 133, 136
Autry, Gene, 61, 63
Avalon, Frankie, 245
Awards, 82

"Baby, We're Really in Love," 289, 290, 291
Bailes Brothers, 69, 78
Bailey, Deford, 88
Bands: and country singers, 94–96
Banjo, 88–89
Barron, Blue, 66

"The Battle of Armageddon,"
295
Beach, Freddie, 54
Beatles, 85
"Be Careful of Stones That You
Throw," 293
"Be Honest with Me," 61
Bennett, Tony, 117, 118
Benny, Jack, 151
Bergen, Polly, 117–18
Berle, Milton, 151, 153–54
Berry, Chuck, 250
"Beyond the Sunset," 225, 279
Big Jeff, 102–3
Billboard, 67, 82, 130, 172, 199,
220
"Black Belt," 3, 56
Blacks, 21, 81; HW's appeal to,
74–75; HW's attitude toward,
161. *See also* Tee-Tot
"Blue Love (in My Heart)," 295
Blues, 74, 81–82
"The Blues Come Around," 267
"Blue Yodels," 111
"Boil Them Cabbage Down,"
274
Bonano, Sharkey, 151
Bonanza Productions, 238
"Bonaparte's Retreat," 117
Boone, Claude, 97
Bowling, 162
Bradley, Owen, 119
Brown, Bud, 260
Browning, Gov. Gordon, 91, 92
Buddy Lee Attractions, 257
Buck, "Cousin Louis," 101
Burns, Jethro, 215
Butler County, Ala., 3–5, 258
Butrum, Hillous, 94, 97, 98,
100, 112, 145–47, 169, 189,
248, 257
Buttons, Red, 241

"Cajun Baby," 244, 260
"California Zephyr," 298
"Calling You," 64, 263
Canada, 149, 180–81
Candido, Candy, 151
Cannon, Henry, 135, 181
Canton, Ohio, 212–14

Cardwell, Jack, 15, 25, 148,
229–31
Cardwell, Rev. Oscar D., 24–25,
36
Caress, Jay, 257
Carr, Charles, 213–14, 216–17
Carson, Jenny Lou, 61–62
Carter Family, 28, 43, 85
Cash, Johnny, 85, 141, 242, 256
Cash Box, 67, 82
Castle Studio (Nashville), 79,
263, 264
Charles, Ray, 85, 118, 141, 245,
250
Clay, Henry, 69–70
Clifford (WSM porter), 95
Clooney, Rosemary, 124
Cohen, Herb, 259
"Cold, Cold Heart," 57, 106,
116–18, 147, 155–56, 157,
167, 185, 216, 284, 287, 290
Columbia Records, 117
Como, Perry, 85, 86, 156
"Cool Water," 298
Cooper, George, 119–20
Copas, Cowboy, 98
Corbin, Curly, 50–51
Corbin, Everett, 246
Coronet, 129
"Cotton Eyed Joe," 276
Country & Western Spotlight,
248
Country music: publishing of,
59–62, 123–24; and personal
contact, 68; fans of, 85–86;
singers and politics, 91–93,
251; and bands, 94–96; HW
on, 107; and showmanship,
142–47; stars and wholesome
image of, 159
Country Music Association, 253
Country Music Foundation
Press, 262
Country Music Hall of Fame and
Museum, 122, 253–54, 257
The Country Music Story, 98–99
Crabb, Alfred Leland, 90
Craig, Edwin, 93, 197
Cramer, Floyd, 120
"Crazy Heart," 289

Crysel, Dad, 32, 33
Currier/Nast Enterprises, 237

Dallas, Tex., 189
Damrosch, Walter, 88
Dance halls: and liquor, 36–40
Daniels, Jonathan, 5
Davis, Jeanette, 221–22
Davis, Jefferson, 223, 251
Davis, Jimmie, 118; and politics,
  92
Davis, Oscar, 180–81, 203–4;
  and HW's drinking problem,
  58, 205–6
Davis, Sammy, Jr., 241
Dean, James, 229, 245
"Dear Brother," 168, 269
"Dear John," 285, 287
"The Death of Hank Williams,"
  230–31
Dempsey, Jack, 151
Denny, Jim, 70, 204; as adviser,
  103–4; and HW and alcohol,
  171, 172, 179–80, 183, 186;
  and firing of HW, 196–98; and
  HW's second marriage, 204
"Devil's Train," 298
Devine, Ott, 90, 140
Dewitt, Jack, 197
Dickens, Little Jimmy, 98, 225,
  291; on HW as performer, 140;
  and Germany, 149
Disc jockeys, 96
Divorce, 191–94
"Dixie Cannonball," 298
Domino, Fats, 245
Donegan, Lonnie, 118
"Don't Make Me Go to Bed and
  I'll Be Good," 122
Downbeat, 140, 221
Drifting Cowboys, 33–36, 46,
  50–52, 55–56, 59, 63–64, 67,
  73, 75, 151, 169, 175, 191,
  213–16, 263; in stage shows,
  76–78, 145–47; in Nashville,
  94–96, 98; and electric and
  steel guitar, 99–100; car trips
  of, 108–9; and country music
  sound, 121; pay of, 132–33;
  and HW's drinking problem,

178–79, 183–84; and Ray
  Price, 205; after HW's death,
  236–37, 247–48, 257; and
  HW's songs, 247–48
Drifting Cowgirls, 233
Drinking problem. *See* Alcohol
Drugs: and Marshall, 206–9
Duckhead work clothes, 100
Dunkin, Allen, 143
Durante, Jimmy, 151
Durham, Cade, 21–22
Dylan, Bob, 250

Electric guitar, 99
Ellington, Gov. Buford, 91
El Paso, Tex., 195
Embry, Audrey, 252
Embry, Willie, 251–52
Emmet, Judge Richard, 238
Emmons, Buddy, 120
Empire Theater (Montgomery),
  31–32, 251
Ernest Tubb Record Shop, 113
Eshlimar, Billie Jean Jones. *See*
  Williams, Billie Jean
Eshlimar, Harrison, 200, 201
Evans, Ted, 151
"Everything's Okay," 279

"Faded Love and Winter Roses,"
  295
Fans, 244–50
Fibber McGee and Molly, 61
Fields, W. C., 138
"Fingers on Fire," 77, 275
"Fire on the Mountain," 273
"The First Fall of Snow," 295
"First Year Blues," 298
"Fisher's Hornpipe," 277
Fishing, 163
Flatt, Lester, 101
Flying, 135–36
"Fly Trouble," 266
Foley, Red, 1, 2, 63, 84, 140,
  225, 291; and HW's religion,
  160
Folsom, Gov. Jim, 251
"Fool about You," 298
Ford, Mary, 245
Foree, Mel, 62

Foster, Russell, 22
Foster, Stephen, v, 106
Fountain, Pete, 118
Fox, Dr. Vernelle, 173–74
Franklin, Aretha, 141
Franklin, Tenn.: farm in, 157–
58, 192
Franklin Road: house on, 157–
58, 252
Friend, Cliff, 80
Fruit Jar Drinkers, 88
"The Funeral," 128, 279

Gable, Dorothy, 253
Gayle, Willie, 227–28, 251, 259
Georgiana, Ala.: described, 2–5;
HW remembered in, 20–26;
Pan-American through, 64;
HW home for Christmas in,
210–13
Germany, 149–50
Gibson, Garth, 248–49
"Going Home," 298
Gone with the Wind, 242
Grand Ole Opry, vi, 2, 52, 58–
59, 62, 68–69, 73, 94, 132,
157, 193, 245, 261; 1949
appearance on, 1, 83; de-
scribed, 84–86, 89–91, 98,
100–101; history of, 87–89;
and National Life & Accident
Insurance Co., 93; and whole-
some image, 159; and alcohol,
172–73, 191; firing of HW,
196–98
Granger, Farley, 156
Grant, Gogi, 118
"The Great Speckled Bird," 33
Green, Bonnie, 222
Greenville, Ala., 3, 23, 26–30,
64
Gully Jumpers, 88
Guns, 163
Guthrie, Woody, 250
Guy, Erskine, 45
Guy, Lycrecia (stepdaughter),
45, 79

Hadacol Caravan, 150–55, 184
"Half as Much," 289

Halliday, Johnny, 118
Hamilton, George, 143, 240–42
Hancock, Allen, 22
Hancock, Johnny, 22
Handwerger, Sol, 148
"Hank, It Will Never Be the
Same without You," 231
Hank and Audrey's Corral, 157,
192
Hank and Audrey Williams Inter-
national Fan Club, 249
*Hank Williams: From Life to
Legend,* 95, 133, 153, 261
"Hank Williams Meets Jimmie
Rodgers," 231
Hank Williams Memorial Festi-
val, 259
"Happy Rovin' Cowboy," 273,
274, 275, 276
Harper's, 252
Harris, Boots, 33
Hatcher, Indian Joe, 34
Hawkins, Hawkshaw, 215, 229
Hawthorne, H. B., 56, 67
Hay, George D., 87–88
Haymes, Dick, 151, 153
Haynes, Henry "Homer," 215
Hazelop, Dove, 23
Health problems, 175–76
"Heartaches," 61
Heartsill, Flora M., 29
Heather Enterprises, 261
Heidt, Horace, 149
Helms, Don, 40, 50, 52, 55, 70,
94, 97, 98, 144, 145, 146,
194, 199, 247, 257; and steel
guitar, 99–100; on HW's song-
writing, 108–9; on HW as per-
former, 145; and HW's guns,
164; and Las Vegas trip, 179;
on Jack Ruby, 181–82; and
HW's drinking problem, 183;
and heckling, 189–90; and HW
firing, 197; and trip to Canton,
213, 214; and HW's death,
215, 216
"Help Me Understand," 282,
284
Hewlett, Tom, 212
"Hey, Good Lookin'," v, 64,

155–56, 228, 286, 290
Hi-Life (horse), 162
Hill, Lister, 27, 251
Hill and Range publishers, 260
Hirt, Al, 118
Holbrook, Hal, 255
Holly, Buddy, 250
Holmes, Clint, 73
"A Home in Heaven," 286
"Home in San Antonio," 61
Homer and Jethro, 215
"Honky Tonk Blues," 266, 270, 281, 291
"Honky Tonkin'," 64, 65, 118, 264, 267
Hope, Bob, 149, 151, 153
Horses, 162
Horton, Johnny, 214
"A House of Gold," 298
Houses, 157–58
"A House without Love," 271
Houston, David, 134
Howard, Paul, 62, 203, 232
"How Can You Refuse Him Now?" 298
"Howlin' at the Moon," 285
"How's My Ex Treatin' You," 108
How to Write Folk and Western Music to Sell, 112–14
Hunt, Sam, 103, 157
Hunting, 162

"I Ain't Got Nothin' but Time," 298
"I Can't Buy No Likker," 29
"I Can't Escape from You," 298
"I Can't Get You Off of My Mind," 266, 276
"I Can't Help It (If I'm Still in Love with You)," 186, 285, 291
"I Could Never Be Ashamed of You," 294
"I Don't Care (If Tomorrow Never Comes)," 42, 64, 264
"I Dreamed about Mama Last Night," 288
"I'd Still Want You," 288, 289
"If I Didn't Love You," 130

"If You'll Be a Baby to Me," 298
"I Have Other Fish to Fry," 113
"I Heard My Mother Praying for Me," 268
"I Hear That Lonesome Whistle Blow," 185
"I Just Didn't Have the Heart to Say Goodbye," 260
"I Just Don't Like This Kind of Livin'," 272, 280
"I Laid My Mother Away," 107
"I'll Be a Bachelor 'til I Die," 268
"I'll Have a New Body," 275
"I'll Never Get Out of This World Alive," 130, 199, 220, 292
"I Love You Because," 117
"I'm a Long Gone Daddy," 266
"I'm Free at Last," 298
"(I'm Gonna) Sing, Sing, Sing," 109, 298
"I'm Looking Over a Four-Leaf Clover," 66
"I'm Satisfied with You," 266
"I'm So Lonesome I Could Cry," 105, 121, 129, 167, 271, 276
"I'm Sorry for You, My Friend," 289, 290
"I Saw the Light," 72, 141, 195, 215, 224, 225, 251, 265, 276; and monument, 227
"It Just Don't Matter Now," 298
"I've Been Down That Road Before," 110, 288
"I've Just Told Mama Goodbye," 271, 276
Ives, Burl, 118
"I Wanna Live and Love Always," 274
"I Wish I Had a Nickel," 295
"I Won't Be Home No More," 293

"Jambalaya," v, 136, 152, 157, 199, 204, 210, 228, 292

Jazz horn, 25
"Jealous Heart," 62
Jefferson Island salt, 101
Jenkins, Carl, 63, 64, 79, 123
Jenkins, Ray, 184
Jennings, Waylon, 256
"Jesus Died for Me," 298
"Jesus Is Calling," 298
"Jesus Remembered Me," 269
"Joe Clark," 273
Johnny and Jack, 69
Johnny Fair syrup, 73
"John Wesley Harding," 250
Jolson, Al, 154
Jones, Eddie, 224
Jordanaires, 126
Journey's Inn (Camden), 56, 67
"The Journey's Inn Blues," 56
"Just Waitin'," 285

"Kary On," 155
Katzman, Sam, 240, 241
"Kaw-liga," 129–30, 210, 220,
  228, 294
King, Larry L., 252
King, Martin Luther, Jr., 223
King, Nelson, 96, 230
King, Pee Wee, 43, 44, 61, 118
King, Wayne, 37
"KP," 155
Kristofferson, Kris, 256
Ku Klux Klan, 21
KWKH radio (Shreveport), 69,
  198

Laine, Frankie, 118
Lamkin, Edna Curry, 212
Lancaster, Burt, 240
"The Last Letter," 231
"Last Night I Dreamed of
  Heaven," 298
"(Last Night) I Heard You Cry-
  ing in Your Sleep," 265
Las Vegas, Nev., 179
"Leave Me Alone with the
  Blues," 295
LeBlanc, Dudley J., 150–55
LeBlanc Corporation, 261, 272
"Let's Turn Back the Years,"
  291

Lewis, Carolyn, 222
Lewis, Jerry Lee, 108
Lewis, Ramsey, 245
"The Life of Hank Williams,"
  231
Lindeman, Edith, 184–86, 188
Linn, Ed, 45, 46, 81, 104
Liquor. *See* Alcohol
Lister, "Big Bill," 154
"Little Paper Boy," 295
Liuzzo, Viola, 5
"Living It Up and Having a
  Ball," 169
Loesser, Frank, 239
Loneliness, 176–77
"Lonesome Blues," 185
"Lonesome Whistle," 288
"Long Gone Lonesome Blues,"
  110, 278, 280
"The Long Train," 296
"Lost Highway," 269, 274
"Lost on the River," 268
Loudermilk, John D., 115
Louisville & Nashville Railroad,
  2
Louisiana Hayride, 52, 68–78,
  84, 198–200, 206
"Lovesick Blues," 1–2, 76, 80–
  83, 95, 96, 97, 110, 141, 149,
  153, 157, 158, 190, 201, 205,
  206, 258, 268, 273, 275, 280,
  283
"Low Down Blues," 298
Luke the Drifter, 74–75, 127–
  29, 145, 250, 279, 282, 285,
  288, 293
Lund, Art, 66
Lyon, Rev. Henry L., 225
Ly-Rann Music, 238

McAlpin, Vic, 106, 108; and
  HW's songs, 109–11; on
  melody, 111; on Fred Rose,
  130–31; on HW and money,
  138
McAuliffe, Leon, 100
McCluskey, Bob, 131
McFadden, Jack, 132
McGill, Lilly, 27–28
McLean, Don, 258

McNeil, J. C. (cousin), 71;
describes HW, 8; HW's year
with family of, 16–20; and
HW and guitar, 22; on Tee-
Tot, 23–24; sings with HW,
25; on Lilly and money, 34;
on shopping for songs, 43; on
HW's early drinking, 48
McNeil, Mrs. Walter (aunt), 17,
18, 22
McNeil, Walter (uncle), 18, 19,
25
McNett, Bob, 75–78, 94, 98,
247, 257; and electric guitar,
99; and HW's drinking prob-
lem, 183
Macon, Uncle Dave, 88
Malone, Bill C., 99
"Mammy," 154
"A Mansion on the Hill," 60,
130, 249, 267, 275
March of Dimes, 261, 283
Marriage problems, 154, 165–
70, 174; and alcohol, 191
Marshall, Horace R. "Toby,"
206–9, 214, 241
Martha White's Self Rising
Flour, 101
Martin, Grady, 103, 120
Martin, Tony, 151
Marvin, Ken, 136
Mays, Mexican Charlie, 33
"May You Never Be Alone,"
269
"Me and My Broken Heart," 58
"Men with Broken Hearts," 128,
285
"Message to My Mother," 298
MGM: recording contract, 65–
67, 103; recording sessions,
121, 125–27, 264–72, 278–
79, 281, 282, 284–86, 287–
94, 299–303; movies and HW,
156, 240–43, 256; records and
market for HW's songs, 157,
244–47; response to HW's
death, 219–20, 236–37; and
HW's estate, 233. *See also*
Polydor Records
Miller, Mitch, v, 239; on HW's

songs, 106; and "Cold, Cold
Heart," 117; Fred Rose agree-
ment with, 121
Miller, Roger, 108, 250
"Mind Your Own Business," 82,
97, 186, 270, 276
"Minni-Ha-Cha," 130
Miranda, Carmen, 151
"Moanin' the Blues," 282, 283
Mobile, Ala.: HW in shipyards
in, 54–55; HW's show in, 148
Mona Lisa, 247
Money: HW's generosity with,
137–39; HW's attitude toward,
138–39; HW's income esti-
mated, 156–57
Monroe, Bill, 137
Monroe, Marilyn, 176
Montgomery, Ala., 47, 67, 210,
212, 233, 238–39, 242, 251–
52, 259; move to, 30–33
Montgomery *Advertiser,* 29; and
HW's death, 221–22; on *Your
Cheatin' Heart,* 242
Moody, Clyde, 62
Mooney, Art, 66
Moonshine, 15, 38
Morgan, George, 137
"Mother Is Gone," 298
Mother's Best Flour, 100
"Move It On Over," 67, 69, 79,
82, 126, 185, 265
Movies, 156
Music City News, 246
"Music City U.S.A.," 91
"My Bucket's Got a Hole in It,"
29, 127, 159, 272
"My Heart Would Know," 286
"My Love for You (Has Turned
to Hate)," 57, 60, 64, 264
"My Main Trial Is Yet to Come,"
296
"My Old Pal of Yesterday," 25
"My Son Calls Another Man
Daddy," 270, 278
"My Sweet Love Ain't Around,"
267

Nashville: Personality of a City, 90
Nashville, Tenn., 90–91, 178,

252–54; radio in, 100–102;
house in, 157–58, 192–93,
252; museum, 258
Nashville *Banner,* 224
"Nashville Sound," 118–20
Nashville *Tennessean,* 142, 199
National Life & Accident In-
surance Co., 62, 93, 104,
196–97
Nation's Business, 107, 149–50
Nelson, Ken, 105–6
"Never Again (Will I Knock on
Your Door)," 42, 64, 263
New Orleans Municipal Audi-
torium, 203–4, 257
New Orleans Pops Symphony,
257
New York City, 148
New York *Times,* 84, 250
Nichols, Cannonball, 52
"Nobody's Darlin' but Mine,"
92
"Nobody's Lonesome for Me,"
282, 283
"No, No, Joe," 282
"No Not Now," 296
"No One Will Ever Know," 296
Nudie's Rodeo Tailors, 143,
224, 233

Oak Hill, W.Va., 217, 226
Oakwood Cemetery Annex
(Montgomery), 251–52, 259
O'Connell, Arthur, 241
O'Day, Molly, 60
O'Dell, Mac, 102
Oklahoma Cowboys, 98–99
Oklahoma Wranglers, 63
"The Old Country Church," 291
"The Old Home," 298
"The Old Maid and the Burglar,"
99
"Old Man River," 153
Oliver, Susan, 241
"On the Banks of the Old
Ponchartrain," 266
Opryland, 90
Oswald, Lee Harvey, 182
Our Hank Williams, 54–55, 141,
231–32

Owen, Jim, 255–56
Owens, Buck, 101, 132

Page, Frank, 73–74, 78–79, 112,
198, 200
Page, Patti, 118
"The Pale Horse and His Rider,"
286
"Pan American," 64–65, 264,
275
"Pan American Blues," 88
Paramount Theater (Montgom-
ery), 242
Parker, Colonel Tom, 74
Parra, Emile, 151
Pasternak, Joe, 156, 240
Paul, Les, 245
Payne, Rufe. *See* Tee-Tot
"Peace in the Valley," 160, 225
Pearl, Minnie, 1, 86, 144, 181;
on sale of "Prayin' for the Day
When Peace Will Come," 43–
44; on HW as performer, 58,
139–40; on HW and flying,
135–36; and Germany, 149;
on HW's audience appeal, 144–
45; and Hadacol Caravan, 151;
and El Paso performance, 195
Peer, Ralph, 63
Performances: of HW described,
131–47
Persuaders, 134
Pete King Chorale, 245
"Pictures from Life's Other
Side," 288
Pierce, Webb, 74, 159, 199, 225
"Pins and Needles," 61
Pinson, Bob, 256
"Please Don't Let Me Love
You," 296
Politics: and country music,
91–93
Polydor Records, 259
Pop music field, 116–21
Possum Hunters, 88
Powell, Janie, 156
"Prayin' for the Day When Peace
Will Come," 43
Presley, Elvis, 74, 97, 145, 247,
255

Press: and drinking problems, 184–88
Price, Ray, 74, 120, 184, 185, 197, 209–10, 213, 214, 250; on HW's divorce, 193–94; on HW's drinking, 194–95; and Drifting Cowboys, 205
Pride, Herman, 12, 13, 21, 24
Pride, Mrs. Herman, 12
"The Prodigal Son," 275, 296
Pruett, Sammy, 39–40, 50–51, 55, 70, 98, 146; on Lilly, 34–35; and HW and alcohol, 173, 181

Quartarare, Carolyn, 222

Radio: in Montgomery, 32-34; in Shreveport, 73; in Nashville, 100-102, 191. *See also call letters of individual stations*
"Railroad Blues," 24
Rainwater, Cedric, 146, 188
"Ramblin' Man," 287
Rankin, Allen, 29, 32, 109, 128, 140, 184; on HW's voice, 141
Ray, Johnny, 118
"Ready to Go Home," 296
Recording sessions: in Nashville, 79, 120; and Rose, 125–29; and drinking problem, 199. *See also* MGM
Records: sale of, after death, 219–21; as tributes, 229–31. *See also* MGM
Redding, Otis, 141
Reeves, Jim, 74, 253
Reeves, Select, 4
Rehfeldt, Hans-Peter, 248
Reid, Austin, 14
Religion, 159–61
Religious songs, 57, 75
Reporter, 244
Reynolds, George, 63, 197
Richmond, Ind., 184–89
Richmond *Times Dispatch,* 184–88
Ritter, Tex, 242
Rivers, Jerry, 94–96, 109, 145,

146, 257, 261; on studio stars, 102–3; on Fred Rose, 122; and HW and guitar, 125; on travels, 133–37; on "Lovesick Blues," 153; on HW's marriage, 154; on HW's religion, 160; on HW's pastimes, 162, 163; on HW and alcohol, 171, 173, 178, 183, 184; and Las Vegas trip, 179–80; and trip to Ohio, 214; and HW's death, 218; and HW's funeral, 223; and Hank, Jr., 237; and fans, 245, 248
Road trips, 72–73, 96, 109, 133–37, 150–55, 176, 178–82
Robison, Carson, 66
"Rockin' Chair Money," 298
"Rock My Cradle (Once Again)," 298
Rodgers, Cliff, 215
Rodgers, Jimmie, 21, 25, 86, 111, 140, 244, 249, 253
Rolling Stones, 85
"Roly Poly," 298
Roosevelt, Franklin D., 89
"Rootie Tootie," 266
Rose, Fred, 171; meets HW, 59–62; and HW's recordings, 62–67, 79, 125–27; role in HW's life, 66; and "Lovesick Blues," 81; as counselor, 103; as songwriter, 107–8, 117, 129–31; and shaping HW's songs, 116, 121, 129–31; agreement with Mitch Miller, 121; life of, 121–24; and Luke the Drifter, 129; and HW's drinking problem, 183; and firing of HW, 197; and HW's second marriage, 204; and HW's death, 216; after HW's death, 236; and unpublished songs, 243–44; and Country Music Hall of Fame, 253
Rose, Wesley, 59; on "Lovesick Blues," 1, 80, 81; and HW's recording debut, 62; on "Honky Tonkin'," 65; at recording sessions, 66; and per-

sonal contact with audience,
68–69; and HW and Grand Ole
Opry, 83; and HW's drinking
problem, 83–84, 183; on Fred
Rose–HW relationship, 103;
on amateur songwriters, 115;
and pop music field, 116–17,
124–25; on HW as songwriter,
118; on his father and HW,
127; on HW's directness, 142;
and HW firing, 198; and HW's
second marriage, 204; and
HW's death, 216, 218
"Rovin' Cowboy," 272
Royal Crown Cola, 101
Ruby, Jack, 181–82
Rule, Jimmy: on HW's songwriting, 105; and *How to
Write Folk and Western Music
. . .* , 112–14; on Fred Rose,
122, 129; and HW and women,
165
Ryman Auditorium (Nashville),
1, 91, 196, 200, 258

"Sally Goodin'," 95–96, 273,
274, 275, 276, 277
Sanders, Charlie, 186–89
Satherly, Art, 63
Schary, Dore, 156
Scruggs, Earl, 89, 101
Seals, Shorty, 33
"Settin' the Woods on Fire,"
199, 292
Shelton, Aaron, 63, 64, 79, 123
Shelton, Rev. L. R., 204
Shelton, Robert, 84, 98–99, 250
"Shenandoah Waltz," 62
Sheppard, Audrey Mae. *See*
Williams, Audrey
Sheppard, C. S., 45
Sherwood, Roberta, 245
Short, Jimmie, 99
"The Short Life of Hank
Williams," 81
Showmanship, 142–47
Shreveport, La., 68–80, 83;
typical show in, 76; after HW's
firing from Grand Ole Opry,
197–201

Simon, Si, 137
Sinatra, Frank, 85
Sincerity: and country music,
107–8
"Sing, Sing, Sing," 109, 298
"Singing Waterfall," 296
Si's Place, 137
"Six More Miles to the Grave-
yard," 42–43, 60, 265
Skip (dog), 162
Skipper, Ed (uncle), 19, 37
Skipper, Erlene, 210
Skipper, John (grandfather), 11
Skipper, Taft (cousin), 10, 13,
17, 30, 37, 233, 259; describes
HW, 8; on "Jambalaya," 152;
and Christmas, 1952, 210–11
Small Town Girl (film), 156,
240
Smith, Carl, 225
Smith, Fay, 99
Smith, Kate, 156, 258
Smithsonian Institution, 257
Smoky Mountain Boys and
Girls, 133
Snow, Hank, 149, 182, 189
"Someday You'll Call My
Name," 296
"The Song of the Dying Cow-
boy," 99
Songs: unpublished, 243–44
"Songs My Father Left Me,"
244
Songwriting, 29–30, 57, 61–62,
105, 117–18, 161, 199; HW's
philosophy of, 32, 42; early
attempts at, 42; method and
style of, 42–44, 78–79, 107–
15, 199; and selling, 43; of
sacred songs, 57, 72, 112; in-
spiration for, 72, 167, 199; of
recitations, 74–75, 127–29; in
Shreveport, 78–79; qualities
in HW's, 105–7
Soul music, 141
Sovine, Red, 74
Stafford, Jo, 118
Stage: personality, 131; influence of Acuff and Tubb, 131;
shows described, 145–47;

movements and Presley, 145
Stapp, Jack, 197
Starr, Kay, 117
Steel guitar, 99–100
"Steel Guitar Rag," 100
Steiner, Charles, 248
Sterling Records, 62–65, 261, 263–64
Stewart, Jimmy, 240
Stewart, Redd, 61, 118
Stewart, Robert B., 235
Stone, Harry, 218; and HW's drinking, 70–71, 83–84; on radio show pay, 101; and firing of HW, 196–97
Stone, Lillian. *See* Williams, Lillian
Stone, W. W., 212
Street singers, 23–24, 25–26
"Studio stars," 102–3
"Sucking Cider through a Straw," 99
"Sundown and Sorrow," 298
Swan, Jimmy, 231
Swearing, 160
"Sweethearts or Strangers," 92
Swindall, Lillian, 222
"Swing Wide Your Gate of Love," 298

"Take These Chains from My Heart," 294
"Talk with Minnie Pearl," 280, 281
Tanner, Elmo, 61
Taylor, Glen, 93
"A Teardrop on a Rose," 298
"Tears on My Pillow," 61
Tee-Tot, 23–24, 26, 28–29, 241
Television appearances, 156
"Tennessee Border," 298
"Tennessee Waltz," 61, 90, 118
Texas Troubadours, 98, 99
"Thank God," 296
"Thank You, Darling," 227
"There'll Be No Teardrops Tonight," 118, 268, 275
"There's a Bluebird on Your Windowsill," 273, 283
"There's a New Star in Hill-

billy Heaven," 231
"There's No Room in My Heart (for the Blues)," 296
"They'll Never Take Her Love from Me," 281
Thigpen, Fred, 20–21, 24, 37
Thigpen's Log Cabin, 37
Thompson, Uncle Jimmy, 87
"Thy Burdens Are Greater than Mine," 277, 297
A Time to Sing (film), 237
"Tobacco Road," 115
"Too Many Parties and Too Many Pals," 128, 279
"Tramp on the Street," 273, 297
Travel: to Europe, 147–49; to Canada, 147–50, 175, 180–81. *See also* Road trips
T. Rex, 85
True (magazine), 237
Tubb, Ernest, 84, 85, 98, 99, 118, 131, 140, 195; on HW, 58; on own voice, 142; and HW's funeral, 225; tribute to HW, 231
Twain, Mark, 255

Uniforms, 143

Vagabonds, 61
Vanderbilt University, 157, 175
Vardaman, James K., 53
Vienneau, Jim, 246
Virginia Rounders, 231
Voice, 140–42

"Wabash Cannonball," 33, 65
Waggoner, Porter, 100
"Wagner," 275
"Wait for the Light to Shine," 298
WALA radio (Mobile), 148
Waldron, Eli, 129, 244
Walker, Billy, 190
Walker, Frank, 65–66, 246; and HW's death, 218–19
"Walking the Floor over You," 118
Wallace, George, 93, 242

"The Waltz of the Wind," 297

Warren, Jim, 21

Waters, "Sneezy," 255–56

Watson, Dr. J. Crawford, 12

Watts, Howard ("Cedric Rainwater"), 146

Waugh, Irving, 191, 197

WCKY radio (Cincinnati), 96

WCOV radio (Montgomery), 30

"Wealth Won't Save Your Soul," 57, 64, 263

"Wearin' Out Your Walkin' Shoes," 298

"Weary Blues from Waitin'," 298

Webb, June, 215

"Wedding Bells," 82, 97–98, 271, 272, 276

Weissmann, Eva, 249–50

"We Live in Two Different Worlds," 298

"We Planted Roses on My Darling's Grave," 297

"We're Getting Closer to the Grave Each Day," 298

"We Remember Hank Williams," 237

"When God Comes and Gathers His Jewels," 57, 60, 64, 263

"When God Dips His Love in My Heart," 284

"When the Book of Life Is Read," 298

"When You're Tired of Breaking Other Hearts," 298

"Where the Soul of Man Never Dies," 273

Whiteman, Paul, 61

Whitt, Wayne, 115

"Why Don't You Love Me," 157, 278, 280, 281

"Why Don't You Make Up Your Mind," 293

"Why Should We Try Anymore," 278

Wiggins, Roy, 100

Williams, Andy, 103

Williams, Ann Autry (grandmother), 5

Williams, Audrey (1st wife), 44–47, 59, 62, 157, 206, 212, 258; and HW's drinking problem, 49–50, 177, 191; as part of HW's group, 56–57, 268, 269, 286; and HW's songs, 97, 199; and money, 107, 138; and cars, 133; and Germany, 149; marital problems of, 154, 174, 182; and bowling, 162; and marriage, 165–70; career of, 167–69; and divorce, 191–94; and HW's wedding to Billie Jean, 204; and HW's death, 227–28; after HW's death, 232–33, 252; and HW's estate, 233, 234, 239; career of, after HW's death, 237–38, 246, 249, 259; and *Your Cheatin' Heart*, 241, 242

Williams, Bill, 172

Williams, Billie Jean (2nd wife), 200–205, 210–14, 226; and Marshall, 208; singing career of, 232; and HW's estate, 233–35, 260; and *Your Cheatin' Heart*, 241–42

Williams, Clarence, 272

Williams, Elonzo H. "Lon" (father), 5–6, 27, 166, 211–12; illness of, 9; on HW's drinking, 49–50; and HW's estate, 233

Williams, Hank (Hiram Hank Williams): stature of, in country and pop music, v, 140, 155, 236, 244–45, 252–54; family of, 5–6, 8–10; birth and childhood of, 6–20; early musical experiences of, 11–12, 17, 20–26, 31–41; personality of, 18–20, 72, 75–77, 87, 137–39, 140, 142–44, 148, 158, 160, 176, 212; and guitar, 20–23, 28–29, 31, 125; as street singer, 25; appearance of, 27, 41, 44, 139, 143–44; first professional performance by, 31–32; as steel guitarist, 35; as fiddler, 35, 95; and dance-hall fights, 38–40;